What they say about So Sue Me!...

"As a practicing physician, I worry about malpractice lawsuits. So do my colleagues. Finally, we have a book that tells us in a simple, straight-shooting style how we can protect ourselves from the lawsuit epidemic affecting every doctor."

C. Johnson, M.D.
Pennsylvania

"Getting sued is frightening. *So Sue Me!* somewhat relieves that fright and the emotional exhaustion that comes from litigation. It is insightful, thorough, practical and enjoyable to read."

Erica Orloff
Florida

"*So Sue Me!*" is must reading for every lawyer or financial advisor who wants their clients' (or their own) wealth safe from our runaway legal system."

Chris Jarvis, CFP
Los Angeles

"Great book! Dr. Goldstein has distilled his forty years of wealth protection experience into an informative, concise and readable work."

J. Curshen
Red Sea Manaement
San Jose, Costa Rica

"Here's a complete encyclopedia of techniques and tactics to safeguard your assets against virtually any danger."

Financial Forum
Florida

"Goldstein is uniquely qualified to advise America's affluent. *So Sue Me!* is loaded with straight-talk advice on this most important aspect of financial planning."

Bill High
North Carolina

"Finally – an easily understandable explanation how anyone can fight back and survive in our insane legal environement."

Atty. Alan Cohn
Florida

SO SUE ME!

How to Protect
Your Assets from
the Lawsuit Explosion

ARNOLD S. GOLDSTEIN, J.D., PH.D.

**GARRETT
PUBLISHING**

Published by Garrett Publishing, Inc.
2500 North Military Trail, Suite 260
Boca Raton, Florida 33431
Telephone: 561-953-1322
Fax: 561-953-1940
E-mail: info@garrettpub.com
Website: www.garrettpub.com

This book is designed to provide accurate and authoritative information on the subject of asset protection. While all of the cases and examples described in the book are based on true experiences, most of the names and some situations have been changed slightly to protect privacy. It is sold with the understanding that neither the author nor the publisher is engaged in rendering legal, accounting, or other professional advice. As each individual situation is unique, questions specific to your circumstances should be addressed to an appropriate professional to ensure that your situation has been evaluated carefully and appropriately. The author and the publisher specifically disclaim any liability or loss incurred as a consequence, directly or indirectly, of using and applying any of the concepts in this book.

Wealthsaver® is a registered trademark of Arnold S. Goldstein & Associates LLC.

Goldstein, Arnold S.
So Sue Me!! Arnold S. Goldstein, JD, Ph.D.
   p.   cm.
Includes bibliographical references
ISBN 1-880539-63-2   978-1-880539-63-7
1. Execution (law)-United States-Popular works.
2. Property-United States-Popular works.
3. D creditor-United States-Popular works.
4. Liability (law)-United States-Popular works. I. Title

                    2006921267
                    PCN

Printed in the United States of America
10 9 8 7 6 5 4 3 2 1

*To my many clients who entrusted to me
their financial security.*

ACKNOWLEDGMENTS

So Sue Me! is the culmination of my life's work as an asset protection attorney. My knowledge has been greatly aided by my association with other professionals who each in their own way, added immeasurably to my skills. I thank them all.

Special thanks to David Mandel, Chris Jarvis, Ben Knaupp and Jonathan Curshen who contributed much to the specialty of asset protection and to some of the ideas and concepts presented in this book. I particularly want to acknowledge Ryan Fowler, another asset protection specialist, who has added much helpful information to various chapters.

Thanks also to my wife Marlene and my office administrator Barbara Schwartz for their tireless efforts in preparing the manuscript; Sheila Alexander for her expert editorial assistance and Vivian Jorquera and Meredith Garniss for their graphic skills. They make a great team!

Finally, I am forever grateful to my many clients who entrusted to me their wealth and financial security. I hope that I have served them well.

CONTENTS

Introduction: The Book A Million Lawyers Don't
Want You To Read   xiii

Part One: ASSET PROTECTION PLANNING

1. Why You Must Lawsuit-Proof Yourself Today   1
2. Building Your Financial Fortress   23
3. Ten Keys To a Great Plan   41
4. Fraudulent Transfers and Other Blunders   55

Part Two: STRATEGIES AND TOOLS

5. Self-Protected Wealth   77
6. Co-Ownership Tips and Traps   101
7. INC. Yourself   119
8. Lawsuit-Proofing With Limited Partnerships   149
9. The ABCs of LLCs   181
10. Trusts That Can Protect You   203
11. The Offshore Advantage   231
12. Debt-Shield Strategies   259
13. A Final Word About Insurance   279
14. Your Next ... (and Most Important) Step   293

Index   295

The Book A Million Lawyers Don't Want You To Read

For four decades I have helped America's affluent protect their wealth from lawsuits, creditors, tax collectors, ex-spouses and other predatory threats. My experience is that while many people know how to make money, far fewer know how to keep their wealth safe and secure.

I truly believe in the concept that each of us must think and act defensively if we are to protect our wealth in what has become a dangerously predatory society. Our world has turned lawsuit crazy. Your wealth is no longer safe.

So Sue Me! is essential reading because America is in the midst of a litigation explosion. We have too many bad laws, too many greedy lawyers, too many sue-crazy litigants and too many juries handing out outrageous awards. It is also about a nation of 'victims' who too frequently use the courts to redistribute wealth to themselves. It is about the destruction of our basic liberties and property rights and a government which arbitrarily grabs whatever it wants from you. It is also about honest, hard-working people who, through their own talents and efforts, accumulated some wealth and are now targets for every sue-happy litigant. Finally, it is about financial security that has become illusory. These are the philosophical underpinnings for this book.

More importantly, *So Sue Me!* is about what you can do and *must* do to keep your assets safe and the steps that you must take to enjoy lifelong financial security. That's why I wrote *So Sue Me!* As your comprehensive armchair advisor, it will show you how to protect *your* net worth from virtually *any* legal or financial threat.

Within its pages are the same proven and practical strategies that you can and must adopt to shelter your assets. These are the tools and tactics that I have used as an asset protection attorney to successfully shield the wealth of thousands of individuals, families and companies nationwide. These same strategies can turn your *vulnerable* wealth into *untouchable* wealth. But keep several important points in mind:

First, protect yourself *before* you get sued. Advance planning is essential. Creditors also have rights, so think about asset protection as a form of insurance – it's something you want to have in place before you need it. Commit to your financial self-defense program *today*. But don't give up even if you are already in trouble. There are still strategies that can work for you. Your wealth isn't lost until it's in your creditor's pocket!

Second, to create untouchable wealth will take time, effort and money. But asset protection is your best investment. A high net worth means little or nothing when it is exposed.

I wrote this book to be a primer on this important subject. Retain an experienced asset protection lawyer to help you design *your* best plan. Nevertheless, this book highlights many different ways that you can protect your assets. *So Sue Me!* will make you a well-informed client and one who can more intelligently choose and work with your lawyer.

So Sue Me! does more than explain asset protection strategies. It shows you these strategies in action. You will see examples that illustrate how others like yourself gained lifetime financial security for their families and how you can too!

Asset protection and wealth preservation involves different strategies – from the simplest to the most complex. There's no one correct formula or 'quick fix.' Though I present the various wealth protection tools to illustrate which *may* be best in specific situations, *your* best strategy will depend on the many factors that are unique to you. I give you the broad overview and general concepts and leave the specifics to your lawyer.

The Newest Wealthsaver Strategies

So Sue Me! can be a vital addition to your wealth protection library:

- You will find scores of *little known* strategies, tactics and tricks. These asset protection secrets can make the difference between bulletproof financial safety and going broke. The latest and newest strategies essential for your financial self-defense arsenal are all here.

- You will get straight talk, not textbook theory. I tell you what *really* works, what *doesn't* and *why*. You will get the same inside information as if you were in my office paying me hundreds of dollars an hour for this advice.

- You will also see how to avoid making the common mistakes and errors that you may be making right now – mistakes which can undermine your financial security!

- You will find resources – where to go for more help and how to learn more about this vital subject.

- You will find the information easy-to-understand without legalese or confusing technical jargon.

Essential for Everyone With Vulnerable Wealth

So Sue Me! isn't only for the rich and famous. This book is for *anyone* with a few bucks in the bank, some equity in their home and their future security tucked away in their retirement account. I chiefly aim the book to middle-class folks, the people who I help every day and who worked hard for their assets. These are the people who may not recover from a devastating major lawsuit. Nevertheless, you must read this book whether you:

- Are wealthy or have only a few assets that you would hate to lose.

- Are now unprotected against lawsuits or consider yourself fully protected. I show you how to design your first plan and improve upon any existing asset protection plan.

- Have never been sued, are now struggling with a lawsuit or have been sued before and want better protection before you are sued again.

- Need to protect your own wealth or a client's wealth. (If you are a lawyer, financial advisor or accountant, you do share responsibility to safeguard your client's wealth.)

- Need to shelter your personal assets, your business or professional practice.

- Are starting out in life and want to secure your future wealth or are in your twilight years and want to shelter your nest egg or your children's inheritance.

- Want to shield yourself not only against lawsuits but also divorce, the IRS, bankruptcy or other financial threats.

I'm Only a Phone Call Away

Finally, I wrote this book to begin a relationship. I enjoy learning from my many clients and readers who share their experiences with me. My asset protection clients are indeed my greatest teachers!

Let me hear from you. How did you enjoy the book? What ideas can you suggest for my next edition? What experiences can you share with my future readers? Most importantly, how can I help *you* and your family achieve lifelong financial security?

ONE ■ ■ ■

Why You Must Lawsuit-Proof Yourself Today

One lawsuit can ruin you. When it happens to someone else it's a statistic. When it happens to you, it's a nightmare. Take my word for it.

Or ask John Mathews and his wife Millie. They had a good life with a nice home, money in the bank, a solid portfolio of stocks and bonds, a six-figure IRA and a profitable Chicago plumbing supply business. They worked hard and within a few years hoped to retire to Florida and enjoy a financially secure retirement.

But life is unpredictable. John discovered that one day when he was sued by an ex-partner from a minor business deal that ended years earlier. A sinking feeling consumed John as he read the lawsuit. The outrageous misdeeds that John allegedly committed during their short partnership were all lies.

Then came the shocker: John's ex-business associate demanded millions in 'damages.' Suddenly, John's life soured. The ridiculous claims and insane demands for millions were unbelievable. John's anger quickly turned to fear as he realized that this was one lawsuit for which he had no liability insurance.

John was confident that once he saw his attorney all would be well. Undoubtedly his lawyer would assure him that he had little to worry about. But, John's lawyer gave him no consolation. The lawyer agreed that the case against John seemed shaky, but it was always possible John *could* lose. His lawyer didn't expect the ex-partner to be awarded much money even if he did win his case, but John was also being sued for punitive damages. His lawyer reminded John that "You just never know what a jury will do." All John's lawyer could be certain of was that it would cost John thousands of dollars in legal fees to defend this case and that it could take years to resolve – years of legal fees, aggravation, worry and uncertainty for John and Millie.

John left his lawyer's office with the lawyer's words ricocheting in his mind: *"You just never know what a jury will do."* John's worries turned to panic. What if he *did* lose the case? What would happen to his assets? Would he and Millie lose their home? Their investments? Their savings? Could they lose their business? Was John's retirement account safe? Could John be forced into bankruptcy and lose *everything*?

John wondered if it was too late to protect himself. How could he shield his assets to keep them safe no matter how this lawsuit ended? Could John better shelter himself from this and future lawsuits?

John was only one more lawsuit target. Like a lot of people, he suddenly and unexpectedly realized that he too could lose everything in the legal lottery he was about to play.

It Can Happen to You

I tell you about John and Millie Mathews not because their story is unusual. Quite the opposite. Thousands of such stories happen every day. I know. For forty years I earned my living protecting people who shared similar tales with me. Their fears always come down to those same nagging questions: "What will happen to my assets if I *do* lose this lawsuit? How can I protect myself before I lose everything?"

As you might expect, my clients include sports icons, movie stars and industry moguls. But most are everyday folks whose life story is not unlike the Mathews'. Every morning they awake, put in a hard day's work and aspire to build financial security for themselves and their families.

They too knew about lawsuits. They too had heard the maddening stories about others who were wiped out by a lawsuit or some other financial disaster. But these terrible things only happened to *others*. It couldn't happen to *them*. *Until it does!*

Some of these now poorer but wiser souls showed up at my office too late. The sheriff had already auctioned their home, carted away their furniture or seized their bank account. I could give them little or no help.

Fortunately, most sought my assistance in time. They wanted their wealth protected *before* they were sued or other problems arose. These clients we could protect. Still, most people don't think much about asset protection *until* they're sued.

Why, I continue to ask, do nine out of ten Americans have no lawsuit protection aside from their liability insurance? What I find even more amazing is that so many successful people carefully scrutinize their every business deal, demand the best business and investment advice and even micro-plan their vacations; yet they do absolutely nothing to fortify their wealth against lawsuits and the hundreds of other financial pitfalls that *everyone* faces during their lifetime. Why is this?

"Procrastination is the main reason," says Jim 'The Hammer' Shapiro, author of *'Sue the Bastards'* and a New York personal injury lawyer who won tens of millions in judgments against hapless individuals and businesses. "Few people have lawsuit protection high on their agenda until they are hit with a lawsuit. Then they sweat. But once they are sued, they'll find it much harder to protect themselves. The procrastinator is always my most vulnerable target because their assets are so easily picked. The 'deep pocket', vulnerable defendants are who *I* want to sue!"

> The well-protected are less inviting targets for a lawsuit. The bottom line is that wealth is good. Vulnerable wealth is bad.

Procrastination is most people's obstacle to timely defensive planning. Think about it. Only one in five adult Americans have even written a simple will, yet what is more certain than death? Little wonder so few people think to protect themselves *before* they are sued.

Americans are not risk-takers. We just don't always see things from the right perspective. For example, about fifty million lawsuits will be filed this year while there will be fewer than five million injuries and deaths from car accidents. You are ten times more likely to get sued than to injure or kill someone in a car accident. Would you drive without car insurance? You would be ten times as foolish not to become lawsuit protected. New civil lawsuits this year will be eighty times the number of residential fires. Undoubtedly you insured your home against fire, yet you probably have done little or nothing to safeguard your home against a lawsuit.

Are You the Next Target?

I have often wondered why I have such passion to lawsuit-proof people. It may be because I have seen so much devastation that a lawsuit can cause. It's also because lawsuits are epidemic. It will only get worse. Each year brings more lawsuits and still bigger awards. Litigation is America's fastest growing business, and few of us will get through life without being victimized by one or more major lawsuits. The fifty million new lawsuits this year is only one dismal statistic. In actuality, there will be many more lawsuit defendants because a lawsuit can ensnare multiple defendants. We don't have precise numbers, but there may be 100 million

> Are you under age 30? Prepare to defend yourself against no less than five major lawsuits over your lifetime, and most likely many more.

lawsuit defendants at any given moment. Whatever the number, it is indisputable that we have too many lawsuits. Nor can we forget the billions paid each year on the mere threat of a lawsuit.

Why has America become lawsuit-crazy? Sociologists, economists, politicians and lawyers have their own theories. From my perch as a practicing lawyer I have my observations. We have too many lawyers and too many needless laws. We have too few judges with the courage or common sense to summarily throw out a blatantly frivolous lawsuit. And we have too many juries who don't rule on the basis of liability. They see their role to redistribute wealth from 'deep pocket' defendants to plaintiffs who win their sympathy.

Most importantly, we have created an incentive for people to sue. For example, any punitive damage claim can enrich a plaintiff who has suffered little or no actual injury with a multi-million-dollar windfall. Why *shouldn't* people sue? A sue-happy plaintiff won't invest a dime of their own in legal fees, because lawyers who will take their case for a contingent fee are everywhere.

> People seeking protection are neither crooks nor immoral. They are taking advantage of the laws designed and intended to protect against life's vagaries.

There is plenty wrong with our legal system. But it's not only the fault of the system – as perverse as it is. The fault is with us as a society. We have become a nation of victims. When things go wrong, as they invariably do, we instinctively point the blame elsewhere. The lawsuit is the natural consequence of our distorted national mindset.

Walter K. Olson explains the phenomena in *The Litigation Explosion*:

"[The lawsuit] clogs and jams the gears of commerce, sowing friction and distrust between the productive enterprises on which material progress depends and on all who buy their products, work at their plants and offices or join in their undertakings. It seizes on former love and intimacy as raw materials to be transmuted into hatred and estrangement. It exploits the bereavement that some day awaits the survivors of us all and turns it to an unending source of poisonous recrimination. It torments the provably innocent and rewards the palpably irresponsible. It devours hard-won savings and worsens every animosity of a diverse society. It is the special American burden, the one feature hardly anyone admires of a society that is otherwise envied the world around."

Amen!

No less outspoken against the lawsuit deluge is Judicial Watch, a Capital Hill non-partisan, non-profit foundation in their observation: "The American legal system is dangerously corrupt. It picks the pockets of hardworking Americans by putting literally billions of dollars into the pockets of greedy lawyers, turning neighbor against neighbor and threatening to derail the rule of law." Nor can you deny the scope of the lawsuit explosion when you consider the statistics:

- The US tort system is the most expensive in the industrial world. US tort costs consume 2.2 percent of the gross domestic product. This is substantially higher than that of any other developed country.

- US legal system costs are growing at four times our economic growth.

- Class action lawsuits have increased 50 percent in only ten years.

- Asbestos claims have doubled in five years. And lawsuits are threatening virtually *every* industry.

- America has one million lawyers, the highest per capita. China, has five times our population, and only 110,000 lawyers.

- America has 70 percent of the world's lawyers and 90 percent of the world's litigation.

- You have one chance in five that you will be sued next year. (One in three if you are a doctor or business owner.)

With so many lawyers it is inevitable that we have so many lawsuits. The mere thought of a million lawyers running around looking for their next victim should signal a clear and present danger to anyone who has exposed assets. You can't blame every lawyer, though. Not every lawyer is in the lawsuit business. And you can still find a plaintiff's lawyer or two who won't file a frivolous lawsuit. They use their good professional judgment about who and when to sue. They don't abuse our judicial system. Yet how many more lawyers *do* throw around lawsuits like confetti? How many lawyers will file *any* lawsuit for a fast buck? How many lawyers *don't* care if their lawsuit is meritless as long as they can extort enough money from some defendant?

> To find a good attorney, call your local bar association or clerk of your local bankruptcy court. They know the veterans who can best help you.

The tide has turned. The *American Bar Association Journal* (the largest US publication for lawyers) in its article *Protect Your Assets Before Lawsuits Arise,* counsels their 300,000 members that asset protection is as critical for *them* as it is for their clients. One trial lawyer interviewed for the article frankly admits, "I don't want people doing to *me* what I do to *them* in court everyday."

The *Wall Street Journal*, responding to the ABA article, argued that since the lawyers realize the legal system is out of control, they should change the system and not merely protect themselves against it. The fact is that our legal system has yet to be reformed, and it won't be any time soon. Don't expect the lawsuit threat to abate. It will only get worse. It's far smarter to join the lawyers who are themselves running for shelter and lawsuit-proof *yourself.*

Playing the Legal Lottery

> From toddlers to executors of the deceased, anyone can sue and no one is immune – not even the President of the United States.

We can't blame only the lawyers. We should never forget that we would have far fewer lawsuits if we had fewer people so willing to sue. Walter Kelly's cartoon character, Pogo Possum, had it right: "We have met the enemy and they is us."

Ask yourself: Why shouldn't people sue when it costs them nothing if they lose but a few hours of their time, and they can gain so much if they win? Why work when they can sue their way to great wealth? Why play the lottery or hit the slots in Las Vegas when their chances to win are so much better when they gamble in court? And as one client philosophized, "Why marry for money when it's so much more pleasant to spend a few hours with a good lawyer rather than a lifetime with a bad spouse?"

Everybody wants a piece of the action and their own chance to win the legal lottery. Kids sue parents, partners sue partners, patients sue doctors, customers sue manufacturers, students sue teachers and parishioners sue clergy.

More frightening than the blizzard of lawsuits is the number of ridiculous cases that wiggle their way through the courts and reach a jury. And it seems that the more bizarre the case, the greater the plaintiff's victory. Scan the newspapers and magazines. Watch TV. Laugh to the stand-up comics. Who can most scintillate and humor us with the day's nuttiest lawsuit? Why has litigation become our favorite form of entertainment?

I chuckled my way through a book with its own macabre brand of lawsuit humor: *Buy This Book or We'll Sue You* (Citadel Press). Its authors, Laura and Attila Benko, compiled scores of true cases that are supposedly more absurd and funnier than fiction. Think for a moment, though: Are these lawsuits really humorous when you consider the great waste of time, money and energy that their defendants expended to defend against them? How funny are these frivolous cases when you consider the aggravation, worry and grief that so many defendants were forced to endure before they could shake themselves free of these nutty litigants and their stupid lawsuits? More disheartening was that some of these whacky plaintiffs actually *won* their case. This again bolsters my argument that our legal system is a legal lottery where even the bad case has a good chance.

The cases are legendary: Consider the 82 year old lady whose MacDonald's coffee landed on her lap while she was driving and juggling her hot coffee between her knees. Our geriatric plaintiff successfully sued McDonald's for millions and also Wal-Mart, who sold her the auto cup holder. What can we say about the New York couple who won ten million dollars from the city after they were struck by a train while having sex on the tracks? There is the Florida drunk who, while climbing a fence, was zapped by a transformer and sued the six taverns that had served him liquor that day – as well as the electric company. Or the Georgia couple who sued Ford after their 3 year old boy died in a Ford van where they locked him up for several hours in 90-degree heat (the parents argued that Ford should feature a safety device to cool parked cars). I could go on endlessly because such insane cases are now commonplace.

I predicted it. The fast food industry is being sued for turning us into a nation of fatties. Cereal producers are also targets. Can the chocolate industry be far behind? Who's next? Who *isn't*?

You might think that these dumb cases are only legal anomalies and the rare curiosities within our legal system. You would be wrong. Hundreds – if not thousands – of equally nonsensical cases are pending in your local courthouse. I know. I protect people from these ludicrous cases everyday. Or take a moment to scan the weekly bar journals. You'll find plenty of other equally far-fetched cases breaking new legal ground. Each story features a grinning plaintiff's lawyer who bagged another defendant.

Lawsuit mongers are abusing our legal system in record numbers. America is the world's lawsuit capital and California is America's lawsuit capital. To stem their litigation avalanche, California created the Vexatious Litigation Act to identify plaintiffs who overload their courts with frivolous lawsuits. Chronic plaintiffs cannot be denied their 'constitutional right' to sue, but they can't sue in California without an attorney. Nevertheless, one chronic 'victim' filed two hundred lawsuits in seven years. The court clerk who identifies the lawsuit junkies (and who was unsuccessfully sued eleven times in two years) admits: "I don't exaggerate when I say I am extremely frightened by these people."

> You do not have to do anything wrong to get sued. You only have to be in the wrong place at the wrong time.

Nor do you have to do anything wrong to get sued – and lose. You only have to be in the wrong place at the wrong time or somehow stumble across some greedy lunatic who is grieved. Voilá! *Your* wealth is soon in *their* pocket!

Perhaps I shouldn't call any case ludicrous. After all, a jury decides whether a case has merit. And what is the law but what a court determines it to be in any given case. That's another problem with our runaway legal system. The law is no longer predictable. No lawyer will speculate where a case will wind up. "You never know what a court will do." That's what every lawyer says. How different is that from predicting what a roulette wheel will do? It's random chance.

Our theories of liability have become so stretched and convoluted that no lawyer really knows the law anymore. Perhaps this explains why some lawyers accept cases that others won't. It's also why no defense lawyer can assure their client that they *can't* lose. Our legal system is indeed a crapshoot where a plaintiff doesn't play with his own chips, and the defendant inevitably loses some of his own.

One Lawsuit Can Wipe You Out

More distressing still, is that even when you can endure the odds of being sued and the uncertainty of whether you will win or lose, you may be hit with a devastating judgment. You can't predict what you can lose in a lawsuit. A plaintiff who wins a few dollars in actual damages may pocket millions more in punitive damages. Any buyer of a defective $20 product can turn it into a class action that can cost the manufacturer millions or billions. One lawsuit can start an avalanche.

> One lawsuit can start an avalanche. Enough nuisance lawsuits can topple the most powerful business or wealthiest family.

Enough nuisance lawsuits can topple the most powerful business or wealthiest family. We have seen this with litigation against tobacco, pharmaceuticals, asbestos and countless other industries that are no longer in business only because they fell victim to a barrage of lawsuits.

This uncertainty of outcome explains why nine out of ten lawsuits are settled. What defendant can go to trial confident of victory? What defendant can foresee what they will lose? What defendant can afford the exorbitant legal fees to get answers to these questions?

So plaintiffs' lawyers effectively use the lawsuit as their weapon to extort a whopping settlement. The economics are always with the plaintiffs. The defendant is coerced to pay 'go away' money, because the defendant who has exposed wealth simply has too much to lose by gambling in court.

Of course, a lawsuit can involve more than money. A lawsuit can attack you personally, particularly when it alleges fraud, racketeering, conspiracy or some other moral lapse. Or a lawsuit may unjustifiably attack your professional competence. Ask a doctor how it feels to be characterized in a malpractice lawsuit as 'negligent, incompetent or reckless.'

I have a leading New York thoracic surgeon as a client. He was sued twice in his 30-year career and will tell you, "You know you did nothing wrong, yet you begin to question your competence. Inevitably your self-confidence and self-esteem drops a few notches." Sometimes it's not about money – it's about your reputation.

Every lawsuit creates some stress and uneasiness. However, a major lawsuit can disrupt your social relationships, cloud your thoughts, dampen your enthusiasm and cause you that nagging sense of insecurity. The essence of the lawsuit was perhaps best voiced by the *Tort Informer:* "The law provides incredible financial incentives to seek out a victim with deep pockets, drag him into court, ruin his reputation, wear him down with endless discovery demands, pay a fortune to defend himself and then extort a settlement. This is not justice in any sense of the word."

Develop the Survivor Mentality

Of course, not every lawsuit is frivolous. You *should* be sued if you breach a lease, default on a loan, negligently rear-end another car or are clearly in the wrong. A plaintiff then has every right to legal recourse.

But should a claim's legitimacy give you any less reason to protect yourself? I don't think so. It's not whether a lawsuit against you is justified, but whether you can afford to lose. One bonafide lawsuit can still wipe you out. That's why you need a financial self-defense plan regardless of the lawsuit. Nor will you be sued only when you do something wrong. You can as quickly be sued when you do everything right.

You may be uncomfortable with the objectives of asset protection. Some folks are. They view asset protection as illegal or immoral, or a way to cheat creditors of their rightful due. But they would be wrong. People who want protection aren't crooks or immoral. They have a strong survival instinct and are only taking advantage of the laws that were intended to protect against life's financial uncertainties and risks.

Asset protection – properly practiced – is certainly not illegal. Of course you cannot commit illegal acts such as perjury, violate bankruptcy laws or fraudulently conceal assets from creditors; and a good asset protection plan neither encourages nor permits these or other illegal acts. Your asset protection plan must be fully compliant with every law. This is basic to sound planning.

> An asset protection plan must be fully compliant with every law.

Do you consider it *ethically* improper to shelter your assets from those who assert a rightful claim? Then consider asset protection as financial self-defense to not only combat frivolous and harassing lawsuits, but also to make you a less likely lawsuit target. You can then live your life more confident that your financial security can't be easily stripped away.

Whatever your ethical or moral concerns about protecting your assets against lawsuits, try this approach: Protect your assets. If you are rightfully sued, then negotiate a fair settlement or pay the claim. When your assets are protected, you have that option. When your assets are exposed, you have no option.

Four Wealth-Destroying Myths

You may think that your wealth is safe – or that you don't need asset protection. If so, you probably deluded yourself with one of the common myths:

Myth #1: "I won't get sued. I'm too careful."
I repeat: You don't have to do anything wrong to get sued. Nevertheless, you may insist, "I have never been sued before and I can't see why I would get sued now."

One lady attending one of my *Wealthsaver* seminars explained her apathy toward asset protection: "I'm a schoolteacher. What legal problems can a schoolteacher have?" True, she may never be sued as a schoolteacher, yet only a year later she was sued for a million plus dollars for negligently handling her mother's estate.

> **Everyone is a potential lawsuit target.**

There are many unforeseeable reasons one gets sued today. A lawsuit need not relate to your work. And no matter how cautious or careful you are, you can only do so much to reduce the odds that you will get sued. It's not only the doctors, real estate developers and business owners. *Everyone* is a potential lawsuit target.

To further prove the point, at this same California *Wealthsaver* seminar, a young man asked, "Dr. Goldstein, what tips do you have to avoid liability?"

I facetiously replied, "Don't get out of bed in the morning."

The young man retorted, "I tried that and got sued for paternity."

That reply brought laughter from all of us. Nevertheless, it goes to show you that no matter how you live your life or what you do for a living, there is ample opportunity to get into legal trouble. So *who* is safe?

Nobody! Professionals, of course, are the most probable lawsuit targets. When a surgery fails, a trial is lost or an investment sours, the patient, client or investor concludes that the professional is to blame. Unfavorable outcomes translate into 'sue the professional'. These plaintiffs 'walk the Yellow Pages' for a lawyer ready and willing to take the case. Others are also high on the lawsuit hit list: Parents of teenage drivers, commercial real estate owners, small business owners, accountants and other business advisors, architects and engineers, corporate officers and directors, directors of charitable organizations, police officers, celebrities, sports figures and the conspicuously wealthy. In actuality, it's not so much what you do for a living as what you own – and whether it is exposed – that determines your vulnerability.

The proverbial little old lady in tennis shoes can also get sued. One 83 year old great grandmother met with me after she accidentally hit the gas rather than the brake and slammed her Lexus through a K-Mart storefront and seriously injured several shoppers. She will be sued for considerably more than her insurance coverage. On the brighter side, this will be her first lawsuit in 83 years. We all run out of luck...*eventually*!

Myth #2: "I don't need asset protection. I don't have enough assets to protect."
And how many times have I heard this line?

How would you feel if you lost what few assets you *do* own? I was talking to a young man about asset protection and he assured me that he was too poor to worry about lawsuits or asset protection. His entire net worth consisted of his $15,000 car and $10,000 in savings. $25,000 is modest wealth.

I asked, "How long did it take you to earn those few assets?"

"About five years," he replied. "I'm a landscape worker and don't earn much."

"How would you feel if someone seized your car and bank account?"

"Devastated."

My business as an asset protection lawyer has taught me that wealth is relative.

If you have any assets, you need protection.

It is not only the rich and affluent who need asset protection. If you have *any* assets, you need protection.

> **You must protect whatever assets are important to you.**

While traveling to give another *Wealthsaver* seminar, I passed through New York's LaGuardia airport and got a shoe shine. The affable bootblack engaged me in conversation and asked what brought me to town. I told him that I was to give an asset protection seminar and he told me about his own financial problems. He was being sued for $100,000 on a bank loan he guaranteed for his son. He then explained that he owned only his Bronx home with a $100,000 equity. To some people, $100,000 is hardly serious wealth. While they would hate to lose it, such a loss wouldn't hurt their lifestyle. But this $100,000 represented this man's entire fortune. How many more shoes must this fellow shine to replace his $100,000 nest egg?

I get calls from people from throughout the country who have creditor or lawsuit problems. Many of these callers have only a few dollars in the bank, a small home equity or perhaps a few investments. But whatever *their* assets, it is precious to *them*. Protecting their few assets is as important to them as protecting a millionaire's millions. You must treat your wealth accordingly and protect whatever assets are important to *you*.

Myth #3: "I don't need protection. I'm insured."

Here's another fallacy. You buy a liability policy and say, "That's it, I'm covered. If I'm sued, my insurance will take care of it."

I can give you many reasons why your liability insurance can never be a complete substitute for asset protection. You may not realize that liability insurance fully covers only about one in three lawsuits. So how do you shelter yourself from the two out of three lawsuits that won't be covered by insurance? Consider the possibilities: You get sued for breach of contract, default on a loan or a family dispute. Think about the thousands of *uninsured* claims that you can encounter. The possibilities are endless.

One physician friend spent years telling me that he didn't need lawsuit protection beyond his five million dollar malpractice policy. You can bet he wished that he had better protected himself after an employee sued him for two million dollars for sexual harassment. And his malpractice insurance didn't shelter his substantial net worth from Medicare's demands that he repay millions that he allegedly overbilled.

Even when a claim is insured, will your insurance *fully* cover the claim? A million-dollar liability policy doesn't mean much when you're sued for two million. And given today's unpredictable and ludicrous jury awards, who can foresee a judgment that they will someday be forced to pay. You will then discover that liability insurance is never your complete answer.

The countless policy exclusions and inevitable loopholes that let your insurance company deny coverage are another issue.

> **Buy whatever liability insurance you can afford, but consider insurance only a starting point.**

Your insurance company won't always defend a claim against you – even when you think your claim is covered. Why else are so many 'bad faith' claims now pending by insureds against their recalcitrant insurance companies?

You can't even be certain that your insurance company will be in business when you need them. I am now trying to protect the assets of scores of physicians in Ohio, New Jersey and several other states now that their insurance company filed bankruptcy. These doctors *thought* that they were protected, but now they're exposed with little or no coverage. Many are presently defending against lawsuits.

I'm not against liability insurance. I advise my clients to buy liability insurance because insurance is a smart first step for asset protection. Buy whatever liability insurance you can afford – but consider insurance *only* your starting point. Liability insurance can't replace a good asset protection plan which can protect you against *any* type or size claim. Only asset protection can give you *complete* financial safety.

Myth #4: "Asset protection is too costly. I can't afford it."
How can protecting your assets be too costly? It's a vital *investment*. The average family can usually build strong protection for no more than they would spend on their vacation. We have sheltered large fortunes for not much more. And you can take many protective steps that would cost you *absolutely nothing*!

I had one short sighted cardiologist complain to me that he didn't have the spare cash to set up the few entities that I recommended to safeguard his three million net worth. He thought my proposed $15,000 legal fee was too costly. Yet this doctor spends $65,000 a year for malpractice insurance which protects him only against malpractice claims – and only for one million dollars. Next year, the good doctor will pay another $65,000 (though his premiums will probably increase) for the same limited protection. In comparison, I could give this physician *complete* protection against *any* lawsuit or any other financial threat – for an *unlimited* amount – and for the *rest of his life,* for less than one-fourth of what he pays each year for his malpractice insurance. So which is the better deal…insurance or asset protection? That's why I say asset protection isn't an expense. It's an investment – a *great* investment!

Tip-Toe Through The Minefield

A lawsuit is, of course, only one of several ways to lose your wealth. It's certainly not the only path to financial ruin. Life is a financial minefield. No matter how carefully you tread, there's danger with every step.

For example, divorce is one of life's most devastating forms of lawsuit, yet how many people think about divorce as a 'lawsuit'. You can be happily married today; still the statistics are that you will someday divorce. And as unlikely as it may seem now, you may go through several divorces.

What would you lose if you divorce? How can you better prepare yourself financially for your next marriage? Your next divorce?

Bankruptcy and creditor problems plague America. What does it matter whether one litigant sues you for $100,000 or twenty sue you for $5,000 each? Your assets are still in jeopardy for $100,000. That's why you must also protect yourself against creditor claims and the possibility that some day you may be bankrupt.

You can legally and safely fortify your assets so you would lose few or no assets if you do someday file bankruptcy.

Here, too, we have dismal statistics. Two million Americans will go bankrupt next year. Most will lose everything they own. How many of these people could foresee their financial problems? How many had the time to protect themselves once they ran into financial difficulty?

It happens. You lose your job. You run up unexpected medical bills. You get into a bad business deal. Who can be certain they won't have financial problems?

Paul, one of my poker pals can tell you his story which illustrates the vagaries of life. For years, Paul ran a successful South Florida construction company. Though he was worth several million, he never gave much thought to asset protection. Paul had plenty of liability insurance and assumed that he was well-protected until a big project turned bad. When his company failed, he ended up personally owing his bank six million dollars. Paul's personal bankruptcy cost him nearly four million dollars – nearly *everything* he owned. Through advance planning, we could have saved Paul's *entire* net worth! I constantly hear similar tragic stories. Paul was *one* of last year's statistics. You may be one next year.

You know how easy it is to get into trouble with the IRS. Tax problems too are increasingly common. Millions of taxpayers get clobbered each year with huge tax bills. Owe the IRS and you will see how quickly your assets

> **Four million Americans are audited annually. Most are clobbered by huge tax bills. When you owe the IRS you will see how quickly assets will vanish.**

can vanish. Did you know that the IRS is now chasing twenty million Americans who owe $10,000 or more? What will these tax delinquents lose? What would *you* lose if the tax collector knocks on *your* door?

The financial minefield is indeed endless. Law enforcement seizures are a new but equally fast growing threat. Federal and local enforcement agencies seize billions in cash and property each year. And they can grab *your* assets without even a trial or advance notice. Commit a minor drug violation or some other minor infraction, and watch your assets summarily auctioned by the police.

These are but a few of the many dangers. There are plenty of others. The bottom line: You must protectively plan if you are to have a fighting chance to keep your assets. Think defensively. Think realistically: Ask *when* – not *whether* – you will encounter financial danger. Since you don't know the answer, be prepared!

Wealthsaver Tips

1. Face the reality that you can face a wealth-destroying crisis from any direction. Only asset protection can make you invulnerable.

2. Asset protection is legal and ethical. It's also smart.

3. Asset protection isn't only for the wealthy. It's for anyone with *any* assets worth protecting.

4. Liability insurance is never a complete solution. It will protect you in only one in three cases.

5. *Nobody* is safe from the lawsuit epidemic. *Anyone* can get sued for *anything*…at *anytime*.

6. Protect what you own as vigorously as you worked for it.

7. A lawsuit is only one financial threat. Divorce, bankruptcy, taxes and hundreds of other hazards endanger your wealth.

8. Don't procrastinate. You don't know when you may get sued. Don't wait until it's *too* late.

TWO

Building Your Financial Fortress

Whatever did happen to John and Millie Mathews? The bad news is that the Mathews lost their case. After several years of tumultuous litigation, John's ex-partner won a $700,000 judgment. With interest and costs, John ended up owing his ex-partner over $850,000.

The good news is that after several months of wrangling, John settled his case for a relatively paltry $45,000 – this small sum notwithstanding that John's and Millie's net worth was over $3 million.

How did we get this great outcome for the Mathews? The answer is simple. The Mathews had foresight. The Mathews came to us some years earlier to shelter their net worth. We created for them what I call *untouchable* wealth.

John can share his experience.

"I underwent several tough months as my ex-partner's lawyer tried every way imaginable to collect on the judgment. But he always came up empty. Everything I owned was fully mortgaged or protectively titled. All I had exposed was a few thousand dollars – equity in my two cars. I was more than lucky. Before I started my business I anticipated that I might one day become a lawsuit target. I then decided to protect myself. If I hadn't thought defensively at the time, I would now be $850,000 poorer."

Asset protection can indeed make the difference between whether you keep your wealth and preserve your financial security or lose what you have worked your lifetime to amass.

> "That which depends on me, I can do; that which depends on the enemy cannot be certain." That is the underlying philosophy behind asset protection.

Of course, the goal of protecting one's assets from life's inevitable risks and dangers is certainly not new. Raiders on horseback once pillaged and plundered treasure while brandishing menacing swords and lancets. The only defense was a secure fortress. That era is long gone, but little has changed. Nowadays the raiders are the lawyers who storm the courthouse with their Mercedes and Bentleys. With their Mont Blanc pens drawn, they are the new ransackers of our wealth. The only way to defend yourself against these legal knaves is to build the strongest possible fortress – your very own *financial* fortress.

A famous Chinese philosopher once commented, "That which depends on me, I can do; that which depends on the enemy cannot be certain." That is the underlying philosophy behind asset protection. You too must follow this tactical maxim if you are to become legally invincible and able to withstand the inevitable assaults on your wealth.

Create Your Own Untouchable Wealth

John and Millie Mathews are not the only folks who have effectively protected themselves by creating untouchable wealth. I have scores of affluent clients who have either completely sidestepped potentially devastating lawsuits or have settled lawsuits for mere pennies. They stayed safe only because they had timely and intelligently protected everything they owned: their home…savings…investments…real estate…business…cars…retirement accounts…etc. They had nothing exposed to their adversaries.

Of course, successful wealth protection doesn't just happen. Whether you can effectively blockade litigants and creditors from grabbing *your* assets depends on a lot of 'ifs'.

You can be fully protected only...

- *if* you protect yourself *before* trouble strikes.

- *if* you use the right strategies and tools for your particular situation.

- *if* you have the professional advisor with the necessary skills to build your best financial fortress.

- *if* you as enthusiastically *shelter* your wealth as you *generated* your wealth.

This chapter will show you the fundamentals of asset protection. In later chapters I will explain the specific firewalls in greater detail, and you'll see how to apply each tool in different ways and to various situations.

A 1, 2, 3 Overview

Asset protection – in simple terms – is a strategy to title your savings, property, business and other assets to shield them from lawsuits and other claims. In essence, asset protection prevents your adversaries from seizing your wealth.

Asset protection's goal to protect your assets from litigants and creditors might seem apparent, but there is more to the definition.

John Mathews views asset protection differently. "Asset protection – at least in my case – was a safety net. It doesn't guarantee that you won't get sued or run into other financial calamities; but if you do, you will lose few, if any assets. Without it you're in 'free-fall'. You're vulnerable and exposed."

> **You must first anticipate financial trouble and accept your vulnerability. Only then will you take asset protection seriously.**

Until recently we had not heard much about asset protection because only America's wealthiest families were traditionally concerned about shielding their wealth. They were the 'deep pocket' defendants who were most frequently sued only because they had significant wealth. The Rockefellers, Kennedys and other social elites of past eras have long relied upon partnerships, trusts, family corporations and a variety of other protective entities to privatize and lawsuit-proof their holdings; however, they seldom referred to their financial maneuvers as 'asset protection'. Undoubtedly, they also planned for tax avoidance and estate planning – or in their case, 'dynasty planning'.

Of course, America's super-rich are no longer the only lawsuit targets. Every middle-income American – such as the Mathews – has the same need to protect their wealth. With the fast-growing lawsuit threat, many more lawyers are protecting their clients, as they should. Unfortunately, too few attorneys emphasize this, and this should not be surprising. Few law schools teach asset protection as a formal course (they too busily teach their budding lawyers how to sue). Only recently have professional seminars and books on the subject come on the scene. John Mathews observed, "Your lawyer may fight like hell to defend you against a lawsuit, but your lawyer probably won't tell you to shelter yourself in the event they lose your lawsuit. A lawyer who walks the litigation tight-rope without giving their client an asset protection safety net, has a client who pays the price when they stumble." John, of course, is absolutely right.

> Learn! Read other books about asset protection. Attend asset protection seminars sponsored by professional associations. You can't be a bystander on the mission of ensuring your financial security.

Why You Need Untouchable Wealth

The ultimate goal of asset protection is to give you and your family lifetime security. You want the comfort that is only yours when you know that you can't lose what you own – regardless of the financial or legal problems that you may someday face. But a good asset protection plan will help you achieve other important objectives as well:

1. Discourage lawsuits

The first important objective of asset protection is to *discourage* lawsuits against you. And you can only discourage lawsuits when you can convince a potential plaintiff that they can't seize your wealth – even if they sue you and win.

By discouraging lawsuits, your asset protection plan simultaneously shields you from the devastating costs of defending against lawsuits. It is far better to discourage a lawsuit than defend against the lawsuit and win. Once you are sued, you will spend plenty of money, time and effort to 'win.' Prevent even one lawsuit and you pay for your asset protection many times over.

Litigation has its economics. Before a potential plaintiff sues, the plaintiff's lawyer will evaluate the case economics. They weigh the costs of suing you against the odds of *winning* and their likely recovery based on your *exposed* assets. In other words – *are you worth suing?*

Few prospective plaintiffs will sue if they doubt they can recover more than they will spend in the process. Lawyers don't spend time on unproductive cases. But even then you may get sued because lawyers know that even a weak lawsuit has some 'settlement value'. And they're usually right. You will probably pay something to make a lawsuit against you disappear. Or you may settle because

> Before a potential plaintiff sues, the plaintiff's lawyer will evaluate the case economics. They weigh the costs of suing you against the odds of winning and their likely recovery based on your exposed assets.

of privacy concerns or want to avoid legal costs. *Every* case has a nuisance value. You may dislike lawyers and litigants because of this extortion, yet it is reality. That's how our legal system works.

Even when you have solid asset protection, someone may sue you 'vindictively'. They have a score to settle. There are other reasons why you may get sued. For instance, you may be a peripheral defendant in a lawsuit. Your wealth – and its vulnerability – won't be initially checked by the plaintiff because you are only one of several or many defendants. It's only when you are the primary lawsuit target that your assets – and your ability to pay a sizeable judgment – will become a key factor in the lawsuit decision.

> It is not whether or not you have assets that will determine whether you get sued; it's whether your assets are exposed. Be prepared to convince a prospective plaintiff that your financial fortress is impregnable.

In sum, it is not whether or not you have assets that will determine whether you get sued; it's whether your assets are *exposed*. If you want to avoid lawsuits, be prepared to convince a prospective plaintiff that *your* financial fortress is *impregnable*.

2. Negotiate a favorable settlement

So you are sued. If you have good asset protection you are in a far stronger position to negotiate a fast, inexpensive settlement. You can negotiate from that position of strength only when your opponent *knows* that you have nothing to lose and they have little or nothing to gain from their lawsuit. Think about it another way: The lawsuit is a plaintiff's way to extort settlement. Asset protection is your equalizer – how you level the playing field.

A plaintiff may not know that you're financially shielded until after you are sued and the attorneys open a dialogue. It is then that a good defense lawyer will sell the proposition that you are judgment-proof and that the plaintiff best settle their case for those few paltry dollars. Your goal is always to settle early so you avoid a lengthy, time consuming and costly court battle.

Few plaintiffs, of course, blindly accept a defendant's representation that they are indeed judgment-proof. To favorably settle their case, they will want financial affidavits or otherwise seek to verify that you are, in fact, uncollectible.

There is a psychology to winning a favorable settlement. We don't use an 'in-your-face' approach when we discuss our client's protection. We try to present the financial realities that our client has no exposed assets with tact and subtlety. But whatever the style of presentation, you must quickly convince the plaintiff that their chance to recover anything significant is remote. Only then will you make your lawsuit disappear quickly and inexpensively.

3. Reduce insurance costs

A good asset protection plan can also save you money on liability insurance. For example, I seldom promote asset protection as a substitute for liability insurance, but insurance can be too costly for high-risk professionals and business owners. Asset protection can supplement their insurance or be a substitute.

Buy whatever liability insurance you can afford. Insurance can be costly (and yes, it does attract lawsuits); nevertheless, insurance is invaluable in risk management programs. If you can afford insurance, it should be

> You must quickly convince the plaintiff that their chance to recover anything significant is remote. Only then will you make your lawsuit disappear quickly and inexpensively.

your primary defensive weapon. Asset protection would be your secondary safeguard. Your strategy is then to convince the plaintiff to settle within the policy limits and forego further claims against you. You can more readily achieve this only when your assets are insulated.

4. Improved financial planning

A good asset protection plan can also help you save estate and income taxes, improve your estate plan and, perhaps even enhance your investments. Asset protection is an absolutely essential component to any financial plan.

The need for asset protection often forces people to do their estate and tax planning.

5. Become judgment-proof

Of course, the ultimate purpose of asset protection is to *safeguard* your wealth under a worst-case scenario – you are sued and lose. And the odds are that you *will* someday be sued. That's when you need protected assets. This is when your asset protection plan faces its test.

This doesn't suggest that by becoming judgment-proof you can cavalierly dismiss the inevitable problems when you have a judgment against you. A plaintiff's lawyer can resourcefully pursue even the best protected defendant. A determined plaintiff may endlessly attempt to seize your assets and the plaintiff can drag you through the courts to find your assets. Nor can you protect every last asset. 'Loose change' assets will for one reason or another become exposed to your creditor.

> **Remember, asset protection must not only protect assets, but also discourage others from pursuing them.**

More frequently, you will benefit from your asset protection plan only after the plaintiff wins a judgment and has exhausted all collection remedies. Some plaintiffs won't settle until then – notwithstanding earlier assurances that you are judgment-proof.

Even with formidable asset protection, *every* case has some settlement value. You won't want an outstanding judgment hanging over your head for twenty or more years. A plaintiff may force you into bankruptcy. And you can't expect a judgment against you to enhance your credit rating.

The success of your asset protection plan then is not whether you will avoid paying *something* if you are sued. You probably will pay '*something*' to make your case go away. You don't want to lose *significant* assets. When we review a case, we measure our success with one question: "What more could we have done to get a better outcome?" When we have done everything possible, we have passed the litmus test.

Three Pillars of Protection

Let's start with the basics. How *can* you protect your assets? For what is to some a complex mystery boils down to three basic strategies or what I call 'The Three Pillars of Protection.'

1. Own exempt assets. The first and simplest strategy is to own as many assets as possible that have either federal or state statutory protection from lawsuits and creditors. These are *exempt* assets. You would conversely own few (or no assets) that are not exempt or self-protected. You will see this strategy in Chapter 5.

2. Title your assets to one or more protective entities. When you title your assets to one or more protective entities, you will – in one way or another – prevent your judgment creditor from seizing those assets. We explore the numerous protective entities and arrangements in Chapters 6 through 11.

3. Encumber or equity-strip your assets to reduce your assets economic value to your creditor. In sum, fully mortgage your exposed assets and protect the loan proceeds. I more fully cover this in Chapter 12.

It's that simple!

Every important strategy in this book (and that I use to judgment-proof my clients) follows one or more of these three basic strategies – or protective pillars.

But these are only the *fundamental* legal concepts. There is more.

Eight Firewalls

Within these three 'protective' pillars are eight specific firewalls that we frequently use in our planning. Each 'firewall', in its own way insulates assets from creditors. These eight essential firewalls are:

1. Federal and state exemptions (Chapter 5)

2. Co-ownerships (Chapter 6)

3. Corporations (Chapter 7)

4. Limited partnerships (Chapter 8)

5. Limited liability companies (Chapter 9)

6. Domestic trusts (Chapter 10)

7. Offshore entities (Chapter 11)

8. Debt-shields (Chapter 12)

Each firewall has its own unique characteristics; strengths and weaknesses, advantages and disadvantages, applications and instances where they would not be used. Think about these firewalls as you would colors on an artist's palette: Colors differ and some may be more popular than others, however, each is necessary for artistic perfection. That perfect portrait needs their right application. Similarly, only an experienced asset protection attorney can expertly blend these various firewalls into your *ideal* plan.

Countless Wealthsaver Opportunities

Not every asset protection firewall can be so neatly categorized.

There are literally hundreds – or thousands – of variations on the theme, and there are numerous other protective entities that we could discuss. But most entities and strategies – at least conceptually – fall within one of these eight firewall categories. For example, limited liability partnerships and limited liability limited partnerships are variations on limited partnerships and limited liability companies. The professional limited liability company (PLLC's) is another variation.

Nor does every possible firewall neatly fall within one of these eight categories. For example, you may use exposed cash to buy a deferred annuity that will create a future income stream for you. While your future annuity payment may be claimed by creditors, what is it worth to a creditor who must wait years to collect?

Nor can we discuss *every* possible firewall. *So Sue Me!* isn't a technical treatise. I only want to present the more common strategies. Read the asset protection texts that I have written for lawyers and you'll find advanced methodologies and far more sophisticated legal and financial strategies. These invariably complex arrangements can oftentimes provide financial as well as protective benefits. Moreover, asset protection is not static. Asset protection planners are constantly inventing newer strategies and tactics to perfect the science, and, as diligently, collection lawyers try to find ways to pierce these new strategies. Our strategies, oftentimes, are more financial than legal. For example, our plan may employ a number of structured financial products (SFPs) with complex arbitrage arrangements to effectively shift wealth between spouses with different liability exposures. Or we may recommend an insurance-based product to shield a client's wealth.

To counter-balance complex plans, are protective maneuvers that are quite simple – even obvious. For example, you may use exposed cash to prepay certain expenses or to repay a favored creditor. Common sense can often give you your solution when you need to protect modest assets.

Layer Your Firewalls

A good asset protection plan won't necessarily use only one firewall to protect a particular asset. No matter how safe or defensible the particular firewall, there's always *some* possibility that a creditor can pierce it. That's why we frequently 'layer' our protection and use multiple firewalls. This is the 'belt and suspenders' approach to protection. If one firewall fails, others are in position behind it. We always want the opportunity to impose more firewalls if they become necessary.

The ever-present asset protection challenge is to know not only *which* firewalls to use in a given case, but *when* to interpose additional firewalls with an advancing creditor threat. The goal is to stay two steps ahead of a creditor in hot pursuit.

Your asset protection plan may evolve in stages. You would start with a *preventative* plan and advance to a *crisis* plan– if and when it becomes necessary.

If you complete your plan *before* you incur liability, you should need only a good preventative plan or a basic first level of protection. This will not necessarily be your final plan if you are later sued because you may then need a crisis plan to give you maximum safety against that particular threat. We would then add whatever firewalls would be most protective in your specific situation to make you as judgment-proof as possible *before* you walk into the courtroom. This crisis plan probably won't be the same as your preventative plan.

A crisis protection plan is usually more costly and complex than a basic plan. That's one reason we layer firewalls only *after* a legal threat arises. Until we have a specific legal threat to respond to, we cannot prescribe your one best defensive position. How we protect you is greatly influenced by the amount and nature of the claim, the dynamics of the case, what the creditor will likely do to seize your assets should he win a judgment and many other factors that we will soon discuss.

Nevertheless, to start, you want a cost-efficient and simple basic plan. Not everyone gets sued. And not every lawsuit is wealth-threatening. A serious lawsuit may be covered by your insurance. Or the case may be quickly and favorably settled. Layering firewalls would then only proceed in lockstep with the threat. To overbuild your plan prematurely causes you to lose flexibility and burden yourself with needless cost and complexity.

Inevitably, your plan must give you the greatest possible level of safety. But no plan is 100 percent guaranteed. If you don't have a present legal problem (or only a possible legal problem), then you would want to know what your ultimate plan would be if it later becomes necessary to implement. My clients who are in litigation want to know how they will get maximum safety. They must know which firewalls we will use, when they would be added and how and why each firewall will work to insulate their assets. Only when they fully understand their ultimate 'game plan' can they sleep soundly.

When you layer or combine firewalls, you exponentially strengthen your final plan. Layering works in asset protection the same way a plywood panel is substantially stronger than the sum of its component layers. To illustrate, an extreme case may combine a limited partnership, offshore trust, Nevis LLC and a foreign annuity into one integrated plan. This interposes a formidable four-layer firewall barrier that should stop *any* creditor. There are

> When you layer or combine firewalls, you exponentially strengthen your final plan.

countless layering possibilities. They create what we asset protection planners call a '*defense-in-depth*'.

The Diversification Strategy

You would also deploy your assets into different protective baskets (layered entities). This too is axiomatic to sound planning – never put all your eggs into one basket. Force your creditor to chase assets dispersed in several different directions and which are protected by different entities. You then severely handicap your creditor. Even if the creditor recovers assets from 'one basket', whatever wealth you have sheltered in your other 'baskets' would remain safe.

Diversification is particularly important if you must protect significant wealth. For example, to protect ten million dollars or more, we would deploy it into several separate protective baskets – which may be quite dissimilar to each other.

By combining layering (or 'defense-in-depth') with divers-ification, we can produce an exceptionally strong shield and an insurmountable obstacle to any creditor.

Counteroffensive Strategies

Remember the old axiom – "The best defense is a good offense." This applies to asset protection as well as other conflicts.

There are a number of ways to impose liability on a creditor who is chasing your assets. For instance, a creditor who gets a charging order against your limited partnership or LLC interest might incur your tax liability. Or a creditor who sues your Nevis LLC or trust may be required to pay a $25,000 bond. These are only two of a number of liabilities that you can impose on a creditor.

Quills work for a porcupine. You want your own 'quills' when a predator pursues *you*.

These counteroffensive capabilities seldom dictate a particular strategy, still, counteroffensive features may influence our choice of firewall. Whenever possible, we want the creditor to have some 'downside' or risk by pursuing our client's wealth. A creditor who is uncertain about what he can recover from you, must be made to realize what he can *lose*.

Customize Your Best Plan

What should be apparent to you is that there is no 'one right firewall', 'one right strategy' or 'one right plan'. You must customize your plan to your specific situation.

There is no 'one-size-fits-all' plan, and we have a problem with 'so-called' asset protection planners – and gullible clients – who peddle or seek that 'one quick fix' or 'magic bullet' for protection.

For example, some planners push Nevada corporations as 'everybody's' asset protection answer. Others recommend only offshore trusts or limited partnerships. These are good firewalls – *sometimes*. But are they *your* right firewall?

Your asset protection planner must give you the widest range of firewalls, because each firewall is only another tool in the planner's toolbox. Since no one firewall is *everybody's* lawsuit-proofing answer, you need a planner who can *expertly* use every protective tool.

For instance, your planner may not employ offshore and domestic (US-based) protective strategies. But, if you have a high net worth, you may need *both* a domestic and offshore plan. And your planner must skillfully provide both. Not every planner has this dual capability.

Other planners protect only specific assets – usually for self-serving reasons. That's how the planner makes money. For example, insurance professionals sometimes pose as asset protection specialists to sell accounts receivable factoring programs to protect this one asset from lawsuits. These programs are usually promoted at seminars targeted to doctors and small business owners. The accounts receivable finances a life insurance policy for which the planner earns a commission. This arrangement may or may not make sense for a particular client, but even when it is a good plan to shelter receivables, how will it protect *other* assets?

The point is that your planner must be prepared to implement the complete arsenal of protective firewalls. Anything less reduces your options and your protection. To customize *your* right plan, your planner must also consider a number of other important factors that will be unique to you and your situation:

- your state laws

- the specific assets you must protect – and their value

- what liability (if any) you need protection against

- whether you are in the preventative or crisis planning stage

- your financial (estate planning, investment and tax) situation

- the strategies that you would be most comfortable adopting

- costs

- your personal situation (age, marital status, etc.).

Only when you expertly blend these various considerations can you customize your plan. Even then it is only your best plan at that *point in time* and against that specific danger.

Update Your Protection

Good asset protection is also a continuous process. You may rush to protect yourself once you are sued or anticipate a lawsuit; however, once the threat passes, your plan may fall into disuse. That commonly happens. But that mistake can be costly.

Your asset protection plan is only your *best* plan when it was designed. Time will change your finances, obligations and personal situations. The laws, available strategies and possible firewalls will also change. These changes may alter your asset protection plan.

That's why asset protection planning must be a continuous process. Review your plan annually, and more frequently with a major event – windfall inheritance, threatened lawsuit, relocation to another state, family change, etc.

Yes, it involves time, cost and effort to enjoy lifelong protection. But that's a small price. If you let your protection erode because it's no longer important to you, you again become vulnerable. That's not what you want. It's smarter to stay safe and secure.

Wealthsaver Tips

1. Asset protection has three primary goals: Discourage lawsuits, settle lawsuits inexpensively and shield your assets from creditor seizure.

2. Your plan may also give you secondary benefits – lower your insurance costs and enhance your other financial goals.

3. The three broad protection strategies are 1) to own exempt assets, 2) title your assets to protective entities and 3) encumber your assets.

4. These three strategies encompass a number of specific 'firewalls'. There are also many other protective options.

5. Use multiple firewalls to maximize your protection.

6. Diversify your assets or employ multiple plans so your assets aren't in 'one basket'.

7. Impose a liability on your creditor. It strengthens your plan.

8. Customize your plan to your specific situation. Keep it updated and protective as possible.

THREE

Ten Keys To A Great Plan

A *good* plan will keep your assets safe from the lawyers. But there is a difference between a *good* asset protection plan and a *great* plan. A *great* plan will give you other benefits and it will be one that is ideal for *your* particular circumstances.

I have reviewed thousands of asset protection plans. There are an endless variety of possible plans (which explains why no two planners are likely to propose precisely the same plan); nevertheless I note that many good plans could have been *great* plans had their planners employed just a bit more thought.

A great plan will do more than give you lawsuit protection. A great plan will provide you *more* benefits at less cost and with less complexity. Unquestionably, your planner must thoroughly understand your overall financial and personal affairs as well as have a good fix on your financial objectives other than liability insulation.

Some plans have fundamental flaws. These flaws may not compromise creditor protection, but may cause adverse tax consequences, impose needless costs or complexity or disrupt other financial objectives.

So, how can you tell a *good* plan from a *great* plan? Follow what I call the *ten keys to great planning*:

Key # 1 - Protect Everything

It would seem obvious that an asset protection plan should insulate *every* important asset, however, many plans don't. These plans shelter only *some* assets. Others remain exposed.

Why does this happen? There are several reasons. You may overlook or fail to bring to your planner's attention certain assets (such as intangibles, copyrights, patents, notes receivable, claims you have against others, etc.). Or you may assume that some assets are exempt or self-protected and do nothing further to protect them. I oftentimes see unsheltered retirement accounts which a client erroneously assumed to have statutory protection. Never assume that an asset is protected. Your advisor should confirm its protection. Or you may protect only your *personal* assets but fail to shield your business or professional practice.

For full protection, you must also look forward *and* backwards. What *future* assets do you anticipate (inheritances, gifts, etc.). How can you protect *these* assets against your *future* creditors? What assets have you previously gifted or transferred that may be reclaimed by your creditor as a fraudulent transfer? We must sometimes recast questionable prior transfers to protect them against a foreseeable judgment creditor.

Your first step then is to identify *every* significant *past, present* and *future* asset that you must properly shelter. Anything less gives you only partial protection. That's not what you want. You need 100% protection.

Click **www.asgoldstein.com** for an asset worksheet to inventory your assets. Estimate the value of each asset and how it is titled (individually, tenants-by-the-entirety, joint tenants, tenants-in-common, in trust, etc.). Specify your ownership share in co-owned assets. Finally, list the liens or encumbrances against each asset to determine the equity in the asset which you must protect. Your planner will need this information.

> A financial profile that reveals exposure is critical information to any creditor.

Some planners may recommend that you leave a 'few assets' exposed so a creditor has 'something' to seize. That's foolish advice. Why give your creditor *any* asset to recover? It will only fuel their war-chest and encourage them to try to recover more. Leave out of your plan only those assets that have no value and cannot be cost-effectively protected. These same assets cannot be cost-effectively recovered by your creditor.

Key # 2 - Start With a Flexible Plan

No one plan will be effective against *every* potential claimant. Asset protection is much like football. Your best defensive line is the one that will best block a particular offensive line.

For example, to protect your assets against a routine civil lawsuit would likely require a different strategy than one we might adopt to protect you against the IRS or divorce. What we might do to protect your assets against a small nuisance lawsuit would logically bear little similarity to a plan where the government or some other powerful litigant sued you for a significant amount.

> For under $500, a creditor can obtain reasonably accurate financial profiles on most people. Forensic accounting firms involved in larger cases can trace millions in assets (wealth often deployed quite deviously and secretively).

Your plan must, first and foremost, protect you against any known or imminent threat. This is the danger that probably prompted you to seek protection in the first place.

You cannot foresee or anticipate future troubles. That's why a preventative plan will give you only your foundation or *basic* protection. We add those firewalls which would most effectively block a specific threat as it appears.

With a flexible plan you can build upon or modify the plan to meet future situations. Therefore, you must understand the limitations of your plan. This is also why you must consult your advisor whenever you are faced with a new threat.

There's also no 'standard' plaintiff. We must anticipate what a particular plaintiff is likely to do to pursue recovery. Unfortunately, we can't do this with great accuracy, and therefore, it's always best to overestimate your adversary.

You also want a flexible plan because your personal situation will change. You must then modify your plan to accommodate those changes. And because we have a constant stream of newer and more effective strategies and opportunities to protect assets, you will want to periodically upgrade your plan.

Conversely, once a legal threat passes, you may want to partially dismantle your plan back to a 'basic or foundation' plan. You may then eliminate 'firewalls' which may be costly to maintain or unnecessary against another future claimant. A *great* plan is a 'modular' plan whose component firewalls can be speedily added, deleted or changed.

Key # 3 - 100% Legal

Not many years ago, attorneys questioned the ethics and legality of asset protection. That has changed. No intelligent lawyer would today question the legality of asset protection planning and what lawyer could question its necessity?

Nevertheless, there is oftentimes that troublesome grey area between legal and illegal asset protection planning. A good planner, for example, won't rely upon secrecy or counsel you to fraudulently conceal your assets, encourage you to commit perjury, violate tax laws, money laundering, bankruptcy fraud or otherwise defraud your creditors. That's not *great* asset protection. You want *legal* protection, not questionable or patently illegal 'protective' strategies that can only get you into bigger trouble. If you question the legitimacy of a proposed plan, talk to another planner. You have too many perfectly legitimate ways to shield your wealth without resorting to questionable practices. Still, many people do wrongly equate asset protection with secrecy or concealing assets. Perhaps they are the people who mostly need to read this book.

We will talk more about these and other planning mistakes in the next chapter, but for the moment, remember that secrecy is never an effective tactic because you can't fully privatize your finances. In today's hi-tech world – aside from hiding your money in a coffee can under the oak tree – a creditor can uncover virtually any asset or financial transaction.

We may, nevertheless, incorporate secrecy into our plans. Financial privacy and a 'low profile' may discourage a plaintiff from suing you. However, a judgment creditor is entitled to honest answers about your finances.

Nor is asset protection about defrauding the IRS. Most asset protection plans are tax neutral. They will neither increase nor decrease your taxes, though certain strategies may save or defer taxes *legally*. Still,

> Remember: Once your creditor obtains the judgment, the creditor is entitled to honest answers concerning your assets. Secrecy then is no longer a protective device.

asset protection promoters may sell pure trusts, offshore entities and other products for their 'tax savings.' Question any plan that supposedly saves you taxes and have your CPA or tax attorney review the plan.

Money laundering is another problem. If you transfer funds obtained through illicit means, you can be charged with money laundering. Planners, banks and other fiduciaries involved in asset protection planning must follow strict due diligence or 'know your customer' rules. Rightly or wrongly, the government imposes this responsibility on us. You need a clean background, proper identification and several reference letters to retain a reputable planner, particularly with offshore asset protection planning. If your planner doesn't do a background check on you, it tells you something about your planner.

Key # 4 - Simpler is Better

Some planners see complexity as the hallmark of a great plan. I don't agree. Simplicity is usually better.

Overplanning is a chronic planning error. While you may want to layer as many protective firewalls as possible to stop a creditor, you can frequently get the same or superior protection with a less complex plan. A simpler plan may not only give you the same protection, but it will certainly save you legal fees. More importantly, a simpler plan will make it easier for you and your advisors to understand your plan. A simpler plan is also less likely to fall into disuse than a complex plan. A complex plan will also cost you higher annual maintenance costs which may prompt its disuse once the legal threat passes.

That's why I suggest that you start with a basic plan and 'layer' your plan on an 'as need' basis. Once the legal threat against you vanishes, you may disassemble your plan back to a basic plan.

There are many simple ways to protect assets. One example, is to convert non-exempt assets into exempt assets. Another is to debt-shield or encumber your assets. Other highly-effective simple strategies can be implemented at minimum or no cost.

Your goal is *not* to trade safety for simplicity. Go for simplicity only when a more complex plan will give you comparable protection. Any marginal protection that you would gain from a more complex plan must certainly exceed its marginal cost.

For example, I have hundreds of Florida clients. I have their wealth sheltered chiefly – if not entirely – by Florida's generous exemption laws. These clients don't need a more complex plan. It is also sometimes easier to 'sell' a simpler plan to a creditor's attorney who well understands that a Florida home is untouchable. Period. On the other hand, a complex plan may encourage the creditor's counsel to suspect that your plan is no stronger than its weakest link – and that the lawyer can find and break that link.

Above all, you must understand your plan. Regardless of whether it's simple or complex, your advisor must explain to you the function of each firewall and how the firewalls fit together. If *you* don't understand your plan, it's either too complex or your advisor is a poor educator. Either can be problematic.

Key # 5 - Keep it Cost-Effective

Cost is as important to you as it is to every client. You want to spend as few dollars as possible on your plan. Though I refer to asset protection as an 'investment', who wants to spend more than what is absolutely necessary to get good protection? Economy and simplicity are twin goals.

While you shouldn't spend more than is absolutely necessary for good protection, you don't want false economy and design a faulty plan that can cost you your assets.

Throughout this book you will see many low cost alternatives to more expensive structures and strategies. For example, the Nevis LLC (see Chapter 11) can provide superior protection when matched against the far more costly offshore trust. Judgment-proofing techniques (exemptions, tenancy-by-the-entireties, etc.) may cost you little or nothing.

How much you spend, of course, will depend on your plan and your planner. Other variables can also affect costs.

You may comparison shop planners, but can you accurately compare? For example, you may find an offshore incorporation service that could set up your foreign entity for less than what an asset protection attorney would charge you, but would the offshore service firm offer the same protective features? Are you simply buying an 'entity' or do you need legal advice concerning the proper use of the entity – or whether this is your *right* entity? And is your offshore provider knowledgeable about asset protection? You see the point. You cannot compare apples and oranges.

The low price provider is often more costly. You can't simply buy 'entities'. You must buy the expertise to know *which* structures and strategies can give you *your* best plan. Again, the artistry metaphor: Throwing colors against a canvas won't create a fine painting. You professionally apply the colors. That's what you pay for and what you should expect when you hire an experienced asset protection specialist.

And to be cost-effective, your plan should also bear some logical proportionality between what your assets are worth against

> You can compare plans and prices from different providers who have comparable credentials and who will provide you comparable services.

the cost to protect them. How much can you logically spend to shelter $100,000? How much more should you spend to protect assets worth ten or a hundred times more?

Key # 6 - Retain Control

Another common asset protection perception is that you must surrender control over your assets. This may be true, but not always. It depends on which firewalls you use.

For instance, we commonly use limited partnerships and limited liability companies, two entities where you can completely control your assets and they will nevertheless stay protected. You can also control exempt assets as well as assets titled with your spouse as tenants-by-the-entirety.

In contrast, you cannot control a trust set up primarily for wealth protection. Even then, we can frequently employ control retention techniques (check Chapter 11) to allay a client's fears about delegating control over their assets to a third party.

A great plan strikes that optimum balance between safety and control. Achieving that balance is not always easy for a planner because clients usually want to control their assets, even when it endangers their plan.

We can usually achieve strong protection without a client losing control over their assets. We have many ways to safeguard assets that we entrust to others. You will expand your planning options once you understand these control retention mechanisms.

How much control you can safely retain over your assets must, of course, be determined by your advisor. It's always wisest to err on the side of caution.

Some debtors have no choice but to give control over their assets to a third party (usually a professional trustee) if they want to safeguard their assets. Any discomfort about relinquishing control must then be outweighed by the reality that their only other option is to have their assets seized by their creditors. Several celebrated asset protection cases (involving offshore trusts) have gone wrong only because the client retained too much control over their assets.

Every asset protection professional wrestles with this 'control' issue. It's a problem. It takes creativity to balance control and safety – particularly when the client is in crisis mode and insists upon retaining control. Then we must educate our client as part of the process. A client with more confidence in his fiduciary will more quickly surrender control. Ultimately, the client must become sufficiently comfortable with the arrangement or we must design an alternative plan. Or we may discharge a client because we can no longer be responsible for a plan that is unlikely to succeed only because the client insisted upon retaining control beyond the safety point.

Key # 7 - Enhance Other Financial Goals

Asset protection is only one financial goal. It isn't your *only* financial goal. Estate, tax, investment planning and other financial goals must fit your asset protection plan. You want a coordinated and integrated financial plan.

For example, you should integrate asset protection with your estate plan. Not surprisingly, many clients who came to our firm for asset protection had no estate plan – not even a simple will. It was their need for asset protection that prompted their estate plan. If you have an estate plan, we would integrate your asset protection plan with your estate plan.

Integrating asset protection with estate planning, also gives your arrangement a more 'innocent' purpose which is particularly important when you do your planning in the face of an existing creditor. Your plan will be more defensible when a judge views your planning as one undertaken for estate purposes, not to thwart creditors.

We can oftentimes accomplish creative results by combining asset protection with estate planning. We can usually improve upon a client's estate plan using one or more of the entities that we use for asset protection.

A *great* asset protection plan may give you some legitimate tax benefits. For example, we primarily use limited partnerships to shelter assets, however, a limited partnership can also save its partners a fortune in estate taxes. I say to avoid promoters who use asset protection to push *illegal* tax schemes (pure trusts, etc.) – and do ask your planner about the tax consequences of any proposed plan – however, a great asset protection plan may help you to lower or defer your taxes.

Investments are, of course, a more distant goal from asset protection. However, your asset protection plan may introduce you to new investment opportunities. It's all part of integrated financial planning. In fact, I consider this financial integration so important that our firm offers our clients an integrated practice. We have financial and estate planning professionals for those clients who want us to design a more comprehensive and better coordinated financial plan.

Key # 8 - Be Comfortable

A great plan is one you can enthusiastically accept. Or at least you should have minimal discomfort. I say this because for some people, re-titling their assets is discomforting. They prefer the status quo.

More than anything else, it's the idea of relinquishing control over assets (as we have discussed) that is the one reason you may resist a proposed plan. We must then find alternative techniques which will let you retain control and still get good asset protection.

When a client won't accept a proposed plan, we present the next safest plan – hopefully one the client will enthusiastically accept. You need a 'psychological fit' between yourself and your plan. For example, my parents were from the Depression era. They considered high finance saving their money in the largest bank in town. How comfortable would they be putting their savings into an offshore trust in a small Pacific Island and where the trustee hailed from still another unheard of country? You see the disconnect? Ultimately, you and your planner must *both* be comfortable with your plan.

An overly complex plan may unsettle you because you don't understand the plan. Complex circles and squares on your lawyer's legal pad may be simple to your lawyer, but what do you really know about limited partnerships, offshore trusts or captive insurance companies? Very little, I suspect. That's why a good planner must educate you as part of the planning process. In fact, that's one important reason for this book as well as my other books on asset protection. It's also why I want my clients to attend my Wealthsaver seminars. My clients must understand what we are doing to protect their wealth – and so should you. *Then* you will be comfortable.

Key # 9 - Limit Your Liability

> **Many strategies in this book are primarily used to contain or minimize liability. Particularly review the chapters on corporations and limited liability companies.**

Your asset protection plan must do more than protect your assets from creditors. A great plan will also *limit* your liability – or insulate you personally from business and other external liabilities. It will limit your creditors to the fewest assets and the assets of the fewest number of entities.

We deploy assets to different protective baskets so that a creditor can target the fewest assets. A plan to shelter a business owner's personal assets is incomplete unless we further limit the creditors of the business to the assets of that one business. Similarly, a *great* plan transfers or shifts liability to a third party.

Key # 10 - Your Plan Must Protect You

All else is meaningless if your plan doesn't achieve its one primary purpose – protecting your assets.

No planner can guarantee the absolute safety of *any* plan (and be wary of any planner who does). However, you want reasonable confidence that your assets can overcome a creditor attack. You want your assets to be as lawsuit-proof as possible. Anything less is *not* a great plan.

I was a pharmacist before I became an attorney. In my former profession I dispensed sleeping pills. My business hasn't changed. I am still in the 'sleeping pill' business. I no longer dispense pills, I now create asset protection plans. But my goal is still the same – to have my clients sleep soundly.

You can't sleep soundly if you have only questionable protection. You want an *impregnable* financial fortress. When you understand why you *can't* lose your assets – you have a truly *great* plan!

Wealthsaver Tips

1. You want more than a *good* plan. You want a *great* plan.

2. Start with a flexible basic plan and build protection on an 'as need' basis.

3. Keep your plan simple and cost-effective.

4. Look for ways to retain control over your assets. You will be more comfortable with your plan.

5. Your plan must do more than lawsuit-proof your wealth. Your plan should also limit your lawsuit exposure.

6. Design a 100 percent legal plan. Don't take shortcuts or violate laws. Criminal consequences can be far more serious than a lawsuit.

7. Match your plan to your other financial objectives – estate, tax and investment planning.

8. No plan is a *great* plan unless you are confident that you are protected.

FOUR

Fraudulent Transfers and Other Blunders

When we talk about asset protection planning, I can also tell you that there are many more things that you can do wrong than you are likely to do right. I see these same blunders time and again, mistakes that can cause you to lose your protection and possibly get you into even bigger trouble. The big three are: 1) Fraudulent transfers, 2) titling your assets to a 'straw' and 3) concealing your assets.

Fraudulent Transfers

You've probably heard the term 'fraudulent transfers'. A fraudulent transfer is certainly the most frequent asset protection planning mistake and it can be your costliest mistake because such last-minute defective transfers will give you illusory protection, not real protection.

Every state has fraudulent transfer laws. Some states call it a *Uniform Fraudulent Conveyance Act (UFCA)* and others the *Uniform Fraudulent Transfer Act (UFTA)*. However, we can interchangeably use *fraudulent transfer* or *fraudulent conveyance* because their provisions are so similar.

A fraudulent transfer allows a judgment creditor to unwind any transfer previously made by a debtor with the result that the fraudulently transferred property can then be seized by his creditor.

You cannot escape debts by simply gifting assets to friends or relatives, or via other equally transparent attempts to shield assets from creditors.

In other words – given certain circumstances – the courts will invalidate and revoke a debtor's prior sale, gift or other transfer. Assets the debtor sold or gave away for less than fair value will then be re-transferred to the debtor for the benefit of the judgment creditor. A fraudulent transfer can then partially or totally destroy your asset protection.

An effective asset protection plan safely titles wealth *beyond* the reach of creditors. Fraudulent transfers are a dangerous obstacle to that goal since creditors *can* unwind or reclaim fraudulently transferred assets even though these assets are no longer titled to you. Judgment creditors frequently apply the fraudulent transfer laws to seize assets previously transferred by a debtor. Fraudulent transfers may have been to a spouse, family member, friend, corporation, partnership, trust or any other third party. Whether the creditor can succeed with a fraudulent transfer claim chiefly depends upon whether the creditor can convince the court that the transfer was simply a last-ditch effort to defraud the creditor.

If your asset protection plan was designed by a good asset protection specialist, you should be able to more readily convince a court that your transfers were not fraudulent. This would defeat the creditor's attempt to recover previously transferred assets. If you fail in court, you lose the very protection that your plan was intended to provide. The successful defense against a fraudulent transfer challenge is often the true test of an asset protection plan.

Think about asset protection as a vaccine, not a cure. The way to avoid fraudulent transfer claims is to protect your assets *before* you have legal trouble. Once you incur a liability – or are sued – many of the protective strategies that I discuss in this book will no longer be effective, just as a vaccine may not work once you are afflicted with a disease. That's why the best asset protection plans are *preventative* – a plan to insulate you against a *future* liability.

You may have hurriedly transferred assets after you were sued – or anticipated a lawsuit. You may have tried to shelter your assets by gifting them to friends or relatives with the tacit understanding that they will return your property after your financial problem ends. These are typical reactions to legal troubles, but they don't always succeed. They may even get you into bigger trouble.

The good news is that while a creditor may, as a matter of law, recover a fraudulently transferred asset, it does not mean that every creditor makes such an attempt. Relatively few fraudulent transfers are recovered by creditors. One reason is that judgment creditors don't always diligently discover fraudulent disposed assets. Another reason is that the amount owed the creditor or the value of the fraudulently transferred assets, may be too small to justify the creditor pursuing recovery. Then there may be too many competing creditors. A recovery by one creditor would not be worthwhile when the creditor must share the recovery proceeds with other creditors. The procedural obstacles to recovery may also be too severe. For example, offshore asset protection strategies impose procedural barriers that make it costly and time-consuming for a creditor to attempt recovery. Your creditor may have theoretical, but not practical legal recourse when the creditor faces too many firewalls. A creditor's *legal rights* to reclaim fraudulently transferred assets becomes academic when the creditor won't assert those rights.

Nevertheless, it's faulty planning to base your asset protection upon the mere hope that your fraudulent transfer won't be discovered or acted upon by a judgment creditor. The best asset protection plan is one where your creditor *can't* recover your assets as a matter of law – and *won't* attempt recovery as a matter of practicality.

Fraudulent Conveyance Fundamentals

Let's make a complicated subject a bit easier to understand? There are two types of fraudulent transfers: 1) Fraud in fact or *actual fraud* and 2) Fraud in law or *constructive fraud*.

In actual fraud cases, the creditor must prove that you actually *intended* to hinder, delay or defraud your creditor. This, of course, is usually difficult for the creditor to prove directly because the creditor must prove your state of mind or you must admit to fraudulent intent. However, courts can instead look for *badges of fraud* from which they can infer fraudulent intent. These common 'badges of fraud' include:

> Since a creditor cannot easily prove your state of mind or force you to confess such fraudulent intent, they usually prove fraudulent intent through circumstances or factors that suggest such intent.

- Transfers to close family members or friends

- Secretive transfers

- Transfers for less than fair value

- When you continue to use or possess the property after the transfer

- Concealed assets

- A transfer made when you incurred a large debt or anticipated a lawsuit

- Transfers that impoverished you and left you unable to pay your debts.

The mere fact that a creditor can establish one or more 'badges' doesn't necessarily mean that the court will conclude that your transfer was fraudulent. These 'actions' only infer fraudulent intent and may help persuade a judge that there was fraudulent intent. These badges, in themselves, are not fraud. Your creditor must still prove fraudulent intent. On the other hand, a court can conclude that a challenged transfer was proper, even when there are one or more of these badges. For example, you can overcome a presumption of fraud when you can justify a transfer as achieving some business, investment or estate planning objective – rather than the attempt to avoid a debt.

Actual fraud cases are difficult for creditors to prove – even when there were several badges of fraud. That's why creditors more often invoke *constructive fraud* claims to unwind fraudulent transfers. Constructive fraud is a gift or sale of property that:

1) is for less than fair value *(or fair consideration)*

2) made in the face of a known or probable liability

3) which leaves you insolvent.

Notice, that with a constructive fraud claim, your transfer can be fraudulent, even when you act innocently and without intent to hinder your creditors. However, a creditor who challenges a transfer must still prove each of the three elements. Look at them more closely:

1. A gift or sale of property for less than fair value: In a constructive fraud case, your creditors must prove that you made the transfer for less than fair value. While a lack of consideration is obvious when you merely gift your assets, proving a sale was for less than fair value can sometimes be difficult to establish, because courts define 'fair' consideration subjectively.

> Criminal sanctions are rare in fraudulent conveyance cases because there is a very fine line between lawful or at least well-intentioned asset redeployment and criminal fraud.

Fair consideration is generally that price which a reasonably prudent seller would obtain when selling property through commercially reasonable means. However, this need not necessarily be the fair market value. 'Fair value' depends largely on the type property. For example, stocks or bonds of publicly traded corporations have a readily ascertainable fair value because they are listed daily on the public exchanges. A debtor, who transfers publicly traded stock for less than its quoted daily price, would be subject to a fraudulent transfer claim, at least to the difference in value.

Other assets are more problematic to value. For example, what is the fair value of real estate, shares in a privately owned business, antiques, vehicles or other assets? These assets may be sold for considerably less than the fair market value as viewed by a creditor. What if the debtor doesn't have enough time to find a buyer who will pay more? Real estate sold for 70 percent of its appraised value satisfied the fair value test, according to several courts. Other difficult-to-value items – such as jewelry or a closely-held business – requires the courts to consider the relevant facts to determine 'reasonable value'. It's always subjective.

2. A gift or sale of property when there is liability: Even when a creditor who challenges a transfer can show that the asset was sold for less than its fair value, the creditor must next show that the transfer was made against a *present* creditor. A transfer of your assets for less than fair value may even be unsafe against a future *probable* liability. But you can safely transfer assets against a future *possible* liability. Nor can we always easily differentiate between probable and possible liability. Courts decide these cases differently. When did the act occur that created the liability? When did the debtor first realize that there can be liability for that act? When did the transfer occur? You can see why courts reach different conclusions as to whether a liability was *probable* or *possible* at any point in time.

A '*present* liability' is usually one that occurs from the moment you have a creditor (incurred a liability). Only later asset transfers can be challenged. For example, if you sign a lease today and gift your assets tomorrow, your landlord can probably recover your gifted

> A 'present liability' is usually one that occurs from the moment you have a creditor (incurred a liability).

assets if you later default on your lease. You didn't need to be in present default on your lease for your transfer to be fraudulent. It is also immaterial whether you were yet sued. The critical date is when your liability arose – not the default or lawsuit date.

Assume that you are a surgeon and negligently leave a sponge in a patient. You are unaware of this error and so is the patient. The following month you innocently gift your assets for estate planning purposes. Two years later the patient discovers your malpractice and sues you. If the patient wins a judgment can she then recover the transferred assets? Probably the patient could recover your assets. It wouldn't matter that both you and the patient were unaware of the potential claim when you transferred your assets because fraudulent intent is not a requirement to a 'constructive' fraudulent transfer claim. What is significant here is that you never know what claims can arise from the past. Thus, any transfer that you make for less than fair value from that date can place you on the wrong end of a fraudulent transfer claim.

3. Your gift or sale leaves you insolvent: Finally suppose that your creditor can show that your transfer was for less than fair value and that you made the transfer when there was a probable liability. The court, may still not unwind your transfer unless your transfer left you insolvent. That means too few assets to pay your debts as they come due. More simply, you can't pay your creditor because you impoverished yourself.

Once you review these three factors to establish a constructive fraudulent transfer claim, you have hundreds of unanswered questions. For instance, is it a fraudulent transfer to exchange non-exempt assets for exempt (protected) assets of equal value? What if you have no present creditor, but transfer your assets when you have a *foreseeable* creditor (i.e. you plan to sign a lease)? We can go on. The point is that the fraudulent transfer laws are complex and they create a gray area of uncertainty because many transfers are neither clearly fraudulent nor conclusively non-fraudulent. A seasoned asset protection specialist can help you to cope with the complexities and nuances of the fraudulent transfer laws and determine whether a transfer is likely to be unwound by creditors and the courts

Some Case Examples

With this background, let's sharpen your judgment with several case examples:

Case 1: Suppose Mark guaranteed a $500,000 business loan from his bank. Shortly thereafter, and while his bank note was in good standing, Mark gifted his assets to his children for estate planning purposes. Several months later, Mark's business unexpectedly failed and the bank sued Mark on the note. Were Mark's gifts a fraudulent transfer?

Answer: Yes. No consideration was paid for the assets because the assets were gifts. The transfer rendered Mark insolvent and without assets to pay the bank. This case highlights this interesting question: Was the bank guarantee a *present* liability? The loan created a contingent liability, but could Mark reasonably foresee the failure of his business and the need to pay his guarantee? The fact that he had the liability (a signed guarantee) would probably be sufficient for the court to rule the gift a fraudulent transfer.

Case 2: Bob resides in Florida. He transferred his home to his sister as trustee in trust for Bob's minor children. Florida residences are fully protected by Florida state homestead laws and they are exempt from

> Conduct the more questionable transfers of personal property in a state with the shorter statute of limitations. Real estate is always considered transferred in the state where it is located.

lawsuits. When Bob transferred his home to the trust, Bob had a $200,000 lawsuit against him and no other assets to satisfy the claim. Was this a fraudulent transfer?

Answer: Bob's transfer of his home would not be a fraudulent conveyance because Bob's creditors could not seize the home *before* the transfer since it was fully homestead protected. Bob's transfer of the home didn't prejudice the creditor. There is no fraudulent conveyance unless their right to the asset is hindered by the transfer.

Case 3: Assume Linda owned $500,000 in non-exempt (unprotected) assets and, facing several lawsuits, exchanged these assets for $500,000 in exempt or legally protected property. Is this a fraudulent transfer?

Answer: This case has a less certain outcome. Some courts rule that it isn't a fraudulent transfer because it is a fair value exchange, notwithstanding that the debtor transferred exposed assets for safe assets. Another common argument is that there was no 'transfer' because Linda owns her assets – albeit in a different form.

Asset protection plans frequently convert non-exempt or unprotected assets into protected or exempt assets. But courts may disagree on whether this is a fraudulent transfer. Examine *your* state laws and cases. This again underscores a major difficulty with asset protection planning: Courts are inconsistent and frequently reverse prior positions. This adds uncertainty concerning the safety of asset protection plans. Your attorney must thoroughly research recent cases in your state to accurately predict what a court will rule on any asset transfer that can possibly be challenged.

Case 4: Assume Sam deeded his $500,000 home to a friend to partially repay a $700,000 debt owed to the friend?

Answer: This transfer would withstand a creditor challenge because repaying an existing debt is fair consideration for a transfer. For instance, Sam could have instead repaid his $700,000 debt and this would not be fraudulent. Property transferred or mortgaged to one creditor to fully or partly satisfy or secure an existing debt is not fraudulent, even when it impairs other creditors. Other creditors may petition the debtor into bankruptcy within three months of the transfer to set aside the mortgage as a voidable preference under bankruptcy law, but the mortgage wouldn't be voidable as a fraudulent transfer.

Case 5: Before filing bankruptcy, Henry transferred his property to his new wife. She, in return, promised to care for him in his later years. Is this a fraudulent transfer?

Answer: Whether this transfer is fraudulent would depend upon whether the transfer was before or after the debt in question was incurred. A transfer made after the debt was incurred could be set aside as fraudulent because the consideration contemplated future services, not services previously or simultaneously rendered. But, the property could not be recovered by future creditors (claims that arose after the transfer) since they couldn't argue that the transfer hindered or delayed their rights to collect as they weren't creditors at the time of the transfer. This general rule has its exceptions.

> **Transferees to questionable transfers must understand that a claim may arise and must be willing to defend against such a claim.**

Hopefully, you now more clearly understand what a creditor must prove for a court to rule a transfer was either actual or constructive fraud. In practice, to defend a transfer, we need only prove the absence of one or more essential factors. The court must then conclude that the transfer was not fraudulent. For instance, we may prove that there was no fraudulent intent; or that the client received fair value; or that there was no probable liability at the time of the transfer; or that the transfer didn't render the client insolvent.

Watch the Statute of Limitations

There's also the timing factor. A creditor must challenge a fraudulent transfer within the time allowed under the state's statute of limitations. Most states require fraudulent transfer claims to be made within four years after the transfer – or one year after actual discovery of the transfer could have been reasonably made by the creditor – whichever date is later.

Under this rule, a fraudulently transferred asset is never completely safe because a creditor can always argue that they only recently discovered a transfer made years earlier. The creditor would then have one additional year to set aside the transfer.

Most states follow fraudulent conveyance statutes which generally imposes a strict 5 year statute of limitations. Later claims are disallowed regardless of when the creditor discovered the transfer. Check your state laws to determine when creditor's recovery claims become time-barred.

Fraudulent transfer actions are also frequently initiated by a trustee in bankruptcy when the bankrupt fraudulently transfers assets before the bankruptcy. Bankruptcy law gives the trustee two years from the first meeting of creditors to commence a fraudulent transfer claim. The fraudulent transfer must also have occurred within the year preceding bankruptcy. However, earlier transfers aren't necessarily safe because the bankruptcy trustee can sue under a state's fraudulent transfer law rather than under bankruptcy law and every state has a longer statute of limitations. Delay filing bankruptcy for as long as possible if you have questionable prior transfers.

Creditor's Remedies

A judgment creditor who asserts a fraudulent transfer has several possible remedies. The creditor can have a court:

- Set aside the transfer and restore title for seizure by the creditor.

- Enjoin further transactions, encumbrances or depletion of the transferred asset (freeze the asset) pending the outcome of the fraudulent conveyance case.

- Award damages against the transferee and supplemental damages from the debtor (the legal costs to recover the asset).

- Appoint a receiver over the conveyed asset that is likely to disappear or be dissipated.

- Recover whatever proceeds the debtor received from the transfer (but the creditor cannot void the sale to a subsequent good faith purchaser who paid fair value).

While these and other remedies are available to a judgment creditor, the courts, to the extent practicable, only try to restore the creditor to his position before the fraudulent transfer. Whether this remedy is practical, of course, depends largely on whether the transferee still holds the assets and whether it has since been altered, destroyed or sold.

Litigants, who have not yet won a judgment, generally *cannot* commence a fraudulent transfer claim. This is a remedy for *judgment creditors*. Nor can *pre-judgment creditors* usually attach assets or restrain your rights to transfer your assets – even if your transfer would be fraudulent. The plaintiff's remedy is to recover assets under the fraudulent transfer laws *after* the creditor wins a judgment.

The law does not obligate a lawsuit defendant to hold assets for the benefit of the creditors, notwithstanding common belief to the contrary. Justice Antonin Scalia, in one notable US Supreme Court case, announced, "A creditor has no cognizable interest in the assets of a debtor prior to obtaining a judgment. Anyone can transfer their assets all day long until the sheriff shows up with a Writ of Execution pursuant to a court order."

Also, contrary to popular misconception, a fraudulent transfer is not a crime. A fraudulent transfer is only a civil remedy, which simply divides *irreversible* transfers from transfers that can later be reversed by the courts. Neither the transferor nor transferee usually become subject to criminal penalties. And, in most cases, there is ample opportunity for the defendant's attorney to argue that the transfer at issue was not fraudulent for several of the reasons that I noted. Even where a defendant loses, a court can only grant the creditor the noted remedies, which is essentially, to unwind the transfer.

The essence of fraudulent transfer law was well articulated in a recent Florida Supreme Court case:

> "A fraudulent conveyance action is simply another creditor remedy. It is either an action by a creditor against a transferee directed against a particular transaction which, if declared fraudulent, is set aside thus leaving the creditor free to pursue the asset or it is an action against a transferee who has received an asset by means of a fraudulent conveyance and should be required to

either return the asset or pay for the asset. A fraudulent conveyance action is *not* an action against a debtor for failure to pay an amount owing from a prior judgment and does not warrant an *additional* judgment against the same debtor because of the fraudulent conveyance. A fraudulent conveyance action is not a lawsuit against a transferor debtor, but it is an action against the property or the transferee holding the property."

Nevertheless, attorneys should not encourage their clients to make transfers that are fraudulent. The objective should be to design a plan that, even in the most extreme case, can be shown to be a non-fraudulent transfer when we apply one or more of the defenses.

Of course, attorneys walk a fine line. On one hand, an attorney has a duty to aggressively defend the client's wealth. On the other hand, counsel cannot go beyond the line and encourage unethical or illegal practices. This is the asset protection attorney's constant dilemma: Defining that fine line on any particular case. Attorneys can also differ in their viewpoint about where that line is. For that reason, one attorney may accept a case that another would decline. An attorney's sensitivity to a potential fraudulent transfer action may also limit the strategies the attorney would use to protect the client's assets.

> The objective should be to design a plan that, even in the most extreme case, can be shown to be a non-fraudulent transfer when we apply one or more of the defenses.

What is clear is that it is never too late to take defensive measures – even once a lawsuit has been filed against you. You will have fewer options than with advance planning – but even the most dire situation has solutions. I again quote the US Supreme Court, "A debtor [who is sued] need not be like a deer frozen in the headlights of an onrushing auto. The debtor still has within his rights the opportunity to attempt to put his wealth beyond harm's way."

Your safest path is to protect yourself before you have a problem. You then have many more planning options and less risk that your transfer will later be challenged. Unfortunately, too many people already immersed in litigation are advised by their attorney that it is too late for them to protect themselves. This is poor advice, and it's hardly different than a doctor advising a patient that it's too late to try to save him because he is already sick. You may have less desirable wealth-saving alternatives once you are sued and you may need to go to greater lengths to shelter your assets, but you do have options.

Avoid Fraudulent Transfer Claims

Your primary goal is to avoid fraudulent transfer claims. So, it is important to not only know some law, but also to use common sense. For starters, avoid any badges of fraud which will only invite suspicion and undue inquiry. Your transfers must pass a creditor 'sniff' test. Some points here:

- **Protect your assets before you have a liability.** It cannot be a fraudulent transfer if you transfer your assets before you incur the liability. That's why we constantly counsel our clients to become judgment-proof before they have financial or legal problems. Your safest strategy is to be liability-free when you protect your assets.

- **Make small, incremental transfers.** They attract less notice than sudden transfers of major assets. Nor should you transfer significant assets to one transferee. When your eggs are in one basket, they are more vulnerable. Scatter your assets. A creditor will then be forced to file numerous fraudulent transfer lawsuits which will require considerably more cost and effort.

- **Avoid insider transactions.** Transfers to family members, friends or close business associates are always suspicious. Even a completely innocent and 'fair value' transaction can appear suspicious to a court or creditors. Use non-family members as trustees, corporate officers or fiduciaries for entities to which you transfer assets.

- **Document that your transfer was innocent.** Your transfer should not have the obvious goal of sheltering assets from present creditors. Your attorney's correspondence, for instance, may instead show that you were engaged in estate planning when he prepared your irrevocable trust. Documents that recite an innocent legal purpose for the conveyance can be persuasive to a court that may otherwise see another motive.

- **Carefully document whatever consideration you receive for your property.** What services were performed? Why are they worth their stated value? If you borrowed money, do you have cancelled checks or can you otherwise prove the validity of your debt?

- **Avoid circumspect actions.** Selling your home? Don't stay on as its tenant. Selling your business? How will your creditors view your staying on as its manager? Selling your boat? Don't keep it at your dock. You get the idea?

- **Verify the value of your property.** You want to establish fair consideration. For example, have your home appraised to prove that you sold it for its fair market value. Are you selling another asset at a low price? Will photographs or an appraisal show defects or other reasons to justify the low price. Assume that the value of any significant and recently transferred assets will be questioned by your creditors.

- **Choose your transferees carefully.** What if your creditor challenges your transfer? Will your transferee defend the transfer? A friendly 'straw' who holds title to your property may not act as you want when he is sued. If your transferee quickly surrenders your asset or otherwise fails to cooperate in defending the case, you will lose your asset by default. Transferees to questionable transfers must also realize that a creditor may sue them and they must be willing to defend against such a claim.

- **Don't publicize your transfers.** Why alert your creditors when you rearrange your financial affairs? This only encourages your creditors to move more swiftly to protect their rights.

- **Employ multiple asset protection strategies.** Why deed your home to some third party when you can also mortgage it to another 'friendly creditor'? Your creditor must then contest both the transfer and the mortgage. Challenging both transactions may be too ambitious and expensive a proposition for your creditor.

Avoid 'Straw' or Nominee Owner Deals

Here's the second big blunder: You may conclude that your easiest and safest option is to title your assets to your spouse, a trusted friend or a relative – particularly when they are a lower lawsuit risk.

Many people erroneously assume that a 'straw' arrangement is their best strategy. For example, one physician client boasted, "I no longer worry about malpractice lawsuits. I titled everything to my wife and she won't get sued." Can asset protection be that simple? Sometimes. And sometimes that can be your most dangerous strategy.

'Straws' may own your property. Friends or relatives are likely candidates. But whatever their relationship to you, your assets are in their name. Of course, the real deal is that you own the asset, but for lawsuit protection, you don't want it titled in your name.

There are obvious pitfalls to these arrangements. First, is the fraudulent conveyance pitfall when you gift your assets to a friend or relative with the tacit understanding that they will return your assets once the danger passes. But what if you re-title your assets to your straw *before* you have creditors?

> If your straw holds title to your assets, their creditors and ex-spouses can claim your assets.

You can't assume that whoever holds title to your property is safer than you from lawsuits and creditors. Nominees have their own marital problems, tax troubles, creditors and lawsuits. If your straw holds title to your assets, *their* creditors and ex-spouses can claim *your* assets. People lose assets – not always to their own creditors – but to their nominees. This is one reason you should never title assets to a straw.

What if your spouse is your straw? The drawbacks here are less severe. Sometimes it is sensible to title marital assets to the less vulnerable spouse. Still, this too raises problems. For instance, you may title your million dollar home and other assets to your spouse for protection on the expectation that your spouse *won't* get sued. Yet this arrangement may cause estate planning and estate tax problems. For example, when assets are titled to *both* spouses, you can more advantageously plan your estates. You both can use credit shelter trusts to maximize your death tax credits. When your assets are titled to your spouse, your spouse can claim only his or her estate tax exemption. The rest of your spouse's estate will be taxed and this may cost your heirs considerably more estate taxes.

Assets titled to one spouse aren't always safe from the other spouse's creditors. Even when the liability arose *after* the debtor titled assets to the spouse, creditors can argue that the debtor-spouse has an equitable or beneficial interest in at least half the property. For example, a creditor can argue that there is a constructive or resulting trust; namely, that the spouse who holds title is in actuality a trustee for the debtor-spouse. This argument will more likely succeed when the debtor-spouse's money was used to buy the property or when his or her income paid the mortgage, maintenance and upkeep on the property. When the money invested in the asset came from the debtor-spouse, then the property is not truly property of the *other* spouse. When a debtor-spouse's assets can be traced to property, his creditors can assert claim to that property. Nor do you want to encourage further litigation by presenting these sloppy issues. A great plan is a totally defensible plan; one free of possible challenges.

Tax problems are significant when the parties are unmarried. For example, one stubborn client told me, "I owned an expensive Los Angeles home and worried about lawsuits. So I titled my property to my 87 year old mother who has never been sued."

Property that you transfer without consideration is a gift. So, this fellow made a taxable gift to his mother. Gifts between spouses aren't taxable; but gifts to others – including mothers – are gift taxable. Inadvertently he incurred a huge gift tax as a consequence of that transfer. Moreover, his real estate will now be included in his mother's taxable estate. When she dies, will his mother bequeath him back his property or will she instead bequeath his house to his siblings? And his mother will pay a huge estate tax on the *son's* house when she does bequeath it back to him. Can you imagine a more foolish way to 'safely' title assets?

Particularly avoid straw deals if you plan bankruptcy. Bankruptcy fraud convictions are common. It doesn't pay for a bankrupt to hide assets. A bankruptcy trustee or court who concludes that you hid your assets with a straw, can easily make a case for bankruptcy fraud, which is a serious crime.

Finally, how do you know that you can trust your straw? You can't be too trusting. I have seen parents who stole entrusted assets from their children and brothers

> A fraudulent transfer can impose liability on the transferee, and in some states, it is a criminal offense.

who double-crossed each other. Your best friend can forget that *your* asset isn't really *his*! So forget straw deals. You have safer ways to protect your assets.

Don't Hide Your Assets

The third big blunder is confusing secrecy or concealing assets with asset protection. Secrecy has less to do with asset protection than with discouraging lawsuits. This is the chief function of financial privacy. But once you're sued, you can't rely upon secrecy because a judgment creditor can compel you to disclose your finances under oath. You cannot be secretive once you are under oath. If you truthfully disclose your assets, you lose secrecy. If you lie and conceal your assets, you commit perjury. That's not *legitimate* asset protection. Your plan must allow you to fully disclose your assets, confident that they will remain safe from your creditors.

It is not only the judgment debtor who must answer questions about his or her assets. So must the spouse. While spousal communication is ordinarily confidential, this marital privilege doesn't extend to proceedings to discover assets. Most states allow a creditor to interrogate a non-debtor spouse about the debtor spouse's financial affairs. This rule prevents using the marital privilege to conceal assets from a judgment creditor. You will want to review probable creditor inquiries with your spouse before any asset discovery deposition to ensure both correct and consistent answers. Alternatively, tell your spouse as little as possible about your finances.

> As a civil remedy, the courts can hold both the transferee and the transferor jointly and severally liable for attorney's fees and costs incurred by the creditor to recover fraudulently transferred property.

A judgment creditor can force you to disclose your financial information in many different ways. Your creditor can examine you in court through depositions or interrogatories. Or the creditor can request that you produce documents. They can also subpoena your records and information from third parties.

A judgment creditor in search of assets has many ways to find them. They can review loan and credit applications, bank records, tax returns, court cases (such as prior divorces that disclose assets) or insurance policies. The paper trail is revealing. Computer technology makes everyone's financial life an open book.

Because asset protection is so common and because the techniques to achieve secrecy so sophisticated, both judgment creditors and prospective litigants increasingly use professional asset search firms to discover hidden or concealed assets. These firms are sometimes hired to determine whether a prospective defendant has enough assets to make a lawsuit worthwhile. These firms quite efficiently track asset transfers from debtors with judgments against them to uncover assets that may then be seized by their creditor clients.

For $1,000, a creditor can get a very accurate financial profile on you. A forensic accounting firm in a larger case can trace the most deviously and secretively deployed wealth. You can't afford a 'hide the assets' game. Your creditor will probably find your assets. You will then most likely lose them.

Wealthsaver Tips

1. Creditors have rights. A creditor can recover assets that you transferred for less than fair value and which rendered you unable to pay your creditors.

2. Only an existing or foreseeable creditor can recover property that you transferred. An existing creditor is any creditor to whom you have a present liability, whether known or unknown, actual or contingent.

3. Actual intent to defraud a creditor is not a necessary element for a creditor to prove. The creditor need only prove that the transfer rendered you unable to pay the creditor.

4. Creditors usually have five years to commence a fraudulent transfer case. Some states impose a four year (or one year after the transfer was discovered) statute of limitations.

5. A fraudulent transfer can impose liability on the transferee.

6. Your best protection against a potential fraudulent conveyance claim is to shelter your assets *before* you have creditors.

7. Avoid sham transactions and don't title your assets to 'straws' or nominees. This can only cause you greater problems.

8. It's not necessarily too late to protect your assets – even if you have already been sued.

FIVE

Self-Protected Wealth

Can you owe creditors $32 million and still live like a king? Absolutely. If you're O.J. Simpson. Or if you use his strategies.

I'm no fan of O.J. Simpson (and he isn't one of my clients); nevertheless, O.J. is a great case study on how anyone can create wealth that is automatically 'self-protected'.

Consider how O.J.'s Miami home is soundly protected by Florida's homestead laws. And how his six-figure annual pension is judgment-proof under both federal and Florida law. Nor can O.J.'s insurance be touched by his creditors under Florida law. And as the head of his household, O.J.'s wages can't be garnished in Florida.

Can it be that simple to owe a fortune and still live the life of a king? O.J.'s firewalls are only the formidable state and federal laws that shield certain assets from lawsuits, bankruptcy and creditors. You too can fortify some or all of your own assets with these same firewalls. Many Americans use their homestead laws, wage and pension exemptions, bankruptcy exemptions and other protective laws that our federal and state governments have enacted to help debtors keep assets safe from creditors' seizure.

How much protection against lawsuits do these laws give you? The answer varies from state to state. Your state exemptions may be extremely valuable in your planning or meaningless. Their effectiveness depends not only upon the type of liability that you need protection against, but the state where you reside.

Start with one note of caution: Protecting yourself with the federal and state exemption laws can seem simple, but it's quite tricky. You definitely need professional assistance so that you can be confident that these laws, will, in fact, fully protect your assets under *your* circumstances.

One major difficulty in using the various exemption laws involves the interplay between the state exemptions and the federal exemptions that would apply under bankruptcy law.

Because of the pro-creditor changes in the new bankruptcy code, many affluent debtors will find that their state law exemptions – the exemptions that apply outside of bankruptcy – are more advantageous. Conversely, the new bankruptcy law better protects other assets – most notably retirement accounts – than do most state laws.

Therefore, a threshold question in exemption planning is whether you expect to resolve your legal problems in bankruptcy or outside bankruptcy. Only then can you determine which exemptions would apply. Nor can you always avoid bankruptcy. Because the new bankruptcy law is more favorable to creditors, more creditors will petition debtors into involuntary bankruptcy so these debtors lose the protection of their more liberal state exemptions.

> Only after you determine whether you expect to resolve your legal problems in bankruptcy or outside bankruptcy can you determine which exemptions will apply.

Nor does every state permit you to apply the federal exemptions, though most states allow a bankrupt to choose between the federal and state exemptions. When you do file bankruptcy, you must choose which set of exemptions you will use, since you cannot combine federal and state exemptions. Although you must choose between the federal or state exemptions where you have the option, some state exemption laws allow you to also apply supplemental federal exemptions which may slightly expand your protection.

Exemptions fall into three categories:

- *Family exemptions:* Many states have family exemptions that you can be eligible for if you are married. These exemptions are intended to protect a family that has a single debtor (or family debtor) as the head-of-household. These exemptions usually allow you to keep more unsecured property if you file bankruptcy.

- *Head-of-household exemptions.* Even if you are unmarried, you may be financially responsible for others who live with you. If you furnish over 50 percent of the support for at least one household member, you may claim more exemptions than could a single person because of the detrimental effect the loss of your property would have on your dependent.

- *Specific property exemptions.* This is the most important category as it shelters specified assets that you own from your creditors. You may choose to exempt from creditor seizure specific assets up to a defined dollar amount.

You can choose the property you exempt within the terms of the exemption system that you elect. If you file bankruptcy and apply the federal exemptions, you and your spouse may each claim the full exemption. You cannot always double your exemptions under state laws.

Your strategy, in either case, is to maximize your exempt property. Generally, the states exempt much the same property as under the federal system, though their exemption limits vary.

You can see that exemption planning cannot be a do-it-yourself project. You must answer a number of questions before you can design your one best exemption strategy. For that, you need both an asset protection attorney and a bankruptcy attorney familiar with your state laws. For the federal and state exemptions, go to www.bankruptcyaction.com/bankruptcyexemptions.htm.

Homestead Protection

For many Americans, their home is their most valuable asset. You may already be somewhat familiar with your state laws that partly or fully creditor protect your home. You may even assume that you can't lose your home in a lawsuit because of your 'homestead protection'. If you live in certain states, you may be correct. Or wrong. Homestead laws run 'hot and cold'. Five state homestead laws *totally* protect the home. However, most state homestead laws do not completely creditor-shield the home. Forty-five states with homestead laws vary greatly in the home equity they do protect. Five states have no homestead protection.

> Homestead protection can even apply to mobile homes or boats when used as a permanent residence. This will also vary among states and must be carefully checked. You may also lose homestead if you title your home in another entity, such as a living trust.

Will your state's homestead laws fully safeguard your home? Understand what we mean by the term 'homestead.' The homestead laws apply only to your home or *primary* residence. Not every property can qualify as your 'home'. The real estate must be your primary residence – property that you own *and* occupy as your home. Specific 'residences' that qualify for homestead protection depends upon state statutes and court interpretations.

For example, not every state homestead protects cooperatively owned apartments, but most do. Or a state may shelter a single-family home, but not a duplex, triplex or other multi-unit structure where you occupy only one unit. Or your state may not shield a mobile home or houseboat, though you occupy it as your 'home'.

Unique situations make interesting cases. One case involved a client who lived on his 48-foot yacht on Miami's Biscayne Bay. But was his boat homestead protected under Florida law? One Florida court held that a houseboat is homestead protected as a 'home'. But would this decision extend to a yacht? Would the court distinguish between a houseboat intended primarily as a residence and a craft designed primarily for cruising? We never found our answer. We used other strategies to protect our client's boat. You can see that state laws don't cover these fine points.

Other restrictions may limit your homestead protection. For example, Florida law protects an unlimited amount of home equity; however, the acreage must fall within certain limits. Lot size is a common restriction in many states.

Once you are certain that your home qualifies for at least *some* homestead protection, you must then determine how much equity your state will protect. Usually, 'not enough'. Most states lawsuit-proof between $5,000 and $50,000 in equity. Massachusetts, a more protective state, exempts up to $300,000. California and several other states also have six-figure exemptions. But when you consider today's rapidly escalating real estate values and the large equity so many people now have in their homes, you can see why small homestead exemption states are nearly worthless for asset protection.

The next question is, how does your state measure 'equity'? Some courts consider the value of your home as your 'equity'. They do not deduct mortgages against your home. This is the exception.

If you are fortunate and live in Texas, Florida or one of the three other states that homestead protects unlimited home equity, your home has an exceptionally strong firewall. For example, a multi-million-dollar Texas or Florida home will be safe even in bankruptcy – if you owned it for at least 40 months prior to the bankruptcy. O.J.'s fully homestead protected Florida home is not only his personal castle, it's also his financial fortress!

> Five states have unlimited homestead protection, but protection may be limited in bankruptcy.

Will your state homestead laws adequately protect your home equity? Compare your statutory protection to your home equity by subtracting your mortgages against your homes fair market value. For example, a $300,000 home with a $150,000 mortgage has a $150,000 equity. If your state homestead law shelters only $20,000 equity, then $130,000 equity is vulnerable to a lawsuit.

Recent federal bankruptcy amendments limit the state homestead exemption to $125,000 if you purchased your residence within the 40 months preceding bankruptcy. Also, the time period that you must live in that state has been increased from 180 days to 730 days. This new bankruptcy amendment prevents debtors from last minute 'forum shopping' to evade creditors before they file bankruptcy.

You also have procedural requirements to follow. Every state imposes requirements to claim homestead protection. Some state residents must file a declaration of homestead. Other states impose a residency period before they grant homestead protection. You can't assume that your home is protected. Have your attorney show you how to comply with your state's procedural formalities.

In a few states, only the head-of-the-household can claim homestead. However, most states allow either spouse to do so. If you are married, be careful. If both spouses file a homestead declaration, their cross-declarations can cancel each other. Again, your asset protection attorney must guide you on these technicalities.

There are other potential traps. For instance, several states forfeit homestead protection if you title your home to a living trust. Yet, estate planners routinely advise clients to title their home to their living trust to avoid probate. These clients are unaware that they may then lose their homestead protection. Check this point in your state.

> If you are married, be careful. If both spouses file a homestead declaration, their cross-declarations can cancel each other.

Nor will homestead shield your home against every creditor. Most homestead laws protect the home only against debts that arise *after* you claim homestead protection. Other creditors can override homestead protection and seize any equity in your home.

These creditors include:

- The IRS (and other federal agencies). If you owe federal taxes, for example, you can lose your home, regardless of where you reside.

- Do you owe state taxes? Your homestead laws may or may not protect your home from state tax claims.

- A spouse in a divorce or a family member challenging their inheritances can override homestead protection.

- A lawsuit for an intentional tort (libel, fraud, deceit, etc.) won't usually be blocked by homestead protection.

- Mortgages or deeds of trust that you voluntarily give as collateral will be unaffected by homestead.

- Unaffected creditors also include those for whose benefit you expressly waived your homestead protection.

You also encounter a few minor disadvantages with homestead protection. If you sell or refinance your home *after* you declare homestead, your bank or buyer may require you to temporarily lift your homestead exemption. However, these minor procedural inconveniences shouldn't dissuade you from claiming homestead protection.

The more significant problem with homestead protection is that it can give you illusory security. For example, if your home has a $30,000 equity and you have a $30,000 homestead exemption, your home is *now* fully protected. But how well protected will your home be in the future? You will build equity (assuming that the value of your home will appreciate) while you reduce your mortgage. If you are sued some years from now, you may have a sizeable equity that would *not* be protected.

Because of these many state limitations, state homestead laws are ordinarily not sufficient to fully protect the family home. For that reason we have clients refinance their home. The goal is to combine mortgages and your state homestead exemption to leave absolutely no equity for a plaintiff to seize.

If you live in a state with an unlimited homestead exemption, a judgment creditor cannot attach your home, cloud its title or otherwise impede your ability to sell or refinance your home.

You also have several ways to build stronger homestead protection.

- If you are married, then the spouse who is most vulnerable to lawsuits should file the declaration. This will maximize *that* spouse's protection.

- If you live in a state with an unlimited (or large) homestead exemption, you might use exposed cash to buy a more expensive home. Or improve your present home. Or reduce your mortgage.

- You can also move to a state with an unlimited or larger homestead exemption – such as Florida or Texas. This is that common asset protection tactic: Convert *nonexempt assets* into *exempt assets*. (But remember the 2 year residency and 40 month pre-filing rule under the new bankruptcy laws. This cannot be a last minute strategy.)

Safeguarding Retirement Plans

Your retirement plan is probably high on the list as another valuable asset. But is it lawsuit-proof? More importantly, how can you shield an unprotected retirement account?

For asset protection, we divide retirement plans into 1) ERISA-qualified plans and 2) non-qualified retirement plans – such as Individual Retirement Accounts.

An *ERISA-qualified plan* is a retirement account that complies with the Employee Retirement Income Security Act of 1974 (ERISA). This law was specifically enacted to protect employees enrolled in benefit plans sponsored by their employers or unions. A key ERISA requirement is that the pension plan be a spendthrift trust or one that prohibits the beneficiary from gifting, anticipating or encumbering the plan's principal or income. The spendthrift provision immunizes your plan from creditor claims.

The more common qualified retirement plans include profit-sharing plans (defined contribution plans), pension plans (defined benefit plans) and 401K plans, or plans where the employee makes voluntary contributions.

Before 1992 conflicting court decisions confused the question about whether ERISA plans were creditor protected. A US Supreme Court decision, *Patterson v. Shumate*, clarified their protection, ruling that ERISA-qualified plans cannot be claimed by creditors – whether in or out of bankruptcy. *Every* ERISA-qualified pension and profit-sharing plan is thus lawsuit-proof. Public pensions (funded by state or federal government) have always been creditor protected.

For an ERISA pension plan to be lawsuit-proof, the company owners *and* at least one other employee must be covered under the plan. For a variety of technical reasons, some plans are not ERISA-qualified. Have your asset protection lawyer or plan administrator review your pension plan on this point.

> To find out whether your pension and profit-sharing plan are qualified under ERISA, and thus protected, ask your plan administrator. Even when your retirement plans are protected, their proceeds are unprotected when commingled with other funds.

Several court decisions have eroded the protection for pensions since *Patterson*. In several cases, the plaintiffs successfully argued that the defendants' 401K did not fully comply with IRS/ERISA. This made the plan unprotected by ERISA. A disqualified plan then had only the protection of a non-qualified plan under the defendants' state law.

Keogh plans with multiple participants usually have the same lawsuit protection as ERISA-qualified pensions. So your Keogh plan is probably lawsuit-proof. A sole-participant Keogh plan is more vulnerable to a creditor who can seize it because the beneficiary/debtor can voluntarily withdraw their funds.

> **Substantial IRAs and Keoghs are as vulnerable as savings. You must then shelter non-ERISA retirement accounts before creditor seizure. Incurring an IRS penalty for early withdrawal may be preferable to losing your entire retirement fund to the creditor.**

There is no ERISA protection for IRAs. Their protection depends upon state law. As with the state exemptions for homestead, insurance, wages, etc., state laws do vary. Many states fully protect non-qualified accounts, yet other states give them little or no lawsuit protection. Most states at least partially protect non-qualified plans. State laws may protect either a statutory amount (i.e., $50,000) or whatever amount a court deems reasonably necessary to support the debtor. There are probably several other limitations or restrictions under your state statutes. Some states further protect only accounts in trust and not distributions to the beneficiary.

Recent changes to the federal bankruptcy law expanded the protection to IRAs whose owners file personal bankruptcy. Under the new rules, IRA funds rolled over from a tax-qualified plan are generally not subject to creditor claims, regardless of the IRA owner's state or the value of the IRA.

The new bankruptcy law also puts IRAs beyond the reach of creditors. Up to $1 million of IRA funds (and earnings) or such larger amount as may be determined by the bankruptcy court as necessary for the debtor's support are exempt. A 'simple' retirement account, a simplified employee pension (SEP) and assets 'rolled over' to the IRA from a qualified plan or another IRA are disregarded under this $1 million limit. Stated differently, the portion of an IRA attributable to assets 'rolled over' from a tax-qualified plan and earnings on those rolled over assets – typically all or a large portion of the IRA assets, *are* protected, even if it exceeds $1 million. This new exemption applies without regard to 1) the state in which the IRA owner resides, 2) whether that state has 'opted out' of the federal bankruptcy exemptions and 3) whether the IRA owner, in his bankruptcy filing, has elected the federal bankruptcy exemptions or the state bankruptcy exemptions.

Prior to this new law, it was unclear whether an individual's IRA was exempt from creditor claims if the individual filed bankruptcy. Because of a confusing mix of federal and state laws and court cases, an individual oftentimes was uncertain whether a 'rollover' IRA (frequently funds rolled over from a tax-qualified plan and earnings on that amount, and often representing the individual's single most valuable asset) would be lost to creditors in bankruptcy. This uncertainty often resulted in huge legal fees and inefficiencies over retirement plan contests.

> State laws that partly or fully shelter annuities, insurance, wages, IRAs, Keoghs and other exempt assets are worthless protectors against the IRS and other federal agencies.

Is *your* retirement plan lawsuit-proof or bankruptcy-proof? This will depend upon several factors:

- Whether your plan is qualified under the Employee Retirement Income Security Act (ERISA),

- Whether state law exempts non-ERISA plans (i.e. IRAs) and for what amount,

- Whether your plan is a pension or welfare benefit plan and whether it is in payment mode or still in trust,

- The creditor claiming the retirement accounts,

- Whether or not you are in bankruptcy.

Several key strategies can help you shelter an *unprotected* retirement plan.

1. Keep Your Money in Your Pension Plan

Don't roll over your pension into a self-directed IRA too quickly. If you roll over your ERISA-qualified funds into a self-directed IRA, in a state that doesn't fully protect IRAs, you reduce or eliminate your creditor protection. Of course, you may not be able to leave your retirement account in your employer's 401K plan. Or you may want to direct your own IRA investments. Base your 'rollover' decision primarily from an investment viewpoint, but consider asset protection when you do decide.

I had one client make this blunder several years ago. Frustrated by excessive administrative costs charged against his partnership's pension plan, he rolled over his pension plan into an IRA so he could day-trade and gain greater returns. What he never realized was that his pension plan was lawsuit protected, while his new IRA was unprotected under his state law. When he was later sued on a bad business deal he lost his $500,000 IRA.

2. Roll Your IRA into a Qualified Plan

If it is smart to lawsuit-proof your retirement funds by keeping them shielded in an ERISA-qualified plan, it may be as wise to roll back your IRA into a qualified plan. Check into this if your IRA was originally a rollover from an ERISA-qualified plan. Or create your own new qualified plan. For instance, you can set up zero percent money purchase plans that are IRS compliant, ERISA-qualified *and* creditor-proof. Similarly, if your pension plan is not fully creditor protected (i.e. a single member plan) and you add one or more beneficiaries, you will create a creditor-proof plan.

3. Invest Your IRA in an FLP or LLC

A favorite strategy is to invest unprotected IRA, SEP-IRA or deferred compensation plan funds into a family limited partnership (FLP) or single member limited liability company (LLC). Your retirement funds would then have 'charging order protection'. I more fully explain this in later chapters. Your plan custodian must agree with this arrangement, and your transfer may be recoverable by your *present* creditor if it is fraudulent. Therefore, don't rely on this strategy when you have an *existing* creditor. However, a single member LLC can frequently protect your retirement funds and you can be its investment advisor.

4. Invest Your IRA Offshore

For stronger protection, move your retirement funds offshore. Your IRA will have more protection than an IRA invested in a family limited partnership or domestic LLC.

You have two options: 1) You can move your retirement account into a sub-trust of a foreign asset protection trust (FAPT) or 2) instruct your fund custodian to invest your IRA for a membership interest in an offshore LLC.

The first alternative – a foreign trust for retirement fund protection – is complex and costly. You can also inadvertently disqualify your plan unless this is set up correctly. Another offshore trust drawback is that appreciating sub-trust assets may not grow on a tax deferred basis.

Many of our clients invest their IRAs into single member offshore LLCs. It is a simpler and less costly procedure than an offshore trust. Essentially, your retirement plan would set up a Nevis or Isle of Man LLC with the appropriate protective provisions (see Chapter 11). Your IRA custodian would invest your retirement funds in the foreign LLC in exchange for full ownership of the LLC. Then no retirement funds would be within the US subject to creditor claims. Your retirement account would now only be a member in the foreign LLC and would only be subject to the charging order remedy. You may be the investment advisor (and even be as co-signatory on the foreign LLC account) *until* you have a judgment creditor. You would then surrender control. Until then you can safely reinvest the foreign LLC's funds in US investments. A US court cannot compel you or your custodian to turn over the funds because the foreign LLC owns the funds, and the foreign manager and custodian control the funds.

If you own a substantial IRA and if your state doesn't fully protect your IRA, then consider this foreign LLC strategy. One impediment: Too few US custodians are familiar with this offshore strategy. We can recommend several qualified custodians to implement your foreign LLC strategy.

5. Terminate Your IRA and Protect the Proceeds

If your IRA is subject to imminent creditor seizure, your most practical solution may be to terminate your IRA, pay the tax (and early withdrawal penalties) and protect the proceeds as you would shelter cash or other liquid assets. Plan dissolution is certainly the most economical option with a small IRA which can't cost-justify a more complex or expensive form of protection.

6. Invest Your IRA into an Exempt Annuity

Annuities, in many states, are exempt from lawsuits. This is some-times true, even in states that don't completely protect IRAs. In these cases, you may safely invest your IRA in annuities, though we don't ordinarily recommend buying annuities through an IRA because you then duplicate your tax deferral. However, buying a self-protected annuity for your IRA can be sensible when asset protection is your primary goal.

7. Relocate to a State That Protects IRAs

If you own a large, unprotected IRA – and have legal problems – you may also relocate to a state that fully protects IRAs. This is the same strategy as homestead 'shopping' where you relocate to a more protective state to shelter your home. But do keep in mind the residency requirement.

Finally, consider using your retirement plan as your safe haven for your extra cash – if your retirement plan is fully creditor protected. You have limitations on how much you can put into your retirement plans for tax deferral, but you can invest more *after-tax* dollars into a lawsuit-proof retirement plan. When you reach whatever amount you can invest annually on a tax-deferred basis, you can pay the tax on your excess contributions. But these funds would still be protected by your plan.

How to Protect Wages

A judgment creditor seizes paychecks through a *wage garnishment*. However, how much of your paycheck your creditor can claim is limited by both federal and state laws.

As with every other state exemption, each state affords wages a different level of protection. Texas and Florida, the two most debtor-friendly states, exempt all wages from creditor garnishment for 'head-of-the-household'; presumably the family member with the larger income who supports other family members. New York, as another example, shelters 90 percent of the net wages. Only 10 percent (in aggregate) can be claimed by a debtor's creditors.

As with the homestead laws, you must comply with your state laws to protect your wages. Your state may require that you segregate your wages in a 'wage exemption' or 'wage earner' account. You cannot commingle wages with unprotected funds if the wages are to remain sheltered.

> Disposable income is defined as the net compensation after deducting all amounts required by law to be withheld.

Does your state offer you less wage protection? The federal Consumer Credit Protection Act (CCPA) limits the amount your creditor can garnish from your wages. The federal CCPA overrides those state laws that provide less wage protection. The CCPA limits the wages a creditor can garnish to the lesser of 1) 25% of the debtor's disposable income per week (*disposable income* is your net paycheck after deducting federal and state withholding and FICA taxes) or 2) the amount by which your weekly disposable income exceeds 30 times the federal minimum hourly wage.

Exempt (protected) wages cannot be garnished by your creditor once you receive it, provided you keep it segregated from your non-wage funds. Commissions, royalties and other forms of income may not fall within the wage exemption.

You can avoid garnishment of wages a creditor can garnish. One option is to form a corporation and direct your income to that corporation. For tax purposes, you can withdraw the money as a loan. This same simple strategy has been successfully used by debtors to temporarily shield their non-exempt wages from creditors; however, it is not a practical long-term solution.

A less common wage protection strategy is to make a wage assignment to a 'friendlier' creditor who would then periodically 'loan' you money. A wage assignment must be in writing and in force *before* the creditor gets *their* garnishment order.

There are several other exceptions to these exemption laws, which, of course, I only summarize. For example, the Child Support Enforcement Act of 1975 overrides federal and state income exemptions for purposes of enforcing alimony or child support orders. Alimony and child support payments are generally not exempt from garnishment by either the payer's or recipient's creditors. Support payments in some states also have a limited exemption.

Are welfare payments protected? Can they be seized by your creditors? They are usually exempt from creditor seizure; but again, state laws are hardly uniform. Some states partially protect welfare payments. Others afford them no protection. Public assistance programs (Aid to Families with Dependent Children or AFDC) can also be unprotected. As with wages, welfare payments lose their protection once the money is received and commingled with non-welfare funds or the money is converted into non-exempt assets.

Public assistance payments – such as aid to the blind and aid to the elderly and disabled – are generally protected. Creditors cannot garnish these payments if these payments are segregated from non-exempt funds. If you use the exempt proceeds to acquire non-exempt assets, you lose protection.

Social Security and dis-ability income payments arc also not necessarily lawsuit-proof. Social Security is not a pension under the Employee Retirement Income Security Act

> **Proceeds of welfare payments are always unprotected once they are received and commingled with non-welfare funds or are converted to other assets.**

(ERISA), therefore, it is not federally protected. Whether your creditor can seize your Social Security check will depend upon your state laws. The IRS can seize your Social Security but as a matter of policy – they seldom do.

As with protecting your IRAs, you will find increased protection for certain types of income under the new bankruptcy law which now fully protects:

- Social security benefits, unemployment compensation and local public assistance payments,

- Veterans' benefits,

- Disability, illness and unemployment benefits,

- Payments under a stock bonus, pension or profit sharing plan, annuity or similar plan on account of illness.

But remember, you only get the bankruptcy exemption if you are in bankruptcy. Otherwise, your state law governs their protection.

Safety with Life Insurance and Annuities

Buy an annuity or life insurance. It may be the simplest way to shelter yourself from creditors. *Every* state partially or fully creditor-protects life insurance. Life insurance exemptions were first adopted in 1841 to protect the financial stability of an insured's dependents and to avoid their dependency on state support. Life insurance can give you lawsuit protection, it can also be an excellent investment alternative. Life insurance is generally seizure exempt (and likely will remain creditor protected well into the future), nevertheless, here too the states vary in their protection for insurance and annuities. Check:

- Will your state partially or totally shield the insurance policy's proceeds from the policyholder's creditors?

- If your state doesn't fully protect your entire policy, how much will it protect?

- Will your state also protect the policy proceeds? Does this protection depend on whether the policy beneficiaries are the policyholder's spouse, children or other dependents?

- Does your state exempt every life policy (term, universal, whole life, etc.)?

- Does your state protect a policy's cash surrender value as well as the policy proceeds? If your policy has a substantial cash value, how much of that cash value will your state exemption protect?

- Is a policy that you buy *after* you have a creditor, protected against that creditor?

If your state doesn't fully protect your insurance, then you need an irrevocable life insurance trust (ILIT). I also recommend an ILIT when the insurance beneficiaries have present or potential creditors, the policy has a cash value, you owe the IRS or you reside in a state that doesn't fully protect insurance. As I explain in Chapter 10, an irrevocable life insurance trust will fully lawsuit-protect both your policy proceeds and the cash value against both your own and your beneficiaries' creditors. Your ILIT can also save you estate taxes if you will have a taxable estate.

Annuities may be similarly protected by the same state laws that protect insurance. But will an annuity be a good investment for you? Ask your investment advisor or financial planner. Buy an annuity only because it's your right investment – not because it's asset protected.

Still, people who buy variable annuities may be partly motivated by the fact that annuities are lawsuit-proof in their state. Annuities have advantages and disadvantages, as will any other investment. But if an annuity can make financial sense for you, then you will get more protection if you buy a foreign annuity. For instance, Swiss annuities provide creditor protection (including protection against divorce, the IRS and bankruptcy) if your spouse or descendents are the beneficiaries (or a third party is an irrevocable beneficiary). Other countries creditor-proof their annuities and life insurance products. The Isle of Man and the Bahamas are two examples. Isle of Man insurance companies excel for several reasons, aside from the fact that several well-rated insurance companies are located in the Isle of Man.

The new bankruptcy law exempts unmatured life insurance policies (other than a credit life insurance contract). It also protects a debtor's interest in a life policy – up to a value of $9850.

More Lawsuit-Proof Assets

Other assets that you own are probably safe from lawsuits and bankruptcy. Some common examples: Burial plots, wedding rings, jewelry, household furniture, autos, tools of your trade, livestock, health aids, farming implements, funds under 529 plans and similar college programs, and gifts under the Uniform Gifts to Minors Act.

The exempt item list may be expanded in the more debtor-friendly states. These assets are protected up to a certain value. The exemption may not be sufficient to protect an asset worth considerably more than the exemption.

> Swiss law protects Swiss annuities against all creditor claims (including divorce, the IRS and bankruptcy), provided your spouse or descendants are beneficiaries, or a third party is an irrevocable beneficiary.

It is interesting to read the state exemption statutes. Massachusetts law is a throwback to more politically incorrect time. They still exempt 'one wife' from creditor seizure. Of course, some Bay State husbands would wish otherwise.

The federal bankruptcy exemptions are also quite limited in their exemptions. Their exemption list includes residences ($18,450), automobiles($2,950), household items ($9,850), jewelry ($1,225), professional tools ($1,850) and life insurance ($9,850). This is not all inclusive. The bankruptcy law also has a $975 wildcard exemption which you can apply to any asset.

Sheltering Exempt Proceeds

What if you sell or refinance your exempt property? Will the proceeds stay safe from your creditors? For example, if you sell your homesteaded home, how can you safely shelter the proceeds?

You have options. One is to transfer the proceeds from one exempt asset to another. For example, you can use the protected proceeds from selling your homesteaded home to buy an exempt annuity. Or you can invest the proceeds in some other safe harbor – perhaps a limited partnership, LLC, irrevocable trust or some other entity that would safe-keep it from creditors.

Every state protects the proceeds from the sale or refinancing of an exempt asset. Some states protect the proceeds for a specified time (set by statute) or for a reasonable time (determined by the courts). However, to maintain protection, you must segregate your exempt proceeds so that they do not lose their source identity. You always want to identify your funds as coming from exempt assets.

> Every state protects the proceeds from the sale or refinancing of an exempt asset. However, to maintain protection, you must segregate your exempt proceeds.

Exemption Limitations

The exemption laws won't shelter your otherwise protected assets against your most dangerous creditor – the US government. The IRS (and most other federal agencies – such as the SEC, FTC and Health Care Financing Administration [HCFA] etc.) can ignore these exemption laws that are intended to protect assets from *other* creditors. For example, the IRS can seize any home, notwithstanding the state homestead laws. Similarly, state laws that shelter annuities, insurance, wages, IRAs and other assets won't protect you against federal agencies. There are only a few assets (with negligible value) that are protected against the IRS. Moreover, state exemptions may not protect you from state claims.

Nor are exempt assets safe in divorce. For example, a divorce court can award your spouse a share of a retirement account through a Qualified Domestic Relations Order (QDRO). Family law courts can also seize exempt assets to enforce child support.

An asset that is *generally* self-protected under your state law may *not* be protected against *your* creditor in *your* particular circumstances. You can't rely on generalities. You need an attorney thoroughly familiar with your state laws.

Turn Vulnerable Wealth into Self-Protected Wealth

You see the obvious strategy. Maximize your protection by converting non-exempt (or unprotected) assets into exempt or self-protected assets. If you live in debtor-friendly states, you have many options. Or you can 'jurisdiction shop' and relocate to a state whose laws are more protective than where you now reside. Or you can exchange assets with a liability-free spouse. Transfer to your spouse your unprotected assets in exchange for *protected* marital assets of equal value.

Transforming non-exempt assets into exempt assets also has its limitations. Statutes or case law, in certain states deem such conversions fraudulent transfers if you have creditors – even when the transfer is a 'fair value' exchange. Florida, for instance, has a rarely enforced, anti-conversion statute. Florida also denies protection to insurance and annuities that are acquired with the proceeds from non-exempt assets when they are purchased *after* you have a creditor. Converting your vulnerable wealth into exempt assets – even against an existing creditor – may nevertheless be permissible in other states.

O.J.-type stories abound in Texas and Florida and in other debtor-friendly states. But it's not only the O.J.s who flock to Florida and Texas to escape their creditors. These two states give good wealth protection through their generous exemption laws, but you can find ways to protect your wealth in any other state – if you can creatively apply their exemption laws.

Wealthsaver Tips

1. Your state homestead laws may protect your home – though your home may require additional safeguards.

2. ERISA-qualified plans are protected from lawsuits and bankruptcy.

3. IRAs and other non-qualified plans are protected against lawsuits only to the extent allowed by your state. They may have greater protection in bankruptcy.

4. Insurance and annuities may be fully or partially protected by your state laws. An irrevocable life insurance trust can shield this asset.

5. The exemption laws will not protect you against every claim – particularly tax claims, divorce or intentional torts.

6. Proceeds from the sale or refinancing of an exempt asset will be protected for a time set by your state law – and if not commingled.

7. Anticipate bankruptcy. Check the new bankruptcy law. It may have diminished or expanded the value of your state exemption laws.

8. Never rely on the exemption laws to shield your assets without the assistance of a qualified asset protection planner.

SIX

Co-Ownership Tips and Traps

Do you co-own assets or property? I don't refer to co-owning legal entities, such as corporations or LLCs, but situations where you and one or several others (probably your spouse or family members) directly title co-owned assets to your personal names. It may be a bank account, your home, investment property, a business, car, boat or any other asset.

Co-owners of property seldom think about their potential liabilities from their co-ownership. They don't always realize whether co-ownership will aid or impede their protecting these co-owned assets from their creditors.

For example, two business partners together own and title their commercial real estate in their own names as tenants-in-common. What if someone gets injured on the property? Whose liable? How could these co-owners have titled this property to reduce their personal exposure? Or what if one co-owner files bankruptcy or loses a lawsuit and has a major judgment creditor? What more could they have done – and *should* they have done – to safeguard their property, each co-owner's interest in the property and their respective personal liabilities from their property ownership?

Or consider an elderly mother with a middle-aged daughter. The mother wants to leave her savings account to her daughter when she dies. She also wants her daughter to be able to write checks on the account if the mother becomes disabled. Mom sets up a joint account in both her name and her daughter's as joint owners. The mother reasons that when she dies, the account will automatically pass to her daughter and avoid probate. It seems sensible. But does the mother foresee the potential pitfalls from a joint bank account? What if the daughter is sued or has creditor problems, tax troubles or divorces? Poof! The joint savings account would go to some stranger.

I commonly see this same problem with married couples. Spouses frequently view co-ownership to be their simplest and most natural way to title their marital property. They too must ask the same questions: Will co-owning their assets expand their liability? Will they gain more or less lawsuit protection? How strong is that protection? Will co-owning assets help or hinder them from achieving their other estate and tax planning objectives? Good questions? This chapter takes that hard look at whether – and when – you should co-own property. You'll also see the potential dangers from and alternatives to co-ownerships.

Co-Ownership Basics

To understand the risks and benefits that arise from the various co-ownership arrangements, you must first know how each type co-ownership is created and functions. Unless I note otherwise, these ownership arrangements can apply to personal property (bank accounts, stocks and bonds, motor vehicles, copyrights, partnership interests, etc.) or real property (land, homes, condos, buildings, etc.). These co-ownerships are oftentimes called *tenancies*. 'Tenancy', in this context, doesn't suggest a lease and tenants. It is a form of co-ownership.

> Tenancy is a form of co-ownership, and in this context does not suggest a lease and tenants.

There are three types of co-ownership and each has its own features:

1. Tenancy-in-common:

- This is the most frequently used form of co-ownership between non-family members.

- Each co-owner owns a fractional interest in the property (i.e., if there are three co-owners, each owns a one-third share).

- Each co-owner can transfer or mortgage his or her share of the property without the consent of the other co-owners.

- A co-owner can bequeath her ownership share. The interest does not pass upon death to the surviving co-owner.

- Tenancy-in-common is the *default tenancy* for unmarried co-owners. Unless you specifically designate another type of ownership in the title documents, the law assumes that it is a tenancy-in-common.

2. Joint tenancy:

- Each co-owner owns an *undivided* interest in the property (i.e. if there are three co-owners, each owns an undivided share of the entire property).

- Each co-owner can transfer his interest without the consent of the others. If one joint owner transfers his interest, this severs the joint tenancy and the new co-owner becomes a tenant-in-common with the previous joint owners. For example, assume there are three owners of a property in joint tenancy – A, B and C. Each owns an undivided one-third share. If joint tenant A sells to a buyer, then the buyer becomes a tenant-in-common with joint tenants B and C; however, B and C, between themselves, remain joint tenants.

■ When a joint tenant dies, his or her share automatically passes to the surviving joint tenants. The ownership interest cannot pass through a will. This is called the joint tenant's *right of survivorship*. Under the previous example, if C died, B would automatically inherit C's one-third interest. B would then own two-thirds of the property as tenant-in-common with the buyer, who would own a one-third interest.

■ Most states require joint tenancy to be created by written agreement. The title documents will recite joint tenancy, jointly, jointly with the *right of survivorship* or *joint tenants with the right of survivorship* (JTWROS). In a few states, joint tenancy does not have this automatic right of survivorship. This survivorship right must be expressly stated within the title document.

3. Tenancy-by-the-entirety:

■ This form of co-ownership is available in 25 states. Only a husband and wife can co-own assets as tenancy-by-the-entirety. Tenancy-by-the-entirety is thus a special type of joint tenancy for married couples. As such, it also carries the right of survivorship; that is, the surviving spouse automatically inherits the deceased spouse's interest.

■ Neither spouse can sell, transfer or mortgage the property without the other spouse's consent.

- The tenancy-by-the-entirety remains intact until both spouses agree to change the form of ownership, divorce or one spouse dies.

- Some tenancy-by-the-entirety states restrict it to real estate, such as the marital home. Most states allow a married couple to title any personal and real property as tenancy-by-the-entirety.

Tenancy-In-Common

Each co-owner in a *tenancy-in-common* (or tenant-in-common) owns a divided fractional interest

> **Tenancy-in-common gives neither co-owner creditor protection.**

in the property. This, however, creates a serious lawsuit danger and, correspondingly, gives neither co-owner creditor protection. Let me illustrate the risks from tenancy-in-common. For instance, assume that you and your friend John own an apartment building as tenants-in-common. Either you or John can sell, gift or mortgage your half interest in the building without the other's consent. You are essentially 'partners' in the business of renting apartments, collecting rents, maintaining the premises, etc. The building provides you and John with an income.

Since you and John are tenants-in-common, you each own a separate one-half interest in the building. Your interest is distinct from John's interest. Your creditors cannot claim John's interest. Conversely, John's personal creditors can claim only *his* half-interest in the building. Your half would remain safe from John's creditors. While this outcome may seem to be an acceptable arrangement, particularly if you consider yourself to be the *safe* co-owner, tenancy-in-common can nevertheless cause you huge problems.

One risk is that John's personal creditors can force a sale of the *entire* property to satisfy John's personal debts. Since John can transfer his share of the tenancy-in-common property without your consent, John's creditor can 'step into his shoes' and similarly force the transfer of his interest. You might negotiate to buy John's interest to avoid a forced sale of the entire property, but this may not be practical. For instance, you may not have the money. If the court then liquidates the entire property, you still lose the property – although you will recover half the proceeds from the forced sale.

Suppose John's creditors don't force the sale of the entire property. They could instead bid for and claim John's half-interest in the property. The net result is that you would now have a new partner, John's creditor! It happens.

John's financial problems can thus become *your* problems. Your problems can become John's. That's a *bad* arrangement.

How safe will *your* ownership interest be from your own creditors? You know the answer. If John's creditors can seize his interest, your creditors can seize *yours*.

You can see why co-owning property as tenants-in-common is risky. If either you or your co-owner(s) encounters financial problems, you can lose the property. Or you might lose money. You can avoid this trap. Later chapters will show you better co-ownership arrangements and how you can title your assets through protective entities. If you still insist upon titling your co-owned assets as tenants-in-common, then at least make certain that your co-owners are financially secure. You otherwise risk a forced sale of the assets, a new co-owner or a lost investment.

> When you co-own property as tenants-in-common, both owners are liable for all debts that arise from the co-owned property.

Aside from owning a vulnerable co-ownership interest, a bigger pitfall is that tenancy-in-common *expands* your potential liability. For instance, if John accidentally injures somebody by negligently managing the co-owned property, who gets sued? You and John, of course. You co-own the property and you essentially have created a general partnership. A plaintiff who wins a $5 million judgment (or any amount more than what the property or John is worth), can force *you* to pay. As co-owners, you and John are jointly and severally liable for all debts that arise from the co-owned property. The bottom line: Never co-own property as tenants-in-common.

Joint Tenancy

Joint tenancy is another popular form of co-ownership. There are several key features that distinguish it from tenancy-in-common. One is the right of survivorship. When one joint tenant dies,

> Co-owning assets through joint tenancy is nearly always a mistake. It will significantly increase your lawsuit exposure, frustrate sound estate planning and give you little or no lawsuit protection.

the jointly owned property automatically passes to the surviving joint tenant(s). Jointly owned property then passes outside a will, which avoids the expense and delay of probate. Because joint tenancy avoids probate, financial and legal advisors frequently recommend that their clients jointly co-own their assets when the parties intend the asset to pass to the survivor. Unfortunately, these advisors don't always advise their clients how joint ownership can hurt them. Co-owning assets through joint tenancy is nearly always a mistake. It will significantly increase your lawsuit exposure, frustrate sound estate planning and give you little or no lawsuit protection.

Jointly owned property, whether it is personal property or real estate, creates the same lawsuit and creditor risks as will a tenancy-in-common. It can cause even greater exposure. You have no lawsuit protection — as with a tenancy-in-common. Your creditors can seize your interest in jointly co-owned property. Your co-owner's creditors can seize theirs. You also have the same tenancy-in-common risks. If your co-owner(s) creditors seize his interest in the property, he becomes a co-tenant in common with you. Alternatively, a creditor of any co-owner can force a sale of the entire property to recover the debt owed by the co-owner, although the creditor can only take the proceeds of the debtor joint owner.

Joint ownership has one more twist. It puts you in a 'winner-takes-all' game. You 'gamble' that you will survive your co-owner (joint tenant). Jointly owned property automatically passes upon death to the surviving joint tenant(s), so if the liability-free co-owner dies before the debtor co-owner, the entire property will pass to the debtor. The property can then be claimed by the debtor's creditors.

For example, if you and John own the building as joint tenants, and you die, John's creditors can seize the entire building. Your family would have no further ownership interest in the building and not be entitled to proceeds from any forced liquidation.

The obvious alternative outcome in this 'winner-takes-all' game is that if the safe co-owner (you) survives the debtor co-owner (John), you would then own the building free of John's creditors.

Joint tenancy can also impair good estate planning. For instance, if your estate plan is to gift your property upon your death to your children, you would normally provide for this in your will or living trust. Joint tenancy frustrates this estate planning because property that you jointly own will instead pass by rights of survivorship to your surviving joint tenant(s) when you die. You can't dispose of jointly-owned property through a will or living trust. Beneficiaries that you designate in your will or trust to inherit your interest in jointly owned property would effectively be 'disinherited' since that property will go to your surviving joint tenant(s).

I see this avoidable tragedy every day because many people don't understand this survivorship feature about joint ownership. Their advisors never informed them.

This was the case with a prosperous plumber. In his late 60s, Pat married for the second time. Shortly thereafter, Pat titled his Pennsylvania home, Arizona winter vacation condo and $2 million stock portfolio as joint tenancy with his new wife. Pat died six months later. Who now owns his home, condo and stocks? His new wife, of course. His three children and eight grandchildren inherited nothing, although Pat's will bequeathed to them these same assets.

Let's return to Mildred, our retired Florida widow, who set up a joint bank account with her New Jersey daughter. Despite my advice, Mildred insisted upon a joint ac-

> **Joint tenants are jointly and severally liable for the debts or liabilities that arise from the co-owned asset.**

count in case she got sick and could no longer write out checks for herself. Moreover, she wanted joint tenancy on the account to avoid probate. I told Mildred how she could more safely accomplish her objectives by using a durable power of attorney to give her daughter signing authority on her checking account. A living trust would be the better way to avoid probate. But Mildred was stubborn. How safe is Mildred's $300,000 joint account now that her daughter is divorcing?

Intelligent, well-intentioned people get mired in dangerous joint ownerships because they don't realize their risks. And plenty of folks have no idea how their assets are titled.

And as with tenancy-in-common, joint tenants are jointly and severally liable for the debts or liabilities that arise from the co-owned asset. Why expand your liability?

How are your assets titled? If you own property jointly (or as tenants-in-common), then see your lawyer now!

Tenancy-By-The-Entirety

Are you married? If so, read this section carefully. Tenancy-by-the-entirety is a special type of joint tenancy for husbands and wives in 25 states (chiefly on the east coast).

A few states with tenants-by-the-entirety laws give you no more creditor protection than will a joint tenancy; that is, little or none. However, assets titled to spouses as tenancy-by-the-entirety in other states enjoy comparatively strong protection from lawsuits against one spouse.

These more protective states generally prevent a creditor of only one spouse from claiming that debtor-spouse's interest in property co-owned by the spouses as tenancy-by-the-entirety (T/E). A creditor of both spouses can claim the tenancy-by-the-entirety property. For example, if the husband and wife both guaranteed a bank note, the bank could claim the couple's tenancy-by-the-entirety property. But if only one spouse was sued on a debt, then the T/E property would stay lawsuit-protected from that one creditor. You can see the value of this protection.

Does your state have T/E protection? Check my website www.asgoldstein.com. If your state T/E laws can protect you, then you might re-title your spousal property as tenancy-by-the-entirety. Your attorney can tell you whether tenancy-by-the-entirety titled assets in your state will be shielded without additional protection. Do bear in mind that upon either spouse's death, tenancy-by-the-entirety property automatically passes to the surviving spouse. You cannot bequeath those assets to other beneficiaries. If this is not your intent, then avoid titling those assets as tenancy-by-the-entirety.

There is little uniformity between tenancy-by-the-entirety laws. Florida and New York have strong tenancy-by-the-entirety laws, as do several other states. Spouses in these states may chiefly rely on tenancy-by-the-entirety for lawsuit protection. For instance, a Florida client recently sailed through bankruptcy with over $1 million in assets titled to himself and his wife as tenants-by-the-entirety. The assets were not claimed by the bankruptcy trustee because his wife was not in bankruptcy and she shared none of her husband's liabilities.

However, we are beginning to see some erosion from tenants-by-the-entirety protection. Several bankruptcy courts have recently ruled that a bankruptcy trustee *can* claim the tenants-by-the-entirety interest of the bankrupt spouse. Whether the trustee can then liquidate the debtor-spouse's property follows a balancing test: Will the creditors benefit more from a forced sale than what the non-debtor-spouse will lose? Several appeals courts let the IRS seize tenants-by-the-entirety interest owned by a delinquent spouse taxpayer - though the spouse had no tax obligation.

Nor can tenancy-by-the-entirety protect any asset. Some states limit tenancy-by-the-entirety protection only to real estate. Others limit its creditor-protection only to the

> You should not title vehicles as tenancy-by-the-entirety. If you do, then you and your spouse would both be liable in the event of an accident.

residence. Florida and New York protect *any* asset titled through tenants-by-the-entirety.

If your state has good tenancy-by-the-entirety laws, it will give you good lawsuit protection. You and your spouse may then title everything that you co-own as tenancy-by-the-entirety. Many of my long married clients have titled their home, investments, family business, etc. in precisely this way. However, you should *not* title vehicles or other liability-producing assets as tenancy-by-the-entirety (or any other form of co-ownership). If you do, then you and your spouse would both be liable in the event of an accident.

Unfortunately, most tenants-by-the-entirety states don't fully lawsuit-protect assets that are so-titled. Massachusetts, for example, protects the family home from the creditors of one spouse, but only for as long as the other spouse resides there; not thereafter. Tenancy-by-the-entirety laws offer patchwork protection. You must know precisely what assets the T/E laws in your state will – and won't – protect. You must also know their exceptions and limitations.

Tenancy-by-the-entirety laws are not foolproof even where the law is broadly protective. For example, if you co-own T/E property and your spouse unexpectedly dies while you have a judgment creditor, you would then own the entire property which could be seized by your creditor.

Divorce similarly extinguishes tenancy-by-the-entirety protection. You would expect divorcing spouses to remain sufficiently amicable to transfer tenancy-by-the-entirety property to another protective entity before they divorce (particularly if one spouse has creditors). But this isn't always true. I have seen a number of cases where a divorcing spouse's creditors gained that 'window of opportunity' to seize the debtor-spouse's interest in T/E assets immediately after a hostile divorce. Ex-spouses don't always cooperate in asset protection planning.

Avoid tenancy-by-the-entirety if you don't want to leave your property to your spouse. If you are in a second (or third) marriage and want your assets to go to your children, tenancy-by-the-entirety will defeat this, as will a joint tenancy.

Even when your state's tenancy-by-the-entirety laws give you good protection, spouses should only title their assets as tenancy-by-the-entirety: 1) When the couple wants survivorship rights to the asset; 2) When the spouses have low liability exposure and do not usually incur significant joint obligations and 3) When the couple is reasonably young and they have less concern that one spouse may unexpectedly die and leave the property exposed to the surviving spouse's judgment creditors.

If you and your spouse own property jointly in a tenancy-by-the-entirety state – and if your assets are not now otherwise lawsuit protected – then consider re-titling your assets as tenancy-by-the-entirety.

Community and Separate Property

Community property is a fourth type of co-ownership and it has its own issues. The 9 community property states are: Arizona,

> Community property is any property acquired by either spouse during the marriage.

California, Idaho, Louisiana, Nevada, New Mexico, Texas, Washington and Wisconsin. The laws in these community property states have important differences in construction and interpretation. If you live in a community property state, then have your attorney review your state laws. Specifically, inquire about the rights of creditors to claim community and separate property. I necessarily speak here in generalities. Your community property state may follow different rules.

Community property means that each spouse owns a one-half interest in the community property. Community property is *any* property acquired by *either* spouse during their marriage – other than inheritances or gifts made only to that one spouse. Property acquired by either spouse before marriage or after divorce (or permanent separation, depending on the state) remains that spouse's *separate property*. Debts incurred before marriage or after divorce are separate debts. Debts incurred while you are married are community debts, if they benefited both spouses. Most debts are considered marital debts, though the debt was incurred by only one spouse.

For example, Harry and Wilma, husband and wife, marry in 1995 and divorce in 2005. Harry's boat, which he owned since 1994, will remain his separate property, as will his inheritance from his father, which he received in 1997. The loan on Harry's boat, dating back to 1994, will also remain his separate debt. Whatever Harry earned as an accountant during their marriage will be community property, as will the antique car that he acquired in his name in 1997.

A couple can use a transmutation agreement to legally convert community property into separate property and vice versa. A transmutation agreement must be carefully drafted according to state law and be closely followed by both spouses. A transmutation agreement essentially provides that: "This specified property – and any property that I acquire hereafter is mine alone and [that] property – and any property that you hereinafter acquire is yours." Thus, the agreement divides present community assets as well as the future assets of each spouse into separate property. The effect of this is that the creditors of each spouse can then only claim the separate assets that belong to that debtor-spouse. This is safer than allowing a creditor to seize assets co-owned as community property.

A transmutation agreement lets you accomplish what you can accomplish with a prenuptial agreement, except that you can write a transmutation agreement before or during marriage. A prenuptial agreement must be executed *before* you marry.

Married couples in community property states frequently sign transmutation agreements to divide their community property into separate property. Why allow one spouse's creditors to claim the other spouse's assets?

A transmutation agreement prepared *after* you have a creditor, presents some risk, as it may be a fraudulent transfer. A *present* creditor whose claim is unsatisfied from the debtor-spouse's separate assets may claim assets fraudulently transferred to the non-debtor-spouse as separate property. Timing is critical. Prepare your transmutation agreement *before* you incur liabilities. Also, record your transmutation agreement in your public registry to provide public notice of the date when your agreement was completed and that your agreement remains in effect.

> Community creditors can claim community property. Certain states let community creditors claim either spouse's separate property.

The next question concerns the assets a creditor can seize in a community property state. The answer depends chiefly on the type debt the creditor is enforcing (a community or separate debt) and the type property the creditor is claiming (community or separate property). It can be difficult to distinguish between community and separate assets and debts. This issue is oftentimes contested in court. Generally, the separate creditors of one spouse can claim that spouse's separate property. Separate creditors can also usually claim community property – as well as the separate property owned by the other spouse - if the debt was incurred for necessities (food, shelter, clothing, utilities, etc.) – or that the debt benefited both spouses.

Community creditors (creditors of both spouses) can claim community property. Certain states let community creditors claim either spouse's separate property. For example, California's community property law – and most community property states – employ rules that are most favorable to creditors. Creditors may satisfy their debts from *any* property over which the debtor-spouse has management control. For instance, a California creditor may seize the separate property of the debtor-spouse as well as the community property – since both spouses presumably equally manage and control the community property. You may have different results in another community property state.

> If you live in a community property state, protect both your separate and community property.

You can see that the safety of community and separate property from creditors is cloudy. Usually, the separate and community property of both spouses are vulnerable. If you live in a community property state, then protect both your separate *and* community property. Title separate property apart from the community property or you may lose your separate property to your spouse (in divorce) or to your spouse's creditors during your marriage.

Co-Owned Assets Increases Liability

Co-ownership expands liability. For example, if you co-own an auto or boat and have an accident, you and your co-owner would share liability regardless who caused the accident. You may recall my 83 year old client who accidentally rocketed her car through a K-Mart window and seriously injured several shoppers. She has been sued for millions. To compound the problem, the car was titled to both her and her husband. Her husband is now defending himself against these lawsuits. Her husband owns substantial assets and may be forced to pay a hefty settlement despite my best efforts to protect him. While the couple owns most of their property as tenants-by-the-entirety, this won't protect them because both spouses are liable to the same plaintiffs.

Aside from the non-existent (or questionable) asset protection and the expanded liability from co-owning assets, there are other disadvantages:

- When one co-owner dies, the IRS may tax the entire value of the jointly owned property for estate tax purposes – unless the surviving co-owner can prove his contribution (this applies only to property co-owned by non-spouses).

- Co-owners cannot always transfer their ownership interests without the consent of the co-owners. This restriction can prevent the timely transfer of property, whether for asset protection, estate planning or other reasons (i.e., you want to sell or gift your interest). For example, one optometrist client is struggling to pay his small optical chain's $400,000 SBA loan. His major asset is a one-third interest in a million dollar commercial property that he co-owns as tenants-in-common with two uncles. I can't convince my client's uncles to re-title the property to an LLC to keep *everyone* safer. After all, nobody's chasing *them!* We used a more costly method to protect my client's one-third interest.

■ One co-owner's death can temporarily impede the other owner's use of the asset. For example, it's not unusual for jointly owned bank accounts to be frozen throughout probate. This can sometimes take years. Another client owns valuable waterfront property with a partner as tenants-in-common. His partner was hit with a $700,000 IRS tax lien which clouded the title to the property. They can't sell the property until they resolve the IRS claim.

These everyday problems from co-ownerships happen only because more people *don't think* about these potential problems. Consider those important questions *before* you title assets in your name and with a spouse or anyone else.

You can overcome every disadvantage from personally co-owning assets by titling collectively-owned assets to a protective entity – i.e. a corporation, limited liability company or limited partnership. The asset will then be safer from *your* creditors and your co-owner(s). You also won't be personally liable for whatever debts and liabilities the asset may generate.

Wealthsaver Tips

1. Co-owning assets may better protect assets or it may expand your liability and the possible loss of the assets. It depends upon the asset, the type co-ownership and your state law.

2. Tenancy-in-common gives you no asset protection. One co-owner's creditors can disrupt the tenancy and force the sale of the co-owned asset.

3. Upon the death of one co-owner, jointly owned property automatically passes to the co-owners. This can avoid probate, but not estate taxes. Jointly owned property will pass free of claims against the deceased co-owner.

4. Jointly owned property isn't protected from the creditors of a co-owner, although it may be procedurally more difficult for a creditor to seize a co-owner's interest.

5. Tenants-in-the-entirety in 25 states is a joint tenancy between husband and wife. With property titled this way, it may have some immunity from the creditors of one spouse. The protection depends upon state law.

6. There are two limitations with tenancy-by-the-entirety. Its protection terminates upon divorce or the death of either spouse. It also won't protect you against IRS claims, and may not fully protect you in bankruptcy.

7. Community property can be seized by your creditor – if their claim arose after you married. A husband's and wife's separate property (assets owned before marriage) can be claimed only by their respective creditors. Community property is generally unprotected.

SEVEN

Inc. Yourself

The chief purpose of a corporation is to insulate personal assets (or the assets of other businesses) from the debts of the incorporated business. This purpose may also be achieved by forming a limited liability company (LLC). Since both entities achieve this end, the word 'incorporation', as used in this chapter, means forming either a corporation or LLC for running your business; however this chapter's description of corporations does not include a description of LLCs, unless otherwise noted. Furthermore, note that unlike the LLC, the corporation is a comparatively poor entity to hold or protect personal assets.

There are two major drawbacks with using the corporation as a personal asset protector: 1) When you transfer assets to and from the corporation, you create tax consequences and 2) personal creditors can seize the shares that you own in the corporation, as well as any obligations due you from the corporation. The limited liability company and limited partnership (LP) overcome these corporate disadvantages and so play a far more important role in personal asset protection planning.

The ABCs of INCs

The mere mention of a corporation usually brings to mind Microsoft, General Motors or some other Fortune 500 company, yet more than 25 million corporations are owned by individuals or families to operate their own small businesses. They may also use corporations for other tax, estate planning or asset protection purposes. Many more people each year now discover the advantages of owning their own corporation. Incorporating is a small expense and brings big dividends.

It is easy to understand the concept of a corporation and how you can most effectively use this for asset protection.

A corporation is a legal entity that is authorized to conduct business or own assets as though it were a natural person. However, unlike a natural person, a corporation has a perpetual existence.

> A corporation is a legal entity that is authorized to conduct business or own assets as though it were a natural person.

It is owned by shareholders who invest in the corporation and share in its profits. Here are some important features of a corporation:

- **Created by state law.** Each state sets its own requirements to establish and maintain a corporation. Some state laws, however, are more corporate friendly than others.

- **Distinct legal entity.** A corporation is a separate legal entity; it is separate in every way from its shareholders. For example, the corporation enjoys the same constitutional rights as a natural person. Similarly, assets titled to a corporation are owned by the corporation, not its corporate shareholders.

- **Limited liability of shareholders.** This, of course, is the key benefit of incorporating. A corporation protects the personal assets of its stockholders, officers and directors from the debts of the incorporated business. Since a corporation is a legal entity distinct from its shareholders, its shareholders have no personal liability for the debts of the corporation. Shareholders can only lose their investment in the corporation (what they paid for their shares or loaned to the corporation) if the corporation is sued, cannot pay its debts or files bankruptcy.

- **Unlimited existence.** Unless the corporate articles state otherwise, the corporation can last in perpetuity. A stockholder's death does not terminate the corporation.

- **Centralized management.** Shareholders do not manage the corporation. Its board of directors, elected by the shareholders, set corporate policy. Daily operations are the responsibility of the corporate officers, who are appointed and supervised by the board (although the president may be elected by the shareholders).

- **There can be any number of shareholders.** Shareholders own the corporation and elect the board. The board of directors must have at least one director, although some states require more. One individual can, in most states, be the corporation's only shareholder, director and serve every requisite office (president, secretary and treasurer).

In Business? Incorporate!

If you go into business by yourself, your choice is between a sole proprietorship, corporation or limited liability company (LLC). If your business has more than one owner, your choice is between a general partnership, limited partnership, corporation or LLC. (While you can always operate through a limited liability company, which I will discuss in a later chapter, for now, let's consider the LLC the same as a corporation as a liability insulator.)

Before I make my case for the corporation, let me first make my case *against* a sole proprietorship or general partnership, and to a lesser extent against the limited partnership. Let's begin with definitions. A sole proprietorship form of organization exists when you operate your business without creating a formal legal entity such as a corporation or LLC. When you operate your business as a sole proprietorship, there is no legal separation between you and your business. You have personal liability for *every* business debt.

It is amazing in these litigious times that so many small businesses still function as sole proprietorships. Consider that 4 out of 5 small businesses fail within their first several years, and you can see that their owners needlessly gamble their family's financial security on the success of their venture. When their business fails, as most will, their owners will likely end in financial ruin, as their business creditors grab their personal assets.

> General partners are jointly and severally liable for every partnership liability.

The general partnership is an even more dangerous form of business organization because the general partners are jointly and severally liable for every partnership liability. Partners in a general partnership can easily lose their personal wealth to creditors if the business or the other partners have too few personal assets to satisfy the partnership obligations. You can lose your wealth even if your partner created the liability.

As you can see, a major disadvantage with both the sole proprietorship and general partnership is that they create 'inside out' liability. Creditors of the proprietorship or partnership can go 'outside' the business to satisfy their claims from the owners' personal assets.

There is also 'outside in' exposure. An owner's personal creditors can seize his business assets to satisfy his personal debts. In the case of the general partnership, a partner's personal creditors can force the liquidation of the partnership to claim his equity in the business.

Limited partnerships are not as bad off as general partnerships or sole proprietorships. However, by itself the limited partnership is a fatally flawed business entity, although it remains a powerful means of protecting personal assets. The problem with using a limited partnership to run a business is that the partnership's manager(s) (called 'general partners') have no limited liability. This means that a general partner's assets may be reached by a creditor to satisfy the partnership's debts. Fortunately, the limited partners, who are non-managing partners that have merely contributed assets to the partnership, have limited liability in a manner similar to that of an LLC or corporation. However, because of the lack of limited liability for general partners, a limited partnership should only run a business in the following circumstances:

- The general partner is a corporation or LLC. That way, the owners of the corporation or LLC (as a general partner) are not liable for partnership debts.

- The limited partnership engages in business activities that would never expose its partners to liability, such as non-margin investing in the stock market.

Note that there are a few states (such as Texas and California) where a limited partnership pays minimal or even no franchise tax, which taxes an LLC or corporation must pay. In this situation it is often advisable to form an LP with an LLC or corporation as the general partner.

In contrast, a corporation is a separate legal entity distinct from its shareholders since the law looks upon the corporation as a separate person. That is why a corporation (or LLC) can protect your personal assets from the inevitable debts and lawsuits against your business. Because your corporation is its own legal entity, you as its shareholder, director or officer are not liable for the debts or lawsuits against your corporation. If your corporation is sued or cannot pay its debts, you lose only your investment in the business; your other assets remain safe. That is why the corporation is such a powerful wealthsaver.

Business owners frequently start their ventures as sole proprietorships or general partnerships and become concerned about losing their personal assets only when their business is sued or heads towards bankruptcy. If you are sued while you operate as a sole proprietor or general partnership, it is too late to convert your company to an LLC or corporation in order to protect your personal assets from existing lawsuits or other collection attempts for company debts. However, you still have the opportunity to avoid personal liability from future company lawsuits or debts. Incorporate your business and transfer the assets of your proprietorship or partnership to the corporation. Your corporation then reduces the debts for which you have personal liability.

If you presently operate an unincorporated business, incorporate before you get into financial trouble. The smartest strategy, of course, is to incorporate before you start your business.

No business is too small to protect with a corporation or LLC, because no business is safe from lawsuits. Obviously, the larger enterprise has more need for corporate protection if only because it is a larger lawsuit target, but still no business, no matter how small or seemingly safe, is immune from legal and financial disasters. Here is why I say no business is safe. A wealthy widow from my own neighborhood enjoyed spending her weekends selling imported dolls at a local flea market. However, not long ago she sold a defective doll. A customer's 3 year old daughter punctured her eye by dislocating the doll's arm, exposing a large nail. My neighbor is now defending herself (and her not insignificant wealth) against a $5 million product liability claim.

> No business is too small to protect with a corporation or LLC, because no business is safe from lawsuits.

Had she incorporated her tiny kiosk enterprise it would be her corporation, and not her, who would have the liability; her personal assets would not be in jeopardy. Why didn't she incorporate? Her accountant discouraged her. "You don't need a corporation. Why spend money to incorporate to run a 'nickel-and-dime' weekend business?" Bad advice! Had she spent a few bucks to incorporate, she wouldn't be worried sick about losing everything she owns. Incorporating is your best insurance.

More Corporate Advantages

The limited liability that the corporation provides its shareholders is certainly the one key reason to incorporate your business. However, a corporation can give additional benefits that are not always available with other entities:

- Employees can participate in corporate profits and defer their income in corporate retirement plans.

- Corporations frequently enjoy lower tax rates than individual taxpayers.

- Tax brackets may be split among several corporations or you can multiply your tax deductions within the same corporation.

- Social Security payments are 50 percent deductible to the corporation.

- Trusts, limited partnerships, LLCs and other protective entities can own a C corporation.

- It is frequently possible to consolidate the income and losses of one corporation with those of other corporations to reduce your overall income taxes.

- Corporate shares can be donated to maximize your deductible charitable contributions.

- Certain tax deductible fringe benefits may be available only through a C corporation.

- When you liquidate your corporation, you may advantageously defer or reduce your capital gains tax.

Although the advantages of incorporating are significant, it is important to also note that an LLC may be structured so as to have all of the corporate advantages we've discussed thus far, in addition to other advantages corporations do not provide. We will discuss more about the pros and cons of the LLC vs. the corporation shortly. More information regarding LLCs is also available in Chapter 9.

Saving Taxes with an S Corporation

The S corporation gives you the same limited liability protection as does the C corporation. Business owners frequently select S corporation designation to avoid the double taxation of a regular or C corporation. However, because the S corporation's shareholders are the only ones subject to tax (unlike a C corporation, the S corporation itself pays no tax), many people erroneously think that the S corporation similarly loses the limited liability feature of the C corporation. This is not so. Consider only the tax factor when you decide whether to choose S or C corporation status. This decision is best left to your accountant.

You will find it far easier to lawsuit-proof your stock ownership in a C corporation than an S corporation, because the S corporation must be owned by natural persons or disregarded entities such as a single member LLC. C corporations, limited partnerships, multi-member LLCs and other legal entities, with few exceptions, cannot own shares of an S corporation. This gives you far fewer options to protect your S corporation shares from your personal creditors. However, we'll discuss shortly how one may protect S corporation shares. The S corporation has other key features:

> **Consider only the tax factor when you decide whether to choose S or C corporation status.**

- The S corporation has pass-through taxation. Corporate profits are taxed only once when they 'pass through' to the shareholders. The S corporation is thus taxed as a proprietorship or partnership. The corporation itself is not taxed, but its owners are.

- The S corporation is limited to 75 shareholders and all shareholders must be US citizens or residents.

- The S corporation must be organized under US law, have only one class of stock and may not own 80 percent or more of the stock of another corporation. You request S corporation status from the IRS. You can also change from C to S corporation status, within certain rigid IRS guidelines.

Corporations vs. LLCs: Which Entity is Better for Running a Business?

As well as being generally superior for personal asset protection, the LLC has evolved to eclipse the corporation as the preferred business entity in most circumstances. While the corporate structure remains useful for very large companies, it has the following drawbacks over LLCs:

- **Statutory inflexibility.** Corporate laws are generally comprehensive and less flexible than LLC laws. Corporate by-laws generally have limited leeway in defining how a given corporation will operate. In contrast, most 'default' LLC laws may be altered by an operating agreement, so as to allow the LLC members to customize their company to best suit their needs. Since corporate laws are written to favor large companies, small and medium companies may find corporate statutory inflexibility a hindrance.

■ **More cumbersome operational requirements.** The corporate decision-making process must adhere to certain complex procedural formalities that many small and medium-sized businesses find cumbersome. Certain corporate decisions require votes by stockholders, which must be duly recorded. Other decisions must be made at formal corporate board meetings, where decisions are voted upon and recorded as reflected in a volume of corporate minutes. Failure to observe such formalities may be grounds for piercing the corporate veil, thus making directors and/or shareholders personally responsible for company debts. Compare this process to the LLC, where managers are given broad leeway to make decisions without following such formalities, except in a few instances as defined in the LLC's operating agreement. Furthermore, LLCs may be structured so as to give the members as little or as much control over operational decision-making as is desired.

■ **Limited Choice of Tax Classification.** A corporation may choose to be taxed only one of two ways: According to the Internal Revenue Code (these corporations are referred to as 'C' corporations) or according to the rules of subchapter S of the same chapter (these corporations are referred to as 'S' corporations.) Compare this with an LLC, which may be chosen to be taxed as a C corporation, an S corporation, a partnership or as a sole proprietorship (which is often referred to as a 'disregarded entity'). For many business owners, both the C and S corporate modes of taxation are undesirable. The C corporation may be undesirable because not only must the corporation pay a tax on its profits, but its stockholders are also taxed when they receive a distribution of profit (which is commonly called a stock dividend). To avoid this 'double taxation', most corporations elect to be taxed as S corporations, where only the owners are taxed on corporate profits (this is known as 'pass-through' taxation). However, a corporation must meet strict criterion in order to qualify for S corporate tax status. Such requirements are often constricting to the operation of a business. An LLC, however, may be taxed as a partnership if it is owned by multiple taxpayers or as a disregarded entity if it is owned by only one taxpayer. Partnership taxation is often seen as preferable to S or C corporate tax status, because of the lack of a C corporation's double taxation and the lack of the structural limitations required to qualify as an S corporation. Furthermore, unlike with corporations, a return of capital from the LLC to a partner/LLC member usually doesn't trigger a tax, and a distribution of profit does not need to be proportional to one's ownership interest in the company. Nonetheless, if an LLC desires to be taxed as either a C or S corporation it may do so, while corporations may not choose to be taxed as a partnership or disregarded entity.

Despite the drawbacks of the corporate structure, there are instances where a corporation is preferred over an LLC. The main benefit of corporations is that ownership of stock may be freely transferred without obtaining the consent of other shareholders or corporate management. This is an essential characteristic of any company that is publicly traded. Therefore, any company that plans on having a public offering should be a corporation. Furthermore, any company that desires easy transferability of ownership or that has a complex equity structure, should seriously consider the corporate form. Finally, some types of business, such as banks, insurance companies or public utilities, are required by law to

> The main benefit of corporations is that ownership of stock may be freely transferred without obtaining the consent of other shareholders or corporate management.

be corporations. Almost any other company, however, would be better off being formed as an LLC or, occasionally, as a limited partnership (LP) or limited liability partnership (LLP).

An LLC is a similar entity to an S corporation since the owners of both entities enjoy limited liability and both entities can be taxed as a proprietorship or partnership to enjoy the benefits of pass-through taxation. An LLC member's risk is also limited to his loss of investment. However, a chief asset protection advantage of the LLC over the S corporation is that the LLC affords you more ownership options. For example, your LLC can be owned by a family limited partnership (FLP), a trust, another corporation, etc. S corporation shares cannot be owned by these entities. Their stock ownership is restricted to individuals. Both estate and asset protection planning become more difficult with S corporation shares.

More importantly, an ownership interest in an LLC is considerably more creditor-protected than are shares in an S corporation, which can be easily seized by a stockholder's personal creditors. A member's interest in an LLC is creditor protected in the same way a partnership interest in a limited partnership is protected. A member's personal creditor is limited only to a charging order against the LLC interest, which gives the creditor only the right to receive distributed profits due the debtor partners.

Finally, because an LLC can choose to be taxed as an S corporation, it is arguable that the S corporation has become obsolete as a business entity. As seen above, corporations are now only suitable for companies that plan on going public or companies that are very large, with a complex equity structure. Because an S corporation's ownership is limited to 75 shareholders, it cannot go public and will almost certainly not have an overly complex equity structure. Therefore, only an extremely rare circumstance would warrant the formation of an S corporation instead of an LLC.

There are still a few possible advantages of an S corporation over an LLC: 1) An S corporation can be more tax advantageously acquired by another business, 2) S corporation owners pay employment taxes only on their salaries, while LLC owners pay employment taxes on all profits and 3) state taxes may (or may not) be lower for an S corporation.

Professionals and Professional Corporations

Although not all states allow professions a choice between professional or corporate structures, physicians, dentists, accountants, lawyers, architects and many other professionals may conduct their practice through a professional corporation. However, the limited liability partnership (LLP) and professional LLC (PLLC) are also becoming a popular organizational alternative. The number of professional corporations (PC) and professional associations (PA) rapidly grew in numbers during the 1980s when, in those pre-tax reform days, a professional could invest more money into corporate pension plans. Few professionals organized professional corporations for liability protection because there were then far fewer malpractice lawsuits. Moreover, professionals traditionally had less concern than business owners about everyday vendors and business debts because they were service providers who incurred few commercial liabilities. Although they knew that they could still be sued personally for malpractice even if they had an incorporated practice, professionals then, as now, viewed malpractice insurance as their traditional liability shield.

Today, the professional corporation is a far more protective tool for the professional. True, a professional can still be personally sued for negligence, but the professional corporation insulates against any personal liability that may arise from an employee's or associate's negligence, as well as contract claims, employee lawsuits, etc. It would be the corporation – not the professional – who would be sued because the corporation would be the employer of a negligent employee or the party responsible for the obligation.

Still, a surprising number of legal, accounting and physicians' groups continue to operate as general partnerships or loose-knit associations. These firms would greatly benefit from incorporating. The professional corporation would insulate each professional from the unlimited personal liability they can now incur because of their organizational structure.

I spend a large part of my time designing safer organizational arrangements for professionals. For example, we may have each professional in a group organize their own professional corporation. Their respective corporations would then form a partnership with each corporation as a partner. If the partnership incurs a liability, the creditors' recourse would be against the partnership assets, and this limits recovery to the assets of the respective partner corporations. In this way each professional's personal assets remain safe.

The professional corporation is not always the professional's best organizational choice. A business corporation may offer the professional one major advantage over the professional corporation: The professional need not own a business corporation, as they must with the professional corporation. A business corporation may be owned by the professional's spouse, another protective entity (such as an LLC, trust or limited partnership) or in some other way that shields the corporate ownership. Other organizational options include the limited liability partnership (LLP), which is particularly suitable for attorneys and accountants.

> A business corporation may offer the professional one major advantage over the professional corporation. The professional need not own a business corporation, as they must with the professional corporation.

In certain states a professional can use either a professional or business corporation; much depends on the specific profession. For example, chiropractors can frequently use a business corporation, although medical doctors are usually limited to the professional corporation by state medical regulations.

Because private practices cannot be publicly traded, if a state allows PLLCs, a PLLC is almost always preferred over a PC. Note, however, that at the time of this writing, some states (such as California) do not allow PLLCs and in such states a professional corporation may be the entity of choice.

Maintain Corporate Protection

Merely operating a business through a corporation does not always mean that some corporate creditor won't try to sue you personally to collect a defaulted corporate debt or try to hold you personally responsible for some corporate mishap. Corporate creditors do sue their owners personally.

These corporate creditors try to pierce the corporate veil to get to their owners' personal assets. They usually claim that their owners are only alter-egos of their corporation. Can they succeed? Possibly. If the owner does not follow basic corporate formalities.

It is not difficult to correctly operate a corporation or any other legal entity. Your one goal is to always treat your entity as independent from you personally and any other entity. If you don't, your corporate creditor can successfully argue that you and your corporation are indeed one and the same and you lose corporate protection. You can avoid such trouble by respecting your entity:

- *Don't commingle assets*: Operate your corporation as a distinct entity, one separate from you personally in every respect. For example, document whatever assets you transfer between you and your corporation. Record all transactions on both your personal and corporate records. Document financial transactions between related corporations or other entities.

- *Sign your corporate documents as a corporate agent*: If you operate through a corporation, your legal documents should say so. Disclose your corporate name and title alongside your signature on all documents.

- *Operate each corporation autonomously*: Do you own multiple entities? The officers or directors of related corporations should occupy different positions, conduct separate corporate meetings and maintain separate corporate books.

- *Keep adequate corporate records*: Business creditors frequently pierce corporations when their records fail to properly document key corporate actions. Record every major director and shareholder vote. You can find inexpensive software to help you instantly prepare your corporate records without a lawyer.

- *Don't voluntarily dissolve your corporation*: If you voluntarily dissolve your corporation, you lose your corporate protection. Pay all corporate taxes and franchise fees. Keep your corporation in good standing. Do not voluntarily dissolve your corporation if it has outstanding debts or these corporate debts automatically become your personal obligations as its corporate stockholder.

Observe all corporate formalities. Does your corporation have its own business address? Telephone number? Do you have cancelled corporate checks to show that your corporation pays its own expenses? Does your corporation have the necessary business licenses? Checking and bank accounts? Each compliance point establishes your corporation as a legitimate entity – one separate from you as its owner. Creditors who try to pierce the corporate veil on the basis that the corporation is only a stockholder's sham alter ego has a difficult burden. Courts only reluctantly dismiss a corporation's important liability protection unless its owners flagrantly ignore corporate formalities.

I usually find a business creditor's lawsuit against the corporate owner to be only an effort by the creditor to force the business owner to defend the lawsuit or settle. That's when you need a combative attorney, someone who will countersue the creditor and his attorney for frivolous bad faith litigation.

Incorporation as a Total Shield

If you are in business, then incorporating is an absolute must if you want outside protection; your only other option is the LLC. While incorporating does not give you complete protection from every business creditor, incorporation is nevertheless an important first step to protect yourself against 9 out of 10 lawsuits.

- *Incorporating protects you from tort claims and business debts.* You shield your personal wealth from the most common lawsuits against your business when you incorporate. For example, negligence claims (slip-and-falls, car accidents, etc.) or claims by employees (responsibility for the acts or omissions of your employees, employment discrimination, etc.). You also shield yourself from corporate contract claims and debts if you did not personally guarantee the contract or debt.

- *Incorporating protects you from customer claims.* Incorporating usually protects you against claims from selling goods or services to your clients or customers. This includes product liability claims, negligence, breach of warranty and employee's malpractice lawsuits, which often bring huge jury awards.

■ *Incorporating won't protect you on personally guaranteed debts.* Those conducting business with a corporation often require that an officer (i.e. president, vice president, etc.) or principal stockholder sign a personal guarantee on the corporation's debt. For example, a landlord may want the owner's personal guarantee on a corporate lease for business premises. If your corporation breaches the lease, the landlord can then sue the owner personally on the guarantee. Debts guaranteed personally for your corporation override corporate protection.

■ *Incorporating won't protect you when you personally cause the harm.* If you personally caused the harm for which someone sues, you are not protected by the corporate shield. For example, if you negligently drive the corporate car and cause an accident, the victim can sue both the corporation and you, because you were personally negligent. Similarly, a physician would be personally sued for his own malpractice, notwithstanding that he was employed by an incorporated group practice.

■ *Incorporating won't protect you as a corporate officer.* This is true for certain tax liabilities and other governmental claims against the corporation for which officers and even directors, in some circumstances, have statutory responsibility.

Avoid Corporate Guarantees

To the extent small business owners guarantee their corporate obligations; it obviously reduces the usefulness of their corporation as a liability insulator.

Major debts, particularly bank loans, inevitably require the small business owner's personal guarantee. However, you can sidestep guarantees demanded by most other creditors (as well as escape liability on existing guarantees) with some common sense and a tougher attitude.

If one supplier demands your guarantee, then find others who won't make your guarantee only another bargaining point for credit. You can locate prospective suppliers who will extend to your corporation at least limited credit without your personal guarantee. That is why I say that when one supplier demands your guarantee, find a more lenient supplier.

> When one supplier demands your guarantee, find a more lenient supplier.

However, understand your creditor's concerns. Try to reduce his risk. You can then more successfully convince your creditor to forego your guarantee. For instance, a supplier who refuses to extend your corporation $20,000 on credit without your personal guarantee may risk $10,000. Perhaps the supplier will accept alternative collateral or a security interest on business assets instead of your personal guarantee or a guarantee from an affiliated corporation.

If you must sign a guarantee, then negotiate for a partial guarantee that limits your exposure. Insist that your creditor cancel your guarantee once your business establishes its own good track record for prompt payment.

Another cardinal rule: Never guarantee an existing debt. Why should you? You gain nothing. Yet, once a business falters, creditors plead, promise, threaten and cajole for the owner's personal guarantee. It would be foolish, however, to risk personal assets to secure an already shaky corporate obligation. Nor can you assume that your business will someday pay its obligations. Companies seriously in trouble seldom fully pay their debts.

Your partners, of course, should sign the same guarantees that you sign. Note that if your partners are less wealthy than you, your creditor will chase you for payment. Creditors pursue the deepest pockets. You want a partner whose pockets are as deep as yours.

If you have already signed numerous personal guarantees, there is a way to extricate yourself from these obligations. To begin, verify which obligations you guaranteed. Many businesspeople do not know which debts are guaranteed. The guarantee may have been part of an original order form or credit application. Ask every creditor whether they have your personal guarantee and request copies.

Next, terminate outstanding guarantees. You can always revoke guarantees for future credit and you should revoke your guarantees to avoid further liability. Also, do not forget to cancel outstanding guarantees for future purchases when you sell your business.

If your business is in financial trouble, you want to float your floundering business while you fully pay any personally guaranteed debts before your company fails. Or secure your guaranteed creditors with a mortgage on the business assets. Your guaranteed creditors will be paid from the liquidation of the business before the non-guaranteed creditors. This greatly reduces the odds that you will be forced to pay these debts from your own pocket.

Your final objective is to negotiate releases from outstanding guarantees. Here you need bargaining power. For example, a creditor who is owed $20,000 may accept $20,000 in return merchandise, $10,000 in cash or a mortgage on business assets in exchange for canceling your personal guarantee. Do you owe your bank? Perhaps they will tear up your guarantee if you agree to help the bank recover more than they could on their own when they liquidate your business. Secured lenders typically need the business owner's cooperation to maximize their recovery. Bargain your cooperation for those concessions that reduce or eliminate your personal exposure.

Secured lenders typically need the business owner's cooperation to maximize their recovery. Bargain your cooperation for those concessions that reduce or eliminate your personal exposure.

Of course, some creditors or lenders who hold your guarantee won't release you for your cooperation. Will this same creditor respond to less friendly overtures? For example, threatening Chapter 11 may forestall foreclosure and this would not necessarily be to your creditor's advantage. You have many bargaining chips to coax creditors to cancel guarantees. Use the 'carrot and stick' approach. It works when you deal with guaranteed creditors.

If you personally paid a guaranteed corporate debt, you also can indemnify and reimburse yourself from your corporation. Set up properly, you can have your corporation give you an indemnification and a security interest on its assets to secure this indemnification. You then have a priority right to be reimbursed from the corporation before your unsecured creditors get paid. Bankruptcy courts frequently set aside 'insider' mortgages when the business goes bankrupt, so you want to secure yourself and or liquidate your business without bankruptcy in this instance.

Why a Corporation Should Not Shelter Personal Assets

This chapter so far primarily discussed outside protection or personal asset protection that a corporation can provide you if you operate an active business; but now let's return to the idea of using your own passive corporation to safeguard your personal assets. This is 'inside' protection. For a corporation to give you inside protection, you must transfer your personal wealth to the corporation. You would no longer personally own your boat, car, paintings, etc., your corporation does. Your personal creditor could not directly claim the assets owned by the corporation. However, they could seize your corporate shares. That's the problem. Whatever ownership interest you have in the corporation, your creditor could seize and control. If you own a controlling interest, your creditor would indirectly control your corporation's assets. This shows that you can never safely use the corporation alone to protect personal assets. You must use it in combination with other asset protection tools to adequately shield your assets.

Nevertheless, a corporation can provide temporary shelter for personal assets. For instance, in one case, a client transferred $100,000 to a Nevada corporation only two days before a creditor won a sizeable judgment against him. Had my client kept the bank account titled in his own name, the creditor would have immediately levied the account. With his funds temporarily titled to a corporate account in another state, the creditor would first have to go through discovery before the creditor could find and seize the corporate shares. Of course, this gave us ample time to create a safer repository for his money.

In sum, the problem with using a corporation to protect personal assets is that you literally 'chase your tail'. While your assets are no longer exposed, your shares are now vulnerable.

> **For asset protection, you must find ways to protectively title your corporate shares. They cannot be owned by you personally.**

For asset protection, you must find ways to protectively title your corporate shares. They cannot be owned by you personally. You have options:

- *Married? Transfer most or all of the corporate shares to your less vulnerable spouse*, who would then control the corporation. One obvious problem with this solution, of course, is that you no longer control the corporation. Consider whether this arrangement meets your personal, estate planning or divorce-proofing objectives.

- *Title the shares with a family limited partnership (FLP).* For example, the husband and wife may become the general partners and control the partnership assets. They may also be the limited partners or other beneficiaries such as children, friends, charities, etc. may be the limited partners. As the general partners, the husband

and wife would then control the partnership that owns the corporation, which in turn would own the assets. Indirectly, the husband and wife, of course, control the assets, but they would not personally own the assets nor the shares of stock of the corporation that owns the assets. Since the assets are now owned by the corporation, they cannot be claimed by the couple's personal creditors, assuming that the transfer of the assets to the corporation was not fraudulent.

■ *Transfer the corporate shares to an irrevocable trust* set up for your children or other beneficiaries. For example, the husband and wife may become the co-trustees and manage the trust that controls the corporation. The couple would indirectly control the corporate assets without directly owning the corporation shares.

■ *Title the shares to an LLC.* As with a limited partnership, a member's personal creditor cannot seize a membership interest in the LLC. Again, you must beware of fraudulent transfer laws if you now have creditors.

■ *Title the shares to an offshore trust or Nevis LLC.* Both the offshore trust and foreign LLC can well-protect your corporate shares. Combine the offshore trust with the limited partnership as the corporate shareholder to substantially strengthen the arrangement. Titling shares of a US-based corporation to an offshore company also 'privatizes' your ownership; however, a judge can force you to surrender your shares in an offshore corporation to your creditor. Therefore, this plan is not recommended, although it is a common arrangement.

■ *Title your shares as tenants-by-the-entirety.* If you co-own your shares with your spouse in a state that adequately protects corporate shares, then tenancy-by-the-entirety may give your stock ownership sufficient protection when only one spouse has creditors.

Each of these strategies is illustrated in other chapters, but for the moment, understand that for your personal corporation to protect your personal assets, you cannot directly own the corporate shares. You must layer your protection with trusts, limited partnerships or other protective entities as the owner of your corporate shares.

Also, when inside protection is your goal, then you want a passive personal corporation. A corporation that engages in business will incur liabilities and you risk losing your personal assets that would be owned by the corporation to any business creditors. Another danger is that corporations used primarily to hold personal assets create serious 'holding' corporation tax problems. C corporations are subject to double taxation. While S corporations are only singly taxed, they cannot be owned by a trust, partnership or any other protective entity. More importantly, the IRS heavily taxes passive income of holding corporations. Another problem with corporations is if you contribute personal assets to a corporation and at a later time wish to take the asset back out, you will likely have to pay tax on the return of capital. Redistributing partnership or LLC assets (where the LLC has not elected corporate tax treatment), however, will not usually trigger any tax.

> Before you set up a corporation for 'inside' protection, review the idea carefully with your accountant for its tax consequences.

As you can see, there are tax traps. Before you set up a corporation for 'inside' protection, review the idea carefully with your accountant for its tax consequences. You will soon understand why limited partnerships, limited liability companies and other entities better protect your personal assets.

To avoid corporate shares from seizure by creditors, many debtors camouflage their ownership interest. Diligent creditors can usually identify corporate shareholders by examining corporate books, tax returns, licensing applications, public records, etc. You can more easily conceal an ownership interest using a Nevada or Wyoming corporation – two states that allow for bearer shares.

Unless you actually possess the bearer shares, you can truthfully deny ownership. If you have already incorporated elsewhere, then your corporation may be owned by a Nevada or Wyoming corporation or a foreign corporation in an offshore privacy haven can be your parent company. International business corporations (IBCs) in several jurisdictions also allow bearer shares or you can register the shares to a nominee 'straw.' Of course, you will need your lawyer to guide you on these strategies so that you do not commit perjury or incur tax problems concerning your corporate ownership. For less visibility and connection to the corporation, resign as a corporate officer or director. Officers or directors of closely held corporations are suspect as having some ownership or financial interest.

'Poison' Your Corporate Shares

When creditors are in pursuit, you can quickly sell any publicly traded stocks or bonds, but what do you do as a stockholder of a privately owned corporation? How can you easily or quickly sell your shares? The answer is that you probably can't. Still, you can make your shares nearly worthless to your creditors.

- **Impose transfer restrictions on your shares.** Corporate restrictions on the transfer of shares generally won't prevent creditor seizure; however, restrictions can discourage a less aggressive or knowledgeable creditor. Restrictions on transfer must be reasonable to be enforceable, but creditors won't usually incur the cost or effort to challenge even unreasonable restrictions.

- **Assess your shares.** If your shares are not fully paid or if the shares are assessable by the corporation, then a creditor who seizes your shares takes them subject to your obligation to pay the assessment. Obviously, a potential assessment by the corporation reduces the value of the shares to your creditor by the amount of the potential assessment. An 'assessment' can be a particularly effective 'poison pill' and I frequently include 'assessment provisions' in corporate documents as an anti-creditor device.

- **Issue irrevocable proxies.** A proxy is an assignment of your right to vote your shares. For example, you may issue a proxy to a relative, etc. A creditor who seizes your shares cannot vote your shares because the voting powers have been irrevocably assigned to the proxy holder. This, too, will significantly lessen the stock's value to the creditor, since the creditor would gain no voting rights in the corporation. If you are sued, you may exchange voting shares for non-voting shares, which will also be of less value to creditors.

- **Dilute your stock ownership.** Why allow a creditor to seize a controlling interest in your business? If you own a controlling interest, dilute your ownership. If and when it becomes necessary, you can have the corporation sell additional shares to other family members or to family controlled entities (trusts, limited partnerships, etc.). A creditor who seizes a minority ownership interest in the corporation cannot, of course, control the corporation. As a minority stockholder, the creditor only has the right to vote his or her shares and await whatever dividends may be declared. It is sometimes wise to spread the stock ownership in a family owned corporation between family members so that no one family member owns more than 49 percent of the voting shares. The by-laws would empower the remaining 51 percent to control the corporation.

- **Pledge your shares.** Another option is to pledge your shares as collateral to a friendlier creditor. If the amount borrowed approximates the value of your shares, your creditor will chase shares with no equity. Chapter 12 shows you many ways to create a friendly mortgage and encumber your shares.

Check Nevada for Incorporating

Corporations are creations of state law and state laws differ, so there may be advantages and disadvantages of incorporating in a particular state. If you determine that incorporation is the way to go, how do you decide where to incorporate? If your corporation operates an active business in only one state, then it is probably best to incorporate in that state where you will do business. If you set up an out-of-state corporation, it must register as a foreign corporation in your home state. This subjects the corporation to your home state laws and to some extent it will nullify the advantages of incorporating elsewhere. If your corporation will not operate a business (a passive corporation) or if you have flexibility as to where to incorporate, then Delaware is a good choice. Most of America's largest corporations are Delaware corporations. Many more corporations, particularly smaller corporations, are organized in Nevada, which has been America's 'incorporation capital'.

Nevada's corporate laws are better than Delaware and all other states, except Wyoming, whose corporation laws follow those of Nevada. The following are advantages of Nevada incorporation:

- Delaware taxes corporate profits while Nevada is tax-free. Delaware is more costly tax-wise if you expect big profits.

- Nevada won't share tax information with the IRS. Every other state, including Delaware, exchanges information.

- Delaware has a franchise tax, but Nevada does not.

- Delaware requires extensive annual disclosures. (Stockholder meeting dates, business localities outside Delaware, number and value of shares issued, etc.) Nevada requires only a current list of officers and directors.

- Nevada corporate stockholders may hold anonymous bearer shares.

- Nevada's corporate officers and directors have far broader protection than do Delaware's. For example, Nevada corporations can eliminate or limit the personal liability of officers and directors for breach of fiduciary duty (other than improper dividend payments). Nevada also has a shorter statute of limitations to sue for improper dividends and offer more opportunities for director indemnification. Delaware director indemnification is at the court's discretion; in Nevada it is an absolute right.

- Nevada allows for broader indemnities to others who incur liability on behalf of the corporation. The use of insurance trust funds, self-insurance and granting directors a security interest or lien on the corporate assets to guarantee their indemnifications are a few examples. For asset protection purposes, the absolute authority of corporate officers and directors to lien the corporate assets to indemnify themselves gives them a priority claim over their corporate assets without the need to prove an exchange of funds. This strategy can be critical for asset protection. Delaware and every other state will invalidate such self-serving legal arrangements. Absent fraud, a Nevada board of directors' decision concerning such financial arrangements is conclusive and cannot be voided by the courts.

■ Many astute business owners now set up Nevada
corporations, so you find many firms who can offer
complete incorporation and resident agent services to their
nationwide clients. Order *How to Establish and Operate
Your Own Nevada Corporation* (Garrett Publishing) to
learn how to quickly and inexpensively form your own
Nevada corporation. For faster, more comprehensive
service, call Nevada Corporate Planners (888-627-7007).
They are a superb and ethical Nevada corporate formation
firm that provides a wide range of corporate and small
business services.

Wealthsaver Tips

1. Operate your business through a corporation (or LLC). Never conduct your business as a partnership or proprietorship or you can lose your personal assets to your business creditors.

2. The C corporation and S corporation feature the same limited liability protection. They differ only in their taxation. The S corporation is taxed as a proprietorship.

3. The Nevada and Wyoming corporations have advantages over corporations chartered in other states.

4. Professionals also need a professional corporation for protection, for the same reasons a business owner requires a business corporation.

5. Operate your corporation as a distinct and separate entity. The courts won't then disregard its protective shield.

6. The corporation is not a good entity to shield personal assets.

7. Protect your shares in a corporation by titling them to limited partnerships, LLCs or another protective entity.

8. There are a number of ways to protect the corporate assets – and your stock ownership.

EIGHT

Lawsuit-Proofing With Limited Partnerships

More astute Americans than ever are forming limited partnerships (LP) to shelter their wealth. There are several very good reasons for the popularity of limited partnerships. The limited partnership ensures continuous succession of property ownership and control over the assets between generations while protecting this wealth from lawsuits, creditors, and to some extent, gift and estate taxation. The versatile limited partnership has helped thousands of families maintain their wealth with optimum protection. Few other legal entities can match the limited partnership's advantages or its many benefits.

The limited partnership or family limited partnership (FLP), although it need not necessarily involve family members, is not a new entity. The limited partnership's long tradition in asset protection, tax and estate planning began in 1916 when the states first adopted the Uniform Limited Partnership Act (ULPA), now revised in some states as the Revised Uniform Limited Partnership Act (RULPA). This long history characterizes the limited partnership's stability, predictability and dependability for achieving so many wealth preservation objectives.

If you attend seminars or read books about asset protection, you will unquestionably discover that the family limited partnership is the cornerstone to many wealth preservation plans.

I organize hundreds of family limited partnerships each year, and I have yet to have a limited partnership fail in protecting a client's assets. That's a strong endorsement for the limited partnership.

If you want to lawsuit-proof your personal assets, you, of course, have a choice of organizational entities to achieve your legal and financial goals. Each entity type has its own unique characteristics and features, and selecting the best entity involves many considerations.

Your range of choices will, of course, also depend greatly upon the intended purpose of the entity. For instance, if the limited partnership is to conduct business, you must evaluate it against the sole proprietorship, limited liability company and corporation.

If your goal is tax reduction, estate planning or asset protection, then you must weigh the limited partnership against various trusts, limited liability companies and other methods to safely title these assets. Alternative entities may be preferable to the limited partnership in certain circumstances. You must consider many factors as you evaluate each possible entity. Compare their advantages and disadvantages and decide which are most important to you.

Limited Partnership Fundamentals

A limited partnership has at least one general partner and one limited partner. The limited partnership's general partner(s) have the same rights and liabilities of a partner in a general partnership, namely the right to manage the partnership. They also have unlimited personal liability for the partnership debts. The limited partners, on the other hand, have no managerial authority and their personal liability is limited to their investment

> A limited partnership has at least one general partner and one limited partner.

in the partnership. In terms of insulation from partnership debts, limited partners have essentially the same protection as corporate stockholders.

However, stockholders in a corporation can lose their corporate shares to their personal creditors. In contrast, a partner in a limited partnership cannot lose his interest in the limited partnership to his personal creditors. Later I explain this point in greater detail, but for now, you can see the significant creditor protection advantage that the limited partnership offers.

General and limited partners in a limited partnership may contribute money, assets or a service, or a combination in return for their partnership interest. The general partner also has complete authority to run the limited partnership.

> **General and limited partners in a limited partnership may contribute money, assets or a service, or a combination, in return for their partnership interest.**

If the limited partnership can incur liability, then the general partner should be a corporation or LLC. A creditor of the limited partnership can then only pursue the assets of the corporation or LLC as its general partner. The assets of its stockholders or members would be safe. The corporation or LLC, owning only a nominal interest in the limited partnership, would only have modest exposure, and whatever assets the corporation or LLC owns can be protected through other asset protection strategies. A corporation or LLC general partner owned and managed by limited partners does not change the situation, because the corporation is a party separate and distinct from its principals.

Limited partnerships operate like general partnerships except that they have limited partners. A limited partner contributes cash or other assets to the partnership and receives distributions based on his or her partnership interest. The limited partner, however, has no direct control over the partnership or its assets. Historically, the limited partner was the 'silent' partner or the partner who did not want his or her identity revealed and did not want to run the company. Instead he or she simply wished to passively invest in the business and receive a profit.

Today's limited partner need not remain anonymous (although such anonymity may still be desirable), but contributes assets to the business and still has no significant say in the affairs of the company. In exchange, the limited partner receives distributions from the partnership and enjoys limited liability. A limited partner's assets cannot be claimed if the company loses money or incurs debt.

While a limited partner cannot give orders or directives to

> While a limited partner cannot give orders or directives to the general partner, a limited partner can provide advisory opinions.

the general partner, a limited partner can provide advisory opinions. The limited partner's name should not be part of the partnership name, nor can the limited partner in any other way create the inference that the limited partner manages the business, although he or she is, in fact, an owner. A general partner may also be a limited partner. In this instance, the individual has unlimited liability arising from the role of general partner.

Limited partners can access the partnership's financial records to the extent that corporate shareholders have the right to inspect corporate records. Limited partners also have the right to other information, such as documents filed with the state and any amendments, copies of the original partnership agreement and any amendments, a list of partners, their addresses, contributions, shares in profits and losses, all partnership income tax returns and any records of the business that are not considered proprietary information.

General partners must furnish the limited partners with the information needed to complete their federal and state income tax returns. Unless the partnership agreement provides otherwise, no limited partner may be required to make additional contributions to the limited partnership and no limited partner in any way has priority rights over any other limited partner. Most importantly, the limited partners have certain voting rights specified in the partnership agreement or under the Uniform Limited Partnership Act (ULPA).

Forming Your Limited Partnership

To prepare a good limited partnership agreement, you need the right assistance. A qualified attorney is essential to prepare an agreement that meets all governmental standards as well as your own personal needs and requirements.

Each partner should consult their own attorneys as you may have conflicts of interest when one professional represents multiple parties. While you may trust your partners, you seldom share the same needs and goals. Your attorney must protect you.

To create the limited partnership, you must file with the state a certificate of limited partnership, also called a certificate of organization or registration statement. Once approved, the state issues a charter or other document acknowledging its formal existence.

Most states have their own form of certificate that can be obtained from the Secretary of State's office. Several states have no form, but require you to file your own prepared certificate containing certain points:

- Name of the limited partnership
- Address of the partnership
- Name and address of the general partner
- Name and address of the resident agent
- General activities or purpose of the limited partnership (in some states a statement of 'any lawful business which may be conducted by a limited partnership' will suffice).
- Mandatory dissolution date.

Some states require additional information, so you should check your state's requirements. The certificate normally does not list the limited partners, nor is the limited partnership agreement filed as a public record.

Once your certificate of limited partnership has been filed and approved, you apply to the IRS for an employer's identification number (EIN) by completing and returning Form SS-4 to the IRS. If you already have an employer identification number for a retirement account or because you have had employees prior to registering as a limited partnership, you nevertheless need a new number because the limited partnership is a new entity. You may also need a tax identification number from your state; check with your state tax department. The simplest way to obtain your number is to telefax the SS-4 application to the IRS. This should bring you a number within a week, as opposed to 4 or more weeks when the application is mailed.

Once the limited partnership obtains its taxpayer ID number (by filing IRS Form SS-4), it should open its own bank accounts and set up recordkeeping. It is important to remember that funds and other assets belonging to the limited partnership must be kept separate and apart from your own funds as well as funds belonging to other entities because it is viewed in the eyes of the law as a legal entity separate and apart from the owner(s). Hence, to avoid potential IRS problems, you must maintain separate records for the limited partnership separate from your personal affairs. As a rule, however, it is not necessary to maintain an elaborate bookkeeping system. Separate bank accounts and bookkeeping that clearly show what you and the limited partnership separately earn and pay out are usually sufficient. A local bookkeeper or accountant can easily set up a convenient accounting and tax system for your partnership.

> To avoid potential IRS problems, you must maintain separate records for the limited partnership separate from your personal affairs.

Transferring Assets to Your Limited Partnership

There is a difference between the assets your limited partnership can own and what assets it should own. The limited partnership is not an ideal entity to hold certain assets, although it would be legally permissible. There are many considerations when you select which assets your limited partnership should own.

If the limited partnership has a specific business purpose, then the limited partnership should own only those assets necessary to fulfill that function. For example, a limited partnership organized to develop real estate should not own unrelated assets, such as personal investments. Obviously you would not use a limited partnership to own your own assets with a number of unrelated partners. Here you would invest only in proportion to the other partners, usually cash or other assets to be utilized to further the business or investment interests of the partnership.

Your limited partnership can possibly protect all, or at least a significant percentage, of your wealth. For instance, your limited partnership can own:

- Cash
- Stocks, bonds and other investments
- Vehicles
- Real estate
- Antiques, art and collectibles
- LLC memberships
- Other limited partnership interests
- Intangible assets (copyrights, patents, etc.)
- Claims against others
- Notes/mortgages, other obligations due you
- Beneficial interests in trusts
- C corporation shares

As a rule, your limited partnership should only own in-come-producing or appreciating assets, which is ostensibly the reason for setting up your limited partnership. Under S corporation rules, the limited partnership cannot own S corporation shares unless it is structured to be taxed as a disregarded entity (which we'll discuss shortly). It also should not own annuities (unless it's considered a disregarded entity for tax purposes), because you would then lose their tax deferral status.

> Your limited partnership cannot own IRAs or other retirement accounts; however, your retirement account can invest its funds in your limited partnership, which then protects your IRA.

Your limited partnership also cannot own IRAs or other retirement accounts; however, your retirement account can invest its funds in your limited partnership, which then protects your IRA.

A limited partnership should not be used to operate a business unless its general partner(s) are LLCs or corporations, since the general partners would incur liability for the partnership debts. The corporation or limited liability company is preferable to operate a business.

Also, do not title your home to a limited partnership A creditor can argue that your home is not an 'investment or business related' asset and this could persuade a court to disregard your limited partnership. You would also lose two tax benefits that are yours when you personally own your home; the deduction on mortgage interest and the capital gains rollover. Still, some limited partnership promoters recommend titling the home to a limited partnership. Generally, that's poor advice. There are better alternatives for protecting your home, such as equity stripping or in certain circumstances, using an LLC or personal residence trust.

Use Multiple Limited Partnerships

Multiple limited partnerships can maximize your asset safety. Even when the limited partnership is your best organizational choice, don't title all your assets to the same limited partnership. Segregate your assets within multiple limited partnerships. If one limited partnership encounters financial or legal problems, it won't jeopardize the assets titled to the other limited partnerships. Remember the axiom, "Never put all your eggs in one basket."

Separate safe or 'no risk' assets from liability-producing or 'at risk' assets. For example, you may title surplus cash, stocks, bonds and mutual funds within one limited partnership because they are 'no risk' assets. They may decrease in value, but they will not create liabilities or creditor problems that would jeopardize these assets.

Commercial properties belong in a separate limited partnership because they are 'at risk' assets that can create liability. For example, a tenant

> Commercial properties belong in a separate limited partnership because they are 'at risk' assets that can create liability.

who sues for negligent maintenance of the building has recourse against the assets held by that specific limited partnership. You would not want to expose your 'no risk' assets to this potential litigant.

I have clients who have deployed their assets amongst ten or more separate limited partnerships. Individuals with extensive commercial property holdings often prefer a separate limited partnership for each property to decrease their exposure as much as possible. Some large property owners have many limited partnerships to match their separate properties. However, it is generally preferable to title investment real estate to limited liability companies which are better liability insulators.

Although segregating assets into separate limited partnerships is highly recommended, the downside is that more limited partnerships means increased maintenance costs. In some situations, a Series LLC (discussed in Chapter 9) may be a viable way to segregate liability between assets, without having to form a multitude of business entities. Another option may be to use a number of irrevocable grantor trusts, such as carefully drafted land trusts, (which are discussed in Chapter 10) to each hold a separate piece of property. The beneficiary of each trust will then be either a limited partnership, Series LLC or normal LLC. Since you only need one limited partnership or other entity, because trusts can be structured so as to be ignored for tax purposes (meaning their activity is simply reported on the trust grantor's tax return) and they are not subject to resident agent or state filing fees, operational and maintenance costs are greatly reduced. Furthermore, once you have a properly drafted trust agreement, setting up a new trust may be a fairly simple process. For example, let's say you have nine pieces of real estate, each held in a land trust, with a limited partnership as the beneficiary of each trust. When you buy another property, you simply use the same pro forma trust document to quickly draft a tenth trust. This 'cookie cutter' arrangement does not need to be registered in most states and thus can be set up very quickly, involving little more than notarization of the new trust and a quitclaim of the property into the trust. This strategy is especially useful in states such as California, which at the time of this writing have a hefty $800 per year franchise tax levied against each limited partnership. With that said, be aware that there are many factors that must be considered when determining whether such an arrangement is beneficial for any particular situation. The help of a qualified professional is essential to the proper implementation of these more advanced strategies.

How the Limited Partnership
Creditor-Proofs Your Assets

The limited partnership has become the cornerstone for protecting domestic (US-based) assets for several reasons. With the limited partnership, you can maintain complete control over your assets as the general partner and indirectly own the assets through ownership of a limited partnership interest. Correctly drafted, assets transferred to the limited partnership become fully protected and beyond the reach of any future creditor, including the IRS and other governmental claimants. Most asset protection attorneys share my view that the limited partnership and the LLC are generally the most advantageous domestic entities for protecting assets, which is why they are the foundation for safeguarding assets situated within the United States.

When considering the limited partnership for asset protection, the two central questions are:

- How does a limited partnership protect assets?

- How much protection does a limited partnership provide?

To answer these questions, you must understand the specific rights and limitations of a partner's personal creditor when that partner's assets are protected through ownership in a limited partnership. Generally, a creditor of a limited partner can attempt to seize only three types of assets:

- the limited partnership interest,

- any profits or distributions payable to the limited partner,

- those assets previously transferred to the limited partnership by that debtor-partner.

Let's examine each possibility:

1. Seizure of the Limited Partnership Interest

A creditor of a limited or general partner cannot seize his limited partnership interest. A judgment creditor of a limited partner can only apply to the court for a charging order against the limited partnership interest. The charging order only gives the creditor the right to claim any profit or liquidation proceeds payable to the limited partner.

The charging order does not make the creditor a substitute partner, nor does it give the creditor any partnership rights except to claim profits or distributions payable to the debtor-partner. For example, the creditor cannot sell or auction the partnership interest, nor can the creditor vote as a limited partner or even inspect the partnership books. In sum, the creditor becomes only an assignee of the limited partnership interest for the purposes of collecting any profits or distributions voted by the general partners and actually paid to the limited partner.

The charging order's central purpose is to protect the partners that are not involved in the debts of the debtor-partner from any undue interference in the affairs of the partnership by that creditor. This is distinguished from a typical corporation where a shareholder's creditors can force the sale of the debtor-shareholder's shares with the buyer becoming a successor stockholder with all the rights of a stockholder. This one distinction makes the limited partnership useful for safeguarding wealth.

2. Seizure of Profits or Liquidation Distributions

If the creditor's right to claim distributed profits or liquidating proceeds due the debtor-partner is his sole remedy, how practical is that remedy? Consider its limitations.

First, partnership profits can be illusive, particularly when the limited partnership is family-owned or the interests of the partners are closely aligned, as is the case for most limited partnerships.

Second, the decision of distributing profits belongs exclusively to the general partners. The creditor cannot force a distribution.

Thus, the limited partnership can simply defer any profit distributions until the charging order creditor loses patience and settles; nor will this deferral strategy necessarily deprive the debtor-partner access to partnership funds.

> The decision of distributing profits belongs exclusively to the general partners. The creditor cannot force a distribution.

The debtor-partner may accept loans, salaries, consulting fees or payments for other assets he may sell to the limited partnership. The debtor-partner can also divert profits to other interconnected entities that may transact business with the limited partnership and thus become a protected conduit for partnership earnings. These funds would not be subject to the charging order because they are not a distribution of profits or proceeds from liquidation.

Third, you can structure your limited partnership to allocate a higher percentage of the profits to the other partners, who nevertheless may own a lesser percentage of the partnership. Thus, you may own, for example, 90 percent of the limited partnership but be entitled to only 10 percent of its profits. This 10 percent would be the only vulnerable profit distribution. Indeed, the opportunities are endless to defeat the creditor from ever receiving partnership profits. A creditor awaiting profit distribution can be in for a long, frustrating, profitless wait.

Of course, the ability to frustrate a creditor may not be so easy if you are only a minority limited partner in a limited partnership with hundreds of investors and an unaffiliated general partner whose interests and agenda may not parallel that of the debtor-partner. Should a partnership generate a constant and substantial profit stream, the creditor's charging order may produce payment. The debtor-partner's only option would then be to sell or encumber his partnership interest or assign future partnership profits to another protected entity – perhaps another limited partnership under his control.

Thus, a creditor is in a far better position when the debtor-partner cannot control or influence the distribution of profits, such as when the limited partnership includes large numbers of unrelated partners. A 2 percent debtor-partner who receives consistently large cash dividends will lose those dividends to a charging order creditor, and, in this instance, the limited partnership becomes far less advantageous an asset protector. Despite this fact, there is a simple strategy that allows us to overcome this problem: Simply place your minority interest in another limited partnership of which you are a majority partner (ideally this of course should be done before creditor threats arise). Although the larger partnership may not withhold distributions, the distributions will go to another protected entity, which someone friendly to you controls. Distributions may then be withheld in order to thwart any attempts to collect on a charging order.

> Few creditors ever get a charging order for one good reason: The charging order creditor becomes automatically liable to pay the taxes on all partnership profits allocable to the debtor-partner — even when the creditor receives no payment or profit distributions from the partnership.

In fact, few creditors ever get a charging order for one good reason: The charging order creditor becomes automatically liable to pay the taxes on all partnership profits allocable to the debtor-partner – even when the creditor receives no payment or profit distributions from the partnership.

Consider the plight of a creditor holding a charging order against a limited partner with a 50 percent partnership interest. Assume that the partnership earns $100,000 in a particular year, with $50,000 allocated to the debtor-partner, who would normally pay the taxes on this $50,000. Instead, the charging order creditor assumes the partner's tax liability, whether or not he receives the distribution. A creditor in a 35 percent tax bracket thus has a $17,500 tax bill each year the charging order is in effect and the debtor-partner has similar allocable profit. Meanwhile, because no profits have been actually distributed, the creditor has a $17,500 tax liability and still has received no cash. Conversely, the debtor would enjoy $50,000 tax-free retained earnings within the limited partnership.

Under IRS Revenue Rule 77-137, the tax obligation becomes entirely the obligation of the charging order creditor and the creditor, not the debtor-partner, receives the K-1 reported to the IRS. Some states even prohibit a charging order creditor from releasing the charging order without the consent of the debtor-partner - a consent the debtor-partner with taxable income may understandably withhold. Thus, the charging order cannot reasonably be seen as an effective weapon, but more realistically as a device that can give the creditor only a tax bill instead of a payment. It is important to note that there is some debate among the professional community as to whether the mere holder of a charging order may be liable for the debtor's share of partnership liability. This is because IRS Revenue Ruling 77-137 states that only an assignee of partnership interest that holds 'complete dominion and control' over the interest would be liable for the debtor's payments on partnership liability. Fortunately, an immaculately drafted partnership agreement will allow the general partner to transfer voting and other rights to the creditor, without jeopardizing the partnership or the debtor's partnership interest, so that the debtor's share of tax liability will properly flow to the creditor. Regardless, there is nothing that would prohibit a general partner from sending a K-1 to the creditor and the mere possibility of receiving tax liability for undistributed profit serves as a prohibitive deterrent against a creditor obtaining a charging order.

3. Recovering Assets Transferred to the Limited Partnership

A third possible remedy is for the creditor to ignore the charging order remedy and instead attempt to set aside any prior transfer of assets from the debtor to the limited partnership. With these assets no longer in the partnership, they would then be unprotected and subject to creditor seizure.

This is frequently a far more threatening possibility than the dangers from a charging order and creditors often recover assets fraudulently transferred to the limited partnership. Of course, a creditor cannot directly claim limited partnership assets because the assets no longer belong to the debtor-partner, but are owned by the limited partnership under a tenancy-by-partnership. That is why if the creditor is to obtain access to the assets, he must first rescind the prior transfer to the partnership as a fraudulent transfer.

Creditors do, of course, have remedies when assets are fraudulently transferred to a limited partnership or any other party. For example, if you owe a creditor $100,000, you might transfer $70,000 in cash to the limited partnership so that the creditor cannot seize your cash. This could constitute a fraudulent transfer and the cash may be recoverable from the partnership (or any other transferee) by the creditor.

The result, nevertheless, is far from certain. Much depends upon how you structure your limited partnership. For instance, if you and your wife each contribute $70,000 and each obtains in exchange a 50 percent partnership interest, then the court may agree that the transfer was a 'fair consideration' exchange because you now own one-half of a limited partnership with assets worth $140,000 or an interest mathematically equal to your original $70,000. However, if you and your wife each contributed $70,000, but you obtained a disproportionately smaller partnership interest – or no interest, then you essentially 'gave away' at least part of your money and at least that portion would be recoverable by your present creditors. Many debtors overlook this point and hurriedly transfer their assets to the limited partnership for a disproportionately small partnership interest because they want little or no interest subject to a creditor's charging order. They probably also overlook the fact that the creditor would pay the larger share of the taxes on partnership profits if they had owned more. This is always poor planning, because a present creditor can then successfully argue that the transfer was without fair consideration and thus a fraudulent transfer.

Even when the consideration is fair, it does not guarantee that a court will not set aside such a transfer made against a present creditor. Many courts find that merely impairing a present creditor from collection is sufficient to constitute a fraudulent transfer, even when the consideration (the limited partnership interest) has a value corresponding to the value of the asset transferred.

Because the law on this point varies between states and individual cases, you cannot assume that any transfer to a limited partnership made against a present creditor is safe. The limited partnership provides more protection than keeping it titled in your name, but appreciably less protection than would an offshore trust, offshore LLC or some other foreign structure that keeps the asset beyond the reach of US courts and any practical opportunity to recover. While liquid assets can be physically transferred offshore and placed beyond the reach of US courts, we have different problems when the assets must remain US-based, as with real estate. Here, when the limited partnership offers questionable protection, the only remedy is to sell or fully encumber the assets (using liens as a debt-shield) and move the proceeds to an offshore trust or comparably protective structure.

> The limited partnership provides more protection than keeping it titled in your name, but less protection than would an offshore trust, offshore LLC or some other foreign structure.

Still, from the debtor's position, the limited partnership shields the partnership assets from all but the most determined creditor. A creditor must overcome numerous barriers before he can recover assets. As a practical matter, few creditors choose to pursue a partnership interest or assets conveyed to the partnership unless the claim and the corresponding assets are exceptionally large.

When the Charging Order May Fail

The statutory limitations of the charging order were once thought to be insurmountable by a creditor. However, although extremely rare, there exist a few instances where a creditor of a limited partnership's or LLC's partner or member was able to gain ownership of their company interest, notwithstanding the statutory limitations of the charging order. Three cases are relevant to this topic. (Because the charging order statutes for LLCs are very similar or even identical to those of limited partnerships, this section applies equally to both types of entities.) The first two cases were decided in California district courts. In both these cases, the court decided to ignore the limitations of the charging order because, the court ruled, charging order protection was originally enacted as a means of protecting the non-debtor partners in the partnership and to insure that partnership business remains uninterrupted, not so that a debtor-partner can escape paying his debts. Because in both cases the partnership interest could be transferred to the creditor without causing an interruption in business, the courts on both occasions decided that charging order restrictions did not apply and the partnership interest was transferred to the creditor. Although the court in one case only allowed this transfer with the other partners' consent, in the other case the transfer was allowed without the consent of the other partners. Despite the fact that

> There exists a few instances where a creditor of a limited partnership's or LLC's partner or member was able to gain ownership of their company interest, notwithstanding the statutory limitations of the charging order.

these cases technically should only hold weight in California, they set a precedent that may be imitated by other courts nationwide.

Another situation in which charging order protection may fail is found in a recent bankruptcy proceeding. In this proceeding, the court ruled that the debtor's LLC membership interest was forfeited to the bankruptcy estate, due to the fact that the LLC's operating agreement was deemed a non-executory contract. Under bankruptcy law, an executory contract would include an agreement wherein the company's partners have ongoing obligations towards the company, such as an ongoing obligation to act as advisors or to periodically contribute cash or other capital. Such an executory contract would be subject to a certain section of the bankruptcy code, which section would uphold the limitations of state or other applicable law (thus allowing the limitations of the charging order remedy to apply). The court makes it clear, however, that if a partnership or operating agreement is non-executory, the company interest would instead be subject to another section of the bankruptcy code, which section would override any other statutory limitations on the bankruptcy trustee's right to the debtor's assets.

In light of the above cases, there is yet another situation wherein charging order protection may be circumvented. That is where all members of the company are debtors to the same creditor. In this situation, the underlying reasons for charging order protection would not apply to the situation at hand, and therefore a court could conceivably disregard charging order restrictions.

To summarize, we can see that the following factors may jeopardize the charging order component of an asset protection plan:

- An LLC's or limited partnership's operating/partnership agreement is non-executory (which is probably only important if the company's owner files or is forced into bankruptcy).

- The forfeiture of a debtor's membership interest to a creditor would not interrupt partnership business.

- All members/partners of the LLC/limited partnership become a debtor of the same creditor.

The solution to this dilemma is to ensure that the operating or partnership agreement is executory in nature. Such an executory agreement, if carefully drafted by a skilled professional, will also cause an interruption in ongoing member obligations towards the company to also cause an interruption in the company's business. This would allow the debtor-member to argue that such an interruption in business prohibits any court from transferring his company interest to a creditor. It goes without saying that there are many considerations that must be made when drafting such an agreement. Such considerations are without the scope of this book and are best left to a competent attorney or asset protection consultant. However we can broadly state that the following obligations will effectively reinforce charging order limitations:

- Ongoing obligations to contribute cash or other capital to the entity;

- Ongoing obligations to contribute non-managerial services (such as advisement services); or

- Ongoing obligations to manage the entity, if appropriate.

Lastly, we must make sure that never, under any circumstance, could all members of the LLC personally become debtors of the same creditor. We could accomplish this by doing one or more of the following:

- Make sure at least one of the LLC members is never exposed to liability. This is best accomplished by making one of the members a trust, LLC or other entity that only engages in 'safe' activities; or

- Make sure that at least one member is not an insider or affiliate of any other member under the U.F.T.A. Also, it is best for this member to live in a different state than the other members. This would make it highly unlikely that this member would ever be personally listed as a defendant on the same lawsuit as another member. With this in mind, make sure that the LLC is *not* member managed. Otherwise, a plaintiff suing the LLC could name *all* of the members as co-defendants, claiming each one was responsible for mismanagement of the LLC, which led to the tort offense.

The Limited Partnership as a Personal Liability Protector

The limited partnership protects limited partners against the debts of the partnership. This remains true, however, only if the limited partners do not actively participate in the management of the partnership as outlined previously, yet it is easy for a limited partner to overstep his bounds and thus incur liability for partnership debts. Therefore, limited partners should fully understand the prohibited activities if they are to remain personally immune. Here the limited liability company has a decided advantage: Its members can freely involve themselves in company affairs without jeopardizing their personal immunity.

General partners are liable for all debts of the partnership, including all tort and contract claims. Therefore, individuals should not become general partners when the partnership has 'liability-producing' assets or activities. In this instance, they may form a corporation or limited liability company – with minimal assets – to serve as the general partner.

Bankruptcy and the Limited Partnership

Bankruptcy can, in numberous ways, cause disruption to the smooth or continuous management of the partnership and, therefore, the general partner contemplating bankruptcy should be replaced in advance.

A common question is whether a limited partner will lose his limited partnership interest in bankruptcy. As discussed earlier in this chapter, the answer depends on how the partnership agreement is drafted. If it is drafted correctly, the answer is generally no. The bankruptcy trustee obtains only the charging order remedy of an individual creditor. However, the trustee may claim any paid-in capital contribution that the bankruptcy partner is entitled to withdraw. Of course, the limited partnership agreement should be carefully reviewed by an insolvent partner, well in advance of bankruptcy.

A general partner's bankruptcy does not transfer the managerial authority to his bankruptcy trustee. Nevertheless, the bankruptcy can, in numerous ways, cause disruption to the smooth or continuous management of the partnership and, therefore, the general partner contemplating bankruptcy should be replaced in advance.

Combining Limited Partnerships and Offshore Trusts

For maximum asset protection, it is often recommended that the limited partnership interests be held by an offshore asset protection trust. Family members can be the general partners and thus control the partnership assets. Upon any threat to the partnership or its assets, the partnership can simply liquidate.

Since the offshore trust would own 95 percent or more of the partnership interest, it would receive a corresponding share of the partnership assets upon liquidation. Obviously, the partnership proceeds entrusted offshore would enjoy considerably greater protection. Moreover, since the trust owns the limited partnership interest, it would not be subject to a charging order from creditors of any family members involved in the arrangement.

Combining Limited Partnerships and Offshore LLCs

It is conceivable that if a general partner becomes a judgment debtor or manages a domestic LLC that is the general partner of a partnership, then under certain circumstances a judge may order the manager to distribute a portion of the partnership's assets to satisfy the judgment. (Remember, that, as discussed earlier, although charging order limitations were once thought to be unassailable, there now exist a few isolated cases which demonstrate to the contrary.) Although the general partner may be changed to a 'safe' onshore individual in advance of a claim being reduced to judgment, the fact remains that as long as the general partner remains inside the US, he is within the reach of the courts. Therefore, an individual who wants the absolute best in asset protection may wish to place the partnership's management outside of the courts' jurisdiction by making the partnership's general partner an offshore LLC. This strategy would allow an onshore person to manage the LLC until creditor threat arises, at which point the LLC's manager is replaced with an offshore individual. After the threat has passed, the offshore LLC's members may vote to replace the offshore manager with a domestic manager again.

Nine More Ways to Maximize Limited Partnership Protection

Aside from the many pointers already discussed, there are several other strategies to bolster the asset protection from limited partnerships:

1) The limited partnership agreement should give the general partners full discretion to withhold distributions of profits for purposes of future investment.

2) The agreement should also specifically restrict the transfer of a limited partnership interest without the consent of the general partner and/or a majority of the limited partners.

3) The agreement should further prevent a limited partner from withdrawing capital contributions without partner consent.

4) The agreement should also carefully specify that a creditor of a limited partner becomes only an assignee of the limited partner's interest and acquires no partnership rights other than the right to distributions. Furthermore, the agreement should allow, in a general partner's sole discretion, a transfer of a limited partner's voting rights, if necessary to ensure that a creditor who obtains a charging order also becomes liable to pay the debtor's share of taxes from partnership profits.

5) A particularly effective strategy is to have a limited partnership agreement allow the general partner to 'assess' the limited partners for a further contribution and to

extend this obligation to any charging order creditor. The agreement could further stipulate that failure to meet such obligations would cause a partner to forfeit his partnership interest, without entitling him to any return of capital he or she had contributed to the partnership.

6) 'High-risk' family members should own a smaller partnership interest, but always proportional to the asset contributions to avoid gift tax consequences or claims of fraudulent conveyance. The agreement should also give the 'low-risk' family member a disproportionately high percentage of the profits.

7) Limited partners may also consider granting an 'option to purchase' the partnership interest back to the limited partnership. Issued well in advance of a creditor claim, it can be an effective way to divert partnership interests.

8) Spouses may consider holding their limited partnership interests as tenants-by-the-entirety in the states where this type of tenancy is recognized. This further protects the interest from creditors of any one spouse.

9) When investing in a large, non-controlled limited partnership or limited liability company, title ownership in a family limited partnership to protect the distributions that you may not be able to avoid.

A well drafted limited partnership agreement can be a formidable barrier to any creditor.

I have few war stories to tell you about limited partnerships. In my many years of practice, I have had only two experiences with charging order creditors. The first case involved a creditor with a $700,000 judgment against my client, who owned a 45 percent limited partnership interest; his family owned the remaining interest. Although the partnership had about $3 million in assets, the creditor sat with his charging order for over 2 years and never collected a dime in profit distributions. Eventually he settled for $50,000. It wasn't a bad outcome.

My second case was more interesting. The creditor was the IRS (yes, a limited partnership is equally effective against the IRS). I never expected the IRS to get a charging order against the limited partnership interest owned by my client and his wife (who had no tax liability). The limited partnership had a $60,000 net income, so my client would have $30,000 in taxable income. We sent the tax liability (Form K-1) to the IRS as the substitute taxpayer for the husband. In essence, the IRS had to pay itself the tax on the husband's $30,000 'phantom income.' A crazy story? Sure, but it makes my work fun. We never again heard from the IRS.

How to Structure Your Family Limited Partnership

> Both partners enjoy exclusive, equal ownership and control of the partnership, just as they enjoyed their assets when titled in their own names. The one difference is that their assets are now fully protected from creditors.

There are typical limited partnership structures for families. Most often, mom and dad form the partnership and contribute various income-producing or business assets in exchange for their respective partnership interests. They can initially receive a small interest in the partnership as the general partners. As such they equally control the partnership, just as they previously controlled the contributed assets. Mom and dad may each also receive, as limited partners, the remaining majority interest in the limited partnership (general and limited partners can be the same parties and both can own an interest in a limited partnership). Thus, mom and dad enjoy exclusive, equal ownership and control of the partnership – and thus the assets contributed to the partnership – just as they enjoyed their assets when titled in their own names.

The one difference is that their assets are now fully protected from creditors.

There are many other ways to structure a family partnership. Perhaps dad has many creditors, so mom becomes the general partner. It would not be to dad's advantage to be a general partner when his creditors could interfere in the partnership. Alternatively, mom and dad could form a corporation or (preferably) a limited liability company, which would be the general partner in the partnership – a particularly good choice if the partnership can incur liabilities for which the general partners are liable. They may subsequently transfer their limited partnership interests. They can gradually gift their limited partnership interests to their children, to a living trust or some other entity, which may also own a part of the limited partnership. Since the limited partnership structure is flexible, the family limited partnership works very well for estate planning and adapts itself perfectly to a systematic gifting program.

> A most attractive tax feature of the family limited partnership is its ability to spread the tax burden between the partners any way you choose.

As stated, a most attractive tax feature of the family limited partnership is its ability to spread the tax burden between the partners any way you choose. For example, general partner dad in a high tax bracket could contribute large amounts of money to a partnership while retaining only a small interest, but full control. The tax burden for this contribution would thus be spread to the limited partners – the kids – who own the majority interest in the partnership. Combining trusts with limited partnerships makes for a powerful family asset protector. However, combining a trust with a limited partnership is a much more complicated structure than using either one alone. A legal or financial consultant should arrange the structure to fully protect your family's assets.

Combining the family limited partnership with the living trust frequently provides a superior estate plan. The partnership, as owner of the family assets, provides asset protection and discounted valuations for estate tax purposes.

The limited partnership interests owned by the partners' respective living trusts allow the partners to bequeath their partnership interest while avoiding probate. In structuring this arrangement between spouses who own the partnership, it is assumed that they will take advantage of the unlimited marital deduction. Upon the grantor's death, the family trust becomes irrevocable, succeeded by two internal trusts: A credit-equivalent bypass trust and a marital trust. This strategy essentially transfers the estate tax liability to the surviving spouse's estate, thus deferring the estate tax.

> **The ability of the limited partnership to reduce estate taxes is its most formidable tax benefit.**

The customary probate complexities and costs are avoided when the partnership interests are owned by living trusts. Delays in completing probate are avoided and creditors need not be notified, allowing disposition economically, quickly and efficiently.

Reducing Estate Taxes

The ability of the limited partnership to reduce estate taxes is its most formidable tax benefit. Assume that an individual has, upon his death, cash in the amount of $3 million and that the estate tax exemption is $1.5 million (be aware that this exemption is increasing each year until 2010, at which point there is no estate tax. Come 2011, however, and the exemption is expected to return to $1 million indefinitely). The estate tax would then be levied on the $1.5 million balance. If these same assets were titled to a limited partnership, they would be subject to a 'discounted valuation.' Possibly the full partnership interests would be valued at $2 million for estate tax purposes, thus eliminating estate taxes on $1 million.

Generally, assets titled to a limited partnership result in a discounted value of 20 to 40 percent compared to their estate tax value when owned outright. This results in a correspondingly lower estate tax. Several factors determine the amount of the allowed discount. The IRS primarily considers: 1) Control the decedent had over the partnership, 2) Marketability of the partnership assets and the ability to quickly liquidate its assets and 3) Accessibility of the partnership interests by the decedent's estate.

On the issue of control, the family may, for instance, decide to have the children become the general partners as their parents age. Divesting control from the parents allows for a greater discount on the value of their partnership interest upon their deaths. Cash and marketable securities support a smaller discount compared to a limited partnership consisting of real estate or stock in closely held corporations.

The question of the limited partnership valuation discount is one that has the rapt attention of – and opposition from – the IRS, who routinely contest a decedent's discount valuation and who systematically petition Congress to disallow the discount. Because tax policies and regulations on the subject are likely to change, get guidance from your tax advisor when using the limited partnership for estate or gift tax planning.

The Limited Liability Partnership (LLP)

Most doctors, lawyers and other professionals carry insurance against malpractice and other types of litigation because claims against these professionals are now a daily occurrence. No professional today, however, can rely solely upon insurance for protection. There are now many other opportunities for professionals to incur liability arising from their practice. The need for sound organizational protection for professionals clearly matches that of the commercial business owner or family with wealth preservation concerns. Enter the limited liability partnership, a special type partnership created for those engaged in professional occupations such as doctors, lawyers, dentists, architects and accountants. It is called a limited liability partnership (LLP) because it closely resembles the limited partnership, although there are important differences between the two. While the limited liability partnership protects the professional partner from both debts incurred by the practice and claims resulting from the malpractice of any other partner, it does not protect the professional partner from personal claims resulting from his own malpractice. Moreover, limited liability partnership assets cannot be directly seized by the professional partner's personal creditors, except when the negligent partner was acting on behalf of the limited liability partnership as his principal.

> **All partners in a limited liability partnership are liable for commercial debts and other partnership actions. However, when a partner is held responsible for malpractice, only the partner is liable.**

Nor can the professional partner's personal creditors easily liquidate his interest in the limited liability partnership, because ownership interest in this type of partnership must usually be owned by professionals from within that profession. This makes the limited liability partnership an excellent option when professionals want to participate in the management of the practice, while still insulating their personal assets from the partnership liabilities.

A limited liability partnership shares common features with other types of partnerships. Like a general partnership, all partners in a limited liability partnership are liable for commercial debts and other partnership actions. However, when a partner is held responsible for malpractice, only that partner is liable. The remainder of the partners are personally shielded from any liability incurred by the professional misconduct of that one partner. Most states that have adopted the Revised Uniform Partnership Act have extended that shield to cover not only tort claims, but contract claims as well.

Despite the continued liability of partners for partnership debts and personal liability if sued for malpractice, the limited liability partnership is a wise choice for professionals since no partner is liable for another partner's inappropriate or negligent practice. This allows high-risk professions to reap the benefits of forming a partnership without sacrificing personal wealth because of another partner's mistakes.

The professional's asset protection improves when they conduct their practice through a limited liability partnership. Conversely, the general partnership is the most dangerous business structure because each partner then has unlimited liability for all partnership debts. Should you still prefer the general partnership structure, each professional operating as a partner in the general partnership should, at the very least, organize his own professional corporation or limited liability company. These respective entities could then become partners in the partnership. While this creates a somewhat more cumbersome arrangement than a simple limited liability partnership, the structure provides certain tax, regulatory and organizational advantages. In a general partnership, the partners are all equally liable for partnership debts. In exchange, the partners enjoy the pass-through tax benefits not found in a corporation. In a limited partnership, all partners except one have limited liability. The general partner remains personally liable for any and all partnership debts.

Remember, a limited liability partnership can help to minimize the risk of its partners, but nothing can completely eliminate that risk. Don't mistakenly think that you no longer need malpractice insurance if you form a limited liability partnership. Also, carefully consider taxes, state regulations for your profession and malpractice insurance when creating your limited liability partnership agreement.

Wealthsaver Tips

1. The limited partnership can be an excellent entity to shelter both personal and family assets.

2. A creditor of a limited partner can only obtain a charging order against the limited partnership interest. This only gives the creditor the right to seize the profit distributions due the partner.

3. LPs are tax neutral. You can move assets into and out of your LP without tax consequences. The LP also pays no taxes on its earnings. This is paid by its partners.

4. General partners – but not the limited partners – are liable for the debts of the LP. For that reason, the LP should not be used for liability-producing activity. Alternatively, a corporation or LLC should be used as the general partner.

5. Separate LPs should own different assets.

6. An LP may save you estate taxes. Check with your estate planner.

7. Whenever you consider an LP, also consider the LLC. The LLC may be preferable - particularly to own real estate.

8. For maximum lawsuit insulation, you need an 'air-tight' limited partnership agreement, one with all the protective provisions.

NINE

The ABCs of LLCs

The limited partnership has been the mainstay of the asset protection planner, but the newer and even more protective limited liability company (LLC) promises to be even a more popular firewall.

You may have noticed that more and more LLCs or limited liability companies are springing up. There's good reason for it. The limited liability company is the first significant new legal entity to emerge since the 1950s and it is already an increasingly favorite for asset protection. The limited liability company was initiated in Wyoming in 1977 to help mining developers attract foreign investors. By 1988, limited liability company legislation began to spread throughout the nation. The incentive for the LLC was that the IRS would let you use the limited liability company as a partnership for tax purposes. As with partnerships, the limited liability company gave you the option of *single taxation.* The limited liability company members would be taxed on the limited liability company's profits. The limited liability company would itself pay no taxes. On the other hand, C corporation profits (not the S corporation) impose *double taxation.* The C corporation is taxed on its income and its shareholders are then personally taxed on whatever distributions they receive from the corporation.

There are other advantages that make the limited liability company a superior business organization in many situations. The LLC is a hybrid entity. It features both the limited liability advantage of the corporation with the favorable single income taxation of the partnership. More importantly, a member's interest in the limited liability company is protected. The member's creditor has only the charging order remedy as you have seen with the limited partnership (LP). Because the limited liability company is comparably protective to the limited partnership, it is equally as useful to title and protect a wide range of assets.

> The LLC features both the limited liability advantage of the corporation with the favorable single income taxation of the partnership.

Moreover, neither the limited liability company managers nor its members have personal liability for the debts of the limited liability company. It can then be an ideal entity to hold liability-producing assets or to conduct a business. Thus, the limited liability company can offer significant benefits over the corporation and other business organizations.

Much of what I say about the limited liability company applies as well to the limited partnership. Considering their similarities, it is not surprising that one lawyer may recommend a limited partnership and another a limited liability company. This doesn't necessarily argue against either since their distinction is so narrow.

Although the limited liability company's organizational, structural and protective features closely follow those of the limited partnership; there are differences in terminology. 'Managers' manage the limited liability company. They compare to general partners in a limited partnership. LLC owners are 'members'. They compare to limited partners.

LLC Advantages and Disadvantages

The limited liability company combines the limited liability advantage of a corporation with the protection for the ownership interest – as with a limited partnership. Yet, there are several reasons why we may prefer an LLC to either the LP or corporation:

- As with the 'S' corporation, you can avoid double taxation with a limited liability company. The limited liability company can avoid the 'C' corporation's corporate income tax – if you so elect. Income from the limited liability company can be singly taxed to its members, as with a partnership. You may also avoid state corporate franchise tax by using an LLC.

- You incur no personal liability with a limited liability company. As with the corporation, LLC managers and members are personally protected from the creditors of the limited liability company – even when its members manage the company. In contrast, general partners of a limited partnership are personally liable for partnership debts. Moreover, the limited partners of a limited partnership cannot participate in managing the limited partnership without incurring personal liability for partnership debts.

The LLC is a strong organizational choice for these two reasons. Still, the limited liability company is not always your best organizational choice. There are still more subtle reasons why we may instead use a corporation or limited partnership:

- The limited liability company may be less frequently adopted by business owners and professionals – only because the limited liability company is a newer entity. Fewer court cases have tested the protection afforded by the limited liability company. Thus, the LLC is less battle-proven than limited partnerships or corporations.

- Limited liability companies do not have the corporate advantage of prior IRS rulings concerning the sale of worthless stock or stock sold at a loss.

- LLC membership interests arguably do not get the same 'discounted valuations' for estate tax purposes as do limited partnership interests. This point, however, must still be clarified by future court cases.

- If you sell 50 percent or more of your ownership in the limited liability company in any one year, it ends the tax advantages of the limited liability company.

- Owners of a limited liability company pay greater unemployment taxes on their earnings than corporate officers.

- You cannot 'go public' with an LLC. To 'go public' you need a C corporation.

Other accounting, tax and organizational issues may influence your decision whether the LLC is your best option. I repeat: There is no one 'perfect entity'. You must consider a wide range of factors when you decide upon your best organizational choice. That decision should involve both your accountant and your attorney.

How the Limited Liability Company Operates

Limited liability company laws between the states vary only slightly because each state's LLC laws conform to the model Uniform Limited Liability Company Act (ULLCA) of 1995. Its provisions are:

- A limited liability company is considered a legal entity – one separate from its members.

- A limited liability company may be for either 'for-profit' or 'non-profit' purposes.

- Some states allow one member limited liability companies; others require two or more members.

- A member interest in a limited liability company is non-transferable without the unanimous consent of the other members.

- A member can transfer his or her interest in future distributions and returns of capital.

- Managers and members of the limited liability company have limited liability. They can lose only their investment if the limited liability company is sued or goes bankrupt.

- A limited liability company can be in existence for a fixed or perpetual duration.

- A limited liability company is dissolved upon: 1) Consent of its members; 2) dissociation of a member; 3) occurrence of a specific event stated in the operating agreement or 4) a fixed dissolution date.

- A limited liability company's operating agreement may not: 1) Unreasonably restrict a member from inspecting company records; 2) eliminate or reduce a member's duty,

loyalty, care or good faith when dealing with or on behalf
of the company; 3) restrict the rights of third parties
or 4) override the legal right of the company to expel a
member convicted of wrongdoing, breach of the operating
agreement or making it impractical for the limited
liability company to continue its business with further
member involvement.

There are other provisions, but these are the most important
characteristics of the LLC.

Unparalleled Tax Flexibility

Limited liability companies are typically taxed as partnerships,
but they may also elect to be taxed as C or S corporations. They
can even be structured as disregarded entities. This means they
are completely ignored for tax purposes (in other words, an LLC's
activities, profits and losses are treated as those of its owner). This
opens unique planning opportunities not available through other
entities. For example:

- Although neither partnerships nor corporations may own
  S corporation stock, a single member LLC that is taxed
  as a disregarded entity can. Thus we can provide a layer
  of protection to prevent S corporation stock from being
  seized if the LLC's owner loses a lawsuit.

- An offshore LLC may also elect to be treated as a
  disregarded entity. As a result, one can benefit from the
  advantages of offshore asset protection, while avoiding the
  reporting requirements imposed upon offshore trusts and

international business corporations (IBCs). Furthermore, a disregarded entity offshore LLC avoids the complex rules and tax traps that can arise from other offshore entities. (I'll discuss offshore limited liability companies in more detail in Chapter 11.)

- If you use a limited partnership or corporation to hold your personal residence, it will disqualify it from the IRS exemption regarding capital gains if the home is sold. This exemption allows for a homeowner to sell their appreciated personal residence free of capital gains tax, for up to $250,000 for a single person or $500,000 for a married couple. Assuming a 15 percent capital gains tax rate, this represents a tax savings of $50,000 to $100,000. There are two criteria that must be met in order to qualify for this exemption: 1) One or both spouses must have owned the home for at least 2 out of the 5 years preceding the sale and 2) the house must be the primary residence during those years. Unfortunately, if a limited partnership or corporation owns the home, the criteria is not met. However, a disregarded entity LLC can hold the residence and still qualify for the exemption, since its activities are treated as those of its owner. (Note that some states require an LLC to have a business purpose. In this case you should pay rent to the LLC that owns the home you are living in. This will ensure the LLC will be respected as a separate legal entity.)

- A disregarded entity LLC's income is reported on the tax return of its owner. If this is a person, then the income is reported on their 1040 return, Schedule C. However, an LLC that holds non-income producing property, and does not generate profit from other activities, will not need to report, at least for federal (and most state) tax purposes. This not only makes such an LLC easier to use, it also makes such an LLC 'anonymous' with the state where it was formed (a feature we'll shortly discuss). It thus becomes an incredible privacy tool. An example of this is if one uses a disregarded entity LLC to buy their personal residence. This purchase can be made without disclosing the LLC owner. Then, even if the owner pays rent to the LLC, because the LLC is disregarded from its owner's activities for tax purposes, the LLC has no gain. Therefore the owner won't be required to list the LLC on any federal tax return.

One may argue that a grantor trust (which we discuss in the next chapter) is also ignored for tax purposes, and therefore as appropriate for protecting a home from creditors. However, most states do not allow a grantor trust to provide asset protection if the grantor (the person that puts assets into the trust) continues to use the property. Therefore, a disregarded entity LLC is a unique entity that both provides limited liability in a wide range of situations, and is also ignored for tax purposes.

Where to Form Your Limited Liability Company

As with a corporation, you must also decide which state it is best to organize your limited liability company. Consider several financial, organizational and legal issues. Where will you operate your primary business? For example, you can register in a state with low organizational fees – such as New Mexico – but if you will chiefly do business in another state, you must nevertheless register in those states. This can increase your filing, registration and administrative costs. Also ask what will it cost to register in the state? What are their annual fees? Will your limited liability company pay state or local income taxes?

It is also important to evaluate five other key points which can differ between states:

- Can the members manage the LLC or must the limited liability company have a separate manager?

- Can the limited liability company merge with other type organizations?

- Can company members be easily admitted or terminated?

- What standards does the state impose on managers for negligence, malfeasance, misfeasance or misconduct? What are the standards for confidence, trust and confidentiality?

- Most importantly, what are the rights of a member's creditors to claim a member's limited liability company ownership interests? For asset protection, the answer to this last question is critical. State laws and court rulings are not necessarily consistent on this vital issue.

Also consider taxation issues. What are the organizational requirements for the LLC to qualify for partnership taxation? Some states allow only multi-member limited liability companies to be taxed as a partnership. Other states allow single-member limited liability companies to elect 'pass-through' taxation.

Some states, such as New Mexico, Indiana and Oklahoma, do not disclose the members or managers of their LLCs. LLCs formed in these states are 'anonymous LLCs'. Used properly, they can provide tremendous financial privacy – even more than that provided by a Nevada corporation.

Unlike corporate law, LLC law allows most of the details regarding the operation of the company to be determined by its operating agreement. In other words, we can decide with broad latitude how the company is structured. This gives us tremendous flexibility from a business, asset protection and estate planning standpoint.

Diversify With a Series LLC

> Your asset protection plan may require you to use a number of limited liability companies to segregate your assets into different entities.

Your asset protection plan may require you to use a number of limited liability companies to segregate your assets into different entities. For example, if you own 5 rental properties, you would title each property separately so that any liability that arises from one property will not jeopardize your other properties. Or you may operate several businesses through different LLCs with the same objective of liability insulation. I have clients who operate over a hundred separate LLCs. These multiple LLCs may be owned by the client personally or through one or more limited partnerships which would be the LLC member (this adds one more layer of protection – as well as an estate tax discounted valuation). Or your LLC may be owned by one or more trusts – particularly living trusts. This is a common arrangement.

One problem with multiple LLCs is that you must form and separately administer each separate LLC. To simplify matters, Delaware and 5 other states have recently established the Series LLC.

A Series LLC lets you establish a series of 'cells' within one LLC. Each cell within the series thus effectively operates as a distinct LLC. Each cell can own different assets, conduct different businesses, have different managers and members and have different operating agreements. Each cell can file one or separate tax returns and operate autonomously from the other cells within the series. What is most important is that the liabilities from one cell remains segregated to the assets of that cell. Consider the Series LLC if you need multiple LLCs. More states will enact Series LLC legislation, which should further popularize the LLC.

> One problem with multiple LLCs is that you must form and separately administer each separate LLC.

The Series LLC is a new entity type and only a few states allow their formation, although they have no problem registering to do business in any state. The question is whether states whose laws do not provide for Series LLCs will respect a Series LLC in regards to its segregation of liability between cells. I feel that the Series LLC will be respected in a non-series state. Still, in these states we advise additional reinforcement of each cell as an extra precaution. For example, if a person owned 10 rental properties in California (a non-series state), they could form a Series LLC with one cell for each property. Instead of placing each property directly in a cell, each property could be placed in a carefully structured irrevocable grantor trust (such as a Land Trust, which is described in Chapter 10), with a Series LLC as the beneficiary. Furthermore, a second non-series LLC that holds little non-trust assets could be the trustee for each trust. If the property is then involved in litigation, the plaintiff would be limited only to the assets of the trust. If the trustee was added as a co-defendant for an act of gross negligence, for example, the trustee would be an entity with little or no attachable assets. And if the trust failed, you would still have the series cell as an extra layer of protection.

As you can see, proper structuring of a Series LLC can be complex. There are currently very few professionals proficient at properly structuring a Series LLC. Therefore, you may need a qualified planner to work in conjunction with your attorney to form your Series LLC.

The Series LLC can be an extremely powerful asset protection tool. Anyone in need of multiple LLCs should consider them.

Limit Your LLC Liability

Limited liability company managers and members have limited liability. Thus the limited liability company compares to a corporation.

However, several states are less protective of LLCs and a one-member limited liability company may expose the single member to the debts of the limited liability company, much as a general partner would incur liability for the debts of a limited partnership. Moreover, this one member/manager must have sufficient personal assets (set by state law) to meet the foreseeable obligations of the limited liability company.

Of course, every business has its lawsuit risks. Your business may default on a debt, an employee may have a car accident, a customer may be injured or a disgruntled ex-employee may sue. Since you'll want to protect your personal wealth from these and other potential business risks, you'll want to organize your LLC in a state that insulates the LLC manager from personal liability.

Fortunately, most states do limit the manager's personal liability. They give outside protection for LLC's managers and members, as the corporation protects officers, directors and stockholders. However, you must follow limited liability company formalities. Only then would the limited liability company's assets be exposed to its creditors and lawsuits and the LLC manager's and member's personal wealth would remain untouchable.

Before you form a corporation, consider the limited liability company with your professional advisor. You will have limited liability, possibly pay less tax and obtain more protection for your ownership interest than you would have as a corporate stockholder.

Because a member, manager, agent and employee of a limited liability company would not ordinarily be personally liable for the debts, contracts or liabilities of the limited liability company (and would have basically the same liability protection as corporate officers, directors and stockholders or limited partnership limited partners – or outside protection),

> With both the corporation and the family limited partnership, you have personal liability for torts that you commit personally, as well as contracts you guarantee and debts where managers have statutory liability.

they can lose only their investment in the limited liability company. However, as with both the corporation and family limited partnership, you have personal liability for torts (negligence, etc.) that you commit personally, as well as contracts you guarantee and debts where managers have statutory liability.

How an LLC Protects Your Personal Assets

Let's look more closely at the LLC's inside protection. Creditors of a limited liability company member cannot seize or force a sale of the member's interest. Nor can the member's creditor vote the interest of the debtor-member. The member's creditors can only get a court charging order remedy to direct the limited liability company to pay to the creditor whatever income or distributions would otherwise flow to the debtor-member. This, you will remember, is the same 'charging order' remedy that a limited partner's creditor has against an interest in a family limited partnership. The creditor gains only the financial rights of the debtor-member, not control rights or ownership rights.

Again, you must note that the charging order will not 1) give your creditor voting rights or 2) force the limited liability company manager to pay distributions to a member or his creditor. The charging order only directs distributions to the creditor rather than the debtor-member.

The charging order may thus be as futile a creditor remedy with the limited liability company as it is with a family limited partnership. If you manage your limited liability company, you will decide if and when you will make distributions. Your judgment creditor cannot replace you as the manager because your creditor cannot vote. And for as long as your creditor has a charging order against you, you can refuse to pay distributions. Nevertheless, you can pay yourself a salary for services and salaries cannot be seized through the charging order. Nor can your creditor garnish loans or other forms of compensation that you may pay to yourself as a manager or member.

You also have the same tax liability 'poison pill' opportunities with the charging order against a limited liability company interest. The charging order creditor may be required to pay your income tax on LLC profits. Since a limited liability company is ordinarily taxed as a partnership, its tax liability automatically passes to its members. The charging order creditor then, under certain circumstances, gets the tax bill for the debtor-member's share of LLC profits. This forces the member's creditor to pay taxes on the member's earnings, even if the creditor has not received any distributions. That's a losing proposition for any creditor.

> **Your creditor cannot garnish loans or other forms of compensation that you may pay to yourself as a manager or member.**

Some professionals argue that the tax bill 'poison pill' wouldn't apply to a charging order creditor unless he or she also had the voting rights of the assigned membership interest. A carefully drafted operating agreement, however, will allow for an assignment of voting rights, while also ensuring that these voting rights do not allow the creditor to replace the manager, force distributions or in any other way compromise the LLC's protection. In this case, there is little doubt that the creditor will be stuck with a tax bill – and no distribution to pay it.

Some states view the charging order as a remedy that is inadequate from a creditor perspective, which it is. As a result, they have passed legislation allowing for the foreclosure of a member's LLC interest, wherein the assignment (charging order) could vest in perpetuity, even after the judgment debt has been settled. In response to this, other business-friendly states, such as Alaska, Arizona and Oklahoma, have passed legislation that forbids such foreclosure.

In reality, the ability to foreclose membership interests is a remedy with a lot of bark and little bite, provided that your LLC is set up properly. A foreclosure will still not allow for a creditor to receive anything more than a right to distributions from the LLC, which as we know the creditor will likely never receive. Furthermore, the receiver of a foreclosed interest will certainly be liable for the taxes on a distribution he will probably never see. This in turn will probably lead to a settlement where the foreclosure is set aside as if it had never happened. Despite this fact, the possibility of a problem that won't go away (in the event of foreclosure) makes the avoidance of LLC membership foreclosures desirable. Thus, you should form your LLC in a state that forbids such foreclosure.

> A foreclosure will still not allow for a creditor to receive anything more than a right to distributions from the LLC, which as we know the creditor will likely never receive.

These charging order's limitations encourage most creditors to settle rather than fight. Why would a creditor elect a remedy that gives them no money, no control and only a tax bill? When your assets are safely titled to a limited liability company, you may reach a faster settlement and avoid the expense, time and hassle of defending the lawsuit.

Unfortunately, the limited liability company also has the same protective deficiencies as the family limited partnership. For example, if you transfer your assets to the limited liability company after you have a creditor, your creditor may possibly recover the assets as a fraudulent transfer.

Profits may be distributed to you (and hence your creditor) when you do not control the manager. You would then not rely on the limited liability company, though your membership interest may then be owned by another LLC that you do control.

And as an LLC member in bankruptcy, your bankruptcy trustee may have greater rights to claim your limited liability company ownership interest than could a judgment creditor holding a charging order.

Should a member file bankruptcy, recent case law has demonstrated that the bankruptcy trustee may also have considerably greater rights to claim the member's limited liability company ownership interest than could be obtained by a judgment creditor holding a charging order. A meticulously drafted operating agreement may curb these greater powers by giving each member an ongoing obligation to render certain services to the company. Such obligations make the operating agreement an 'executory contract', which in turn subjects the LLC to more favorable bankruptcy law. Nonetheless, bankruptcy is the ultimate test of any asset protection plan, and even an immaculately structured LLC is no guarantee that the member declaring bankruptcy will retain his LLC interest.

> As an LLC member in bankruptcy, your bankruptcy trustee may have greater rights to claim your limited liability company ownership interest than could a judgment creditor holding a charging order.

Aside from bankruptcy, we can improve your protection as a limited liability company member by using the same strategies as we would use to maximize protection for your corporate shares or limited partnership interests. For example, we can assess your membership interest, issue voting proxies or grant the LLC options to redeem your membership interest. You may also encumber or lien your membership interest or dilute your membership control having the LLC sell additional ownership interests.

We can also comparably protectively title a membership interest. For instance, limited liability company interests owned by a married couple may title their ownership as tenants-by-the-entirety in those states where this form of marital ownership is creditor-protected. Or an offshore trust can own the membership interests – much as we use offshore trusts as limited partner in a limited partnership. Or a limited partnership may be the member of a limited liability company. This is a particularly good arrangement in those states that better protect a limited partnership interest than a limited liability company membership. We can also use the limited partnership to own a limited liability company to reduce estate taxes as I explain later in this chapter.

Finally, for asset protection, your LLC should have one or more members in addition to the member who is a lawsuit defendant. The courts are more hesitant to expand upon a creditor's remedy when other LLC members would be affected. Some courts will liquidate an LLC for the benefit of a creditor when the debtor is the only member and no other members would be affected.

Limitations of the Limited Liability Company

While we more and more frequently use the limited liability company, there are certain disadvantages that may exclude the LLC from consideration as the best organizational entity:

1. The LLC is not always available to the sole proprietor

Several states require two or more members to form a limited liability company. Therefore on occasion a sole proprietor may not be able to form an LLC. Fortunately, a grantor trust (whose beneficiary is the proprietor) is completely ignored for tax purposes, and can qualify as an extra member for legal purposes. A carefully drafted grantor trust could therefore serve as a second member for the LLC. An additional benefit to this arrangement is that having a second member would also reinforce the limited liability aspect of the LLC, as we've discussed earlier. Notwithstanding the fact that this structure would qualify as a multi-member LLC, the IRS has ruled that such an arrangement would be taxed exactly like a sole proprietorship. Its income would be reported on the owner's 1040 Schedule C income tax return.

2. The LLC is not always available for the professional practice

Many states prohibit an LLC for such professionals as physicians and attorneys. California, for example, prohibits a limited liability company from conducting a professional practice. Don't form a limited liability company to operate your professional practice before you check with your state licensing agency or an attorney familiar with your state's limited liability company and professional regulations.

3. Questionable estate tax benefits

The limited liability company may not save you estate taxes. If you have a taxable estate, then it may be safer to use the family limited partnership if you want a 'discounted valuation' of your estate. Your limited partnership may, however, own one or more LLCs, which would enable you to capture the estate tax discounted valuation.

4. The dissolution dilemma

A final problem is that you may also require the unanimous vote by all LLC members to continue the LLC after the death, bankruptcy, retirement, etc. of one member. One member can then possibly become a holdout and make unreasonable demands on the remaining members to vote to continue the LLC. You can avoid this holdout problem if your LLC operating agreement requires only a majority vote to continue the company.

Assets Your LLC Can Shelter

Your limited liability company can own any asset that you can title to a limited partnership. In practice, I prefer the limited liability company to title more dangerous (liability-producing) assets since limited liability company managers will be fully protected personally from the LLC debts, while the limited partnership's general partner would have personal liability. I use the limited partnership to title and protect 'safe' assets – passive investments, etc. My reasoning: The limited partnership has been battle-tested for nearly a century, whereas the limited liability company is a newer and less tested asset protection entity. A limited liability company is a desirable entity to own:

- Second homes and vacation homes
- Commercial real estate
- Cars, boats, planes, etc.
- Equipment and other physical assets
- Operating businesses.

As mentioned, I sometimes have a single-member limited liability company own a primary residence. I will particularly use the LLC to avoid an attachment of a home by a judgment creditor. You may ask that if both the limited liability company and the family limited partnership can equally protect such a variety of assets, why not title your home to a family limited partnership or multi-member limited liability company to gain the same charging order protection? Some asset protection planners do recommend titling the family residence to a limited partnership, but this has its downside. You would then lose your tax benefits. You can only preserve your family residence tax benefits by titling your home to a single-member limited liability company which is a disregarded entity.

As I previously stated, as a single individual, you have a $250,000 capital gains tax exclusion on profits when you sell your home. If a family limited partnership owns your house for more than 3 out of 5 years, you lose your tax benefit. Of course, you could transfer your home to a family limited partnership for no more than 3 years and then retransfer the home to your own name for at least 2 years, but this is usually impractical.

Our alternative is to have a single-member limited liability company own your home. If you are married, one spouse (usually the less liability-prone spouse) would be that single-member. Since the IRS disregards single-member limited liability companies for tax purposes, the home should, at least for capital gains purposes, be treated as if the home were owned in the name of the individual member. You cannot achieve this tax strategy with a limited partnership, which by definition requires at least 2 owners and therefore cannot be a disregarded entity. Review this strategy with your tax advisor.

It is possible to achieve this same tax strategy with a limited partnership, if you use either a grantor trust or an LLC as one partner, and the trust grantor or LLC owner as the second partner. Because a trust may not provide limited liability as a general partner, it behooves us to instead use an LLC. As you can see, it's pointless to use a limited partnership instead of an LLC, if we need to use an LLC with the limited partnership to achieve our goals anyway. It's much easier to simply use an LLC and a grantor trust.

When an LLC is to hold your personal residence, you must be aware of the home loan's 'due on sale' clause. I am frequently asked by clients about this 'due on sale,' clause (standard in most mortgages), which requires the mortgage lender to consent to any transfer of the property (to a limited liability company or otherwise). Lenders routinely consent to such transfers, unless the lender sold the mortgage to Fannie Mae, the borrower is in default on the mortgage or you are paying lower than prevailing interest rates.

> **When an LLC is to hold your personal residence, you must be aware of the home loan's 'due on sale' clause.**

I have had cases where a lender refused to consent to the transfer, but we nevertheless transferred the property to a limited liability company to sidestep a real estate attachment or creditor seizure. Not once did we have a lender actually foreclose because of the transfer. Further, there are cases that have upheld the right of an owner to transfer property to an LLC or FLP that is owned by the same party – even without the consent of the mortgage holder.

Nonetheless, if it appears that a 'due on sale' clause may cause problems, federal law allows us to transfer the property to a living trust (which may be irrevocable) without triggering the clause. Although a trust usually provides little or no asset protection (particularly if you continue to enjoy use of the property), we can encumber the property with additional liens which act as a 'debt shield' against subsequent creditor claims. Thus we use a trust for privacy and estate planning, we use a debt shield for asset protection, and we can build a solid program that even your lender is happy with. We further discuss liens to protect assets in Chapter 12.

Our overriding strategy is to segregate as many of your assets as possible into separate limited liability companies. For instance, if you own 10 apartment houses, you would title each in a separate limited liability company. Or we would use a Series LLC. Your 10 limited liability companies, or cells in the Series, may be owned by one family limited partnership. Your limited partnership may be owned by your living trust. You can then bequeath your estate without probate while at the same time maximizing the protection for your respective entities. This 'layering' lets you accomplish your different financial objectives. The LLC is usually an essential component to this layering process.

Wealthsaver Tips

1. The limited liability company is a hybrid entity that combines the protection features of the corporation and limited partnership.

2. Managers and members of an LLC have no personal liability for the debts of the LLC.

3. A creditor of an LLC member can only obtain a charging order against that member's interest. The creditor can only claim distributed profits or proceeds due the member.

4. An LLC can operate an active business or protectively own a wide range of personal assets.

5. A single-member LLC may be suitable to own a residence or S corporation shares. It is almost always the preferred entity to own real estate – other than the family home.

6. LLCs can elect to be taxed as C corporations, partnerships or proprietorships (single-member LLCs).

7. For maximum protection, title your assets to separate LLCs. Six states allow Series LLCs where each cell within the LLC acts as its own LLC. This creates a virtual firewall around the assets owned by each cell.

8. Discuss with your advisors the LLC option. It may offer you several important advantages over the corporation or other entities.

TEN ■ ■ ■

Trusts That Can Protect You

When you think 'asset protection', you probably think first about 'trusts'. Trusts and asset protection seem to go together. But is a trust *your* best asset protection option? A trust *may* shelter you, but most trusts will not.

America's wealthiest families have historically relied upon various trusts to protect their wealth from taxes, but now folks from every economic background use trusts for many purposes. Asset protection is one of the more important.

There are many different trusts but only a few are useful for asset protection. The offshore trust is particularly important, and I more fully discuss this special trust in Chapter 11. In this chapter we'll discuss domestic or US-based trusts.

Trust Basics

A trust is created by a *settlor* or *grantor* (the terms are interchangeable) who funds or gives property to the trust. As the trust creator, the grantor sets the terms under which the donated assets shall be managed and distributed.

The grantor names one or more *trustees*. The trustee may be the grantor. The grantor designates the beneficiaries who are to benefit from the trust and receive its income and principal. Certain trusts allow the grantor to be both the trustee and the beneficiary, as is common with the living trust.

Before you consider a trust for asset protection, you must ask:

1) Which trusts can protect your assets from your creditors?

2) Which trusts can protect assets that you bequeath to your beneficiaries from their creditors?

3) How can you improve your trust protection?

4) How much asset protection can you get from the various trusts?

Lawsuit-Proofing Trusts

Not every trust is useful for asset protection. In fact, few are. You need an irrevocable intervivos trust to shelter your assets from your creditors. Any trust – with the right protective provisions – can lawsuit-proof the trust assets from your beneficiaries' creditors.

A trust is either intervivos or testamentary. A living trust – as its name suggests – is created and funded during your lifetime. It is an intervivos trust.

Trusts that you fund upon your death are testamentary. A testamentary trust thus only takes effect upon your death. You would usually create it in your last will or living trust. During your lifetime, your assets remain in your name and would be unprotected against your creditors – unless they have otherwise been sheltered.

Trusts are revocable or irrevocable. You can change or revoke a revocable trust. You cannot revoke or modify an irrevocable trust. Every testamentary trust is irrevocable once you die because you obviously cannot spring back to life to unwind a trust that you set up during your lifetime.

It is important to distinguish a revocable from an irrevocable trust because a revocable trust won't protect you. For protection you need an irrevocable

> **It is important to distinguish a revocable from an irrevocable trust because a revocable trust won't protect you.**

trust. You also need an irrevocable trust that you presently fund – an intervivos trust.

One serious disadvantage from using an irrevocable intervivos trust for asset protection is that once the trust is established and funded, you cannot cancel or modify the trust and reclaim the property you transferred to the trust. You thus lose both ownership and control over the trust assets. That's why we seldom use an irrevocable intervivos trust for asset protection – though such trusts can be useful for estate planning.

The irrevocable trust protects your assets for the same reason that a revocable trust doesn't. A revocable trust will not protect your assets because your creditors can 'step into your shoes' and revoke your trust. For example, assets titled to your revocable living trust are vulnerable to your present and future lawsuits. Nevertheless, a living trust will help you to avoid probate. For lawsuit-proof wealth, you need an irrevocable trust – or another protective entity. Since you cannot revoke or change an irrevocable trust, your creditors have no greater power to unwind your trust and reclaim its assets. And for an irrevocable trust to protect you, it must be presently funded. Until you transfer assets to your trust, they are your assets and can be claimed by your creditors.

There are other limitations with using trusts to shield assets. One limitation is that you cannot settle your trust for your sole benefit. For lawsuit protection, you should have no beneficial interest in the trust. You can, however, retain income rights based on some ascertainable standard (health needs, etc.). Some states disallow self-settled trusts for asset protection. The grantor can neither control the trust nor have any beneficial rights.

Another limitation is that assets fraudulently transferred to the trust can be recovered by present creditors. An irrevocable trust can protect only against future creditors. You should only transfer assets to an irrevocable trust when you are confident that you have no present creditors. But how can you ever be absolutely certain of this? It's more accurate to say that you shouldn't transfer assets to an irrevocable trust if you have the likelihood of a present creditor. A present creditor can recover assets from the trust because the transfer was without consideration. In other words, you received nothing in exchange from the trust.

You can see the limitations with trusts. For protetion, you must use an irrevocable trust, relinquish control and beneficial interest, and still your trust assets may be seized as a fraudulent transfer. Trusts are also set aside when a court concludes that a trust is a sham or that the grantor retained de facto control over the trust.

> The irrevocable trust for asset protection imposes a heavy price. Most people find it too heavy a price.

The irrevocable trust for asset protection imposes a heavy price. Most people find it too heavy a price. There are less draconian ways to become lawsuit-proof.

An irrevocable trust can make sense when 1) you would soon gift the assets to your beneficiaries anyway and 2) you do not foresee needing the assets for your future financial security. Your 'price', then, is not particularly heavy. If you do not foreseeably need the assets, and the trust will now accomplish what you would eventually do – distribute your assets to your beneficiaries (usually your children) at some future time – then, and only then, should you consider an irrevocable intervivos trust for wealth preservation.

Common Trust Pitfalls

You must also avoid three common pitfalls if you do create an irrevocable intervivos trust. First, reserve no power to revoke, rescind or amend the trust, or retain any rights – directly or indirectly – to reclaim property that you transfer to the trust. Attach no strings to the assets that you transfer to the trust. Second, retain no authority on how your trust or its property is to be managed or invested. And reserve no significant power over the trust. You cannot be the trustee, nor should your spouse, relative or personal friend. Courts closely examine relationships between the grantor and trustee to determine whether the trustee is only the grantor's 'alter ego'. Unless your trustee is independent, the courts can ignore your trust and your creditors can claim the trust assets. A corporate trustee – a bank or trust company – won't be considered your alter ego. Their trusteeship will better protect your trust.

Because of these irrevocable trust disadvantages, most people choose other methods to protect their assets. It also explains the popularity of limited partnerships and LLCs which provide excellent asset protection, are revocable, and allow you to control your assets.

Revocable trusts – particularly the living trust – are more common than irrevocable trusts. A revocable trust can help you with your estate planning, but not for asset protection. Creditors can claim assets in a revocable trust as easily as assets titled to you individually. If you can revoke or modify your trust, your creditors can claim the assets for their benefit.

Smart Parents, Spendthrift Kids

You also have to asset protect your children's inheritance. Parents spend their lifetime scrimping, saving and sheltering their wealth, and then leave their fortune to their kids who promptly spend or lose it. Think about a trust to safeguard the assets you will leave to your beneficiaries. They too will have lawsuits, creditors, divorces, etc. How will you protect their inheritance from their financial and legal problems?

You may not want an irrevocable trust to protect your assets from your creditors, but it's frequently smart to set up a trust to protect the assets that you bequeath to your beneficiaries from their lawsuits, creditors and ex-spouses. This is particularly true when the beneficiaries are your children or grandchildren.

Irrevocable trusts can be intervivos or testamentary. With an intervivos trust you transfer some or all of your assets to your trust during your lifetime. A testamentary trust receives your assets upon your death. Your assets are yours and stay vulnerable to your creditors until you die, when title to these assets passes to the trust.

A revocable trust can protect trust assets from your beneficiaries' creditors. Whether you transfer your assets to the trust within your lifetime (an intervivos trust) or upon your death (a testamentary trust), the one difference between a revocable and an irrevocable trust funded within your lifetime is that the revocable trust won't protect you as the grantor. Moreover, assets in your revocable trust will be included in your taxable estate. Assets transferred to your irrevocable trust during your lifetime will be excluded from your taxable estate – provided you live 3 or more years thereafter.

> Nowadays, more Americans with significant wealth rely upon trusts to protect their children's inheritance.

Nowadays, more Americans with significant wealth rely upon trusts to protect their children's inheritance. Why lose their wealth to their children's creditors or ex-spouse? How should you leave your wealth to your kids? It's not a question of how much money you will leave, but when and under what conditions your children will inherit.

Nor is it seldom good planning to gift substantial amounts outright to children during your lifetime. You may make lifetime gifts to your children to reduce your taxable estate, yet you have those same ever-present dangers of your children squandering their gifts and you losing control over these assets. A trust may also not be your right answer. A smarter solution may be to title your assets in a limited partnership with yourself (and your spouse) as its general partner. You can then transfer to your children – through a trust – a portion of your limited partnership interests each year. You reduce your taxable estate as you shift your limited partnership interest to your children's trusts, and your assets will stay safe from your creditors because your assets are titled to a limited partnership. You stay in control of your assets because you would be the general partner. Your children's inheritance will be twice protected – once by the limited partnership and again by their irrevocable trust. When you die, your remaining partnership interest will have a discounted estate tax valuation and you can bequeath this remaining limited partnership interest to your children's trust.

There are hundreds of ways to effectively combine trusts, FLPs, LLCs and corporations to achieve various lawsuit protection, tax and estate planning objectives. The important point is that you can achieve all this while retaining lifetime control over your assets – which should always be an important goal.

Safeguarding Inheritances

For a trust to fully safeguard your beneficiaries' interest in the trust assets, you need the right trust provisions. The right protective clauses will prevent your beneficiaries' creditors from claiming their share of the trust principal or income. The right provisions will also stop the creditor from asserting any rights that the beneficiaries may have to the income or exercise other powers that could forfeit your beneficiaries' protection.

The most important trust clause is the anti-alienation or spendthrift provision which directly protects the trust assets from the beneficiaries' creditors. The anti-alienation clause prohibits the trustee from transferring the trust assets to anyone other than the beneficiaries. This includes the trust beneficiaries' creditors. The spendthrift or anti-alienation clause expressly precludes anyone whose interest is adverse to the beneficiaries (a creditor, ex-spouse, IRS, etc.) from claiming the beneficiaries' share – whether it be the trust principal or income distributions. This is a vital provision for every trust.

The spendthrift clause still won't completely protect the beneficiaries. There are limitations. For example, several states don't enforce spendthrift provisions. A spendthrift clause won't always protect the beneficiaries from bankruptcy, divorce or tax claims. And it won't protect income distributions previously received by the beneficiaries. Or a spendthrift provision may be poorly drafted or narrowly interpreted by the courts. Its protection largely depends on the drafter's skill.

> The spendthrift clause still won't completely protect the beneficiaries. There are limitations.

Another important protective clause is to give your trustee distribution discretion. For example, your trust may provide that the beneficiaries would receive trust distributions at age 25. But would those distributions be safe if a beneficiary then has a judgment creditor? Or what if a divorce is imminent?

With a discretionary clause, your trustee has the right to withhold income and principal distributions that would otherwise be payable to the beneficiaries – if the trustee believes that the distribution would be wasted or claimed by the beneficiaries' creditors. This same discretionary clause can also prevent a wasteful beneficiary from depleting or wasting trust assets. This is always an important consideration when the grantors' children are the beneficiaries. If you have concerns whether money that you entrust for your children will be wasted, then insert a discretionary provision in your trust. Your trustee can then regulate distributions to your children, avoid or minimize waste, and better prevent creditor seizure.

Your child may not be a spendthrift, but what about your child's spouse? These same provisions can safe keep the trust assets if your child dies or divorces. These provisions can also apply to gifts to your grandchildren.

Spendthrift and discretionary clauses combine to protect trust assets from your beneficiaries' creditors, as the trustee can withhold payments to your beneficiaries. A beneficiaries' creditor cannot force a trustee to distribute trust assets to the beneficiaries. The creditor can only claim payments received by the beneficiaries. However, the trustee can directly pay third parties on behalf of a beneficiary which, of course, circumvents a creditor attempting to seize funds from the beneficiaries.

> Spendthrift and discretionary clauses combine to protect trust assets from your beneficiaries' creditors, as the trustee can withhold payments to your beneficiaries.

For more protection, add sprinkling provisions to your trust. Sprinkling provisions are commonly found in trusts that are expected to remain in force for 10 or more years, and where each beneficiary's future income or tax situation is uncertain. The trustee can then modify trust distributions through this 'sprinkling' provision. The trustee can either disburse or retain the principal and income for the duration of the trust. The trustee thus determines what each beneficiary will receive – and when.

The trust grantor would specify criteria for the trustee to follow when making distributions. Required minimum income distributions are recommended when the beneficiary is a spouse or dependent child.

The sprinkling provision adds protection but you still cannot retain the right to modify or revoke your sprinkling trust. As with any other asset protection trust, your sprinkling trust must be irrevocable and you cannot retain control. Moreover, your beneficiary cannot be a trustee. Although legally permissible, the trust assets, in such instances, would become vulnerable to the creditors of your trustee-beneficiary. A trustee, who can distribute trust assets to himself as the beneficiary, gives his creditors the same right to force distributions, which the creditor can then seize.

How would a trust with these protective provisions work? Take the case of Jerry, a New York accountant, who owned $600,000 in mutual funds that he wanted to leave to his two adult children, Steve and Stephanie. Jerry and his wife could live quite comfortably without these funds, and Jerry also wanted to save estate taxes as well as provide some security to his children. Jerry, however, was concerned that his children would unwisely spend their inheritance. So Jerry set up an irrevocable trust with his local bank as the trustee. Jerry's distribution preferences were incorporated within the trust.

Jerry and his wife funded the trust each year with $48,000 in mutual funds as tax-free gifts. Since the trust was irrevocable, neither Jerry's nor his wife's future creditors could seize these funds. The anti-alienation, spendthrift and discretionary provisions protected the trust funds from his children's bad spending habits, as well as from their potential divorces or lawsuits. The net result was that the irrevocable trust protected Jerry's mutual funds from his creditors, let him gift them tax-free to his children, reduced his estate taxes, provided for his children's future (which he intended to do anyway through his will or living trust), and finally, protect the trust funds from his children's creditors. A still better arrangement may have been to combine this with a limited partnership as previously discussed.

Living Trusts

Let's examine the more common trusts and see whether they can help you achieve your legal and financial goals. Let's particularly examine whether they can give you and your beneficiaries good lawsuit protection.

The living trust is America's most popular trust. A living trust helps you avoid the cost and delay of probate. You can also avoid the dangers from jointly owning assets. But a revocable living trust won't lawsuit-protect you.

Though a revocable trust won't protect you, you have the comfort of knowing that you can change or revoke your living trust as often as you can revise your will.

> The living trust helps you avoid the cost and delay of probate. You can also avoid the dangers from jointly owning assets.

But did you know that a living trust can cause you to lose lawsuit protection? Several states have ruled that a homesteaded home transferred to a living trust loses homestead protection. Similarly, assets owned between spouses as tenants-by-the-entirety may lose creditor protection from this type co-ownership when those same assets are instead titled to a living trust.

There are trade-offs between the different ways to title assets. Without a revocable living trust, the court will distribute your assets under your will. This can be expensive, time-consuming and cumbersome. (Probate costs can consume 2-4 percent of an estate and delay estate distributions.) If you bequeath $1 million through your will, your heirs may pay up to $40,000 in probate costs, and your beneficiaries may wait years for their inheritances. A living trust avoids the probate process. Your assets immediately transfer to your beneficiaries.

You can have the best of both worlds. Title your assets to a limited partnership (to lawsuit-proof these assets). Then have your living trust (which avoids probate) own your limited partnership. When you die, your ownership in the limited partnership would immediately transfer through the living trust to your heirs, avoiding probate. During your lifetime your assets would stay creditor-protected by the limited partnership.

Irrevocable Life Insurance Trusts

Life insurance may be another important asset. But life insurance can have a substantial cash value or death benefit exposed to creditors. Even a term policy with no cash value can be a valuable asset in that it will provide your family income and support after you die. But will your beneficiaries get the death benefit or will your creditors? Life insurance can also pay your estate taxes and make funds immediately available to your survivors; thus avoiding the delay and expense of liquidating other assets.

> **Life insurance can have a substantial cash value or death benefit exposed to creditors.**

If you own a large life insurance policy, title your insurance policy to an irrevocable life insurance trust (ILIT). An ILIT is an irrevocable trust specifically designed to own life insurance. As with other trusts, the ILIT has a trustee, beneficiaries and terms for distributions.

Your ILIT would own your insurance policy. The insurance policy beneficiary would be the trust. When you die, your insurer would pay the ILIT trustee, who would follow the trust instructions and distribute the proceeds to the ILIT beneficiaries. Your estate should not be the beneficiary.

An ILIT can be funded or unfunded. An unfunded ILIT's life insurance premiums are not fully paid. You fund future premiums (give annual premiums to the trustee, who pays the premiums). With a funded ILIT, you transfer to the trust a fully paid insurance policy or enough income-producing assets to pay the future premiums.

Whether yours is an unfunded or funded ILIT, your policy premiums must be directly paid from the trust. You cannot directly pay the premiums or you lose both the trust's tax benefits and creditor protection.

The ILIT is irrevocable. It protects the policy's cash value, death proceeds and distributions from the trust to the beneficiaries. If life insurance is not fully creditor-protected by your state laws, then an ILIT is essential protection.

The ILIT – though sometimes important for asset protection – can save you estate taxes. Because the ILIT would own the life insurance policy, the policy proceeds won't be included in your taxable estate nor subject to estate taxes.

Let me illustrate. Assume that you are single and die with a $3 million estate and $1 million of that amount is life insurance. Assume that when you die you have a $2 million death tax exemption. Your estate would then pay an estate tax on $1 million. If the estate tax is 50%, your estate tax would be $500,000. But your ILIT would remove the $1 million life insurance proceeds from your taxable estate. Your estate would save $500,000 in estate taxes because you reduced your taxable estate to zero.

The ILIT also gives you better control over policy distributions than when insurance is owned by you personally. When you personally own insurance, your insurance company directly pays the named beneficiaries when you die. An ILIT not only lets you control who receives the proceeds, but also how and when the policy proceeds will be distributed. For instance, you can specify that the ILIT trustee pays estate taxes and other costs (taxes due on IRAs or other retirement plans probate costs, legal fees, other debts, etc.) before the trustee distributes funds to the trust beneficiaries. Or you can direct your trustee to pay your beneficiaries over a period of months or years. You can add spendthrift, anti-alienation, discretionary distribution and other protective provisions to protect the insurance proceeds from your beneficiaries' creditors. The ILIT can also avoid court interference if a beneficiary becomes incompetent. Insurance companies won't pay life insurance proceeds to an incapacitated beneficiary. They require court instructions. The ILIT avoids this unnecessary complication.

Children's Trusts

Do you want to gift money to you children? Investigate an irrevocable children's trust (ICT). It can reduce taxes and provide asset protection. Property that you transfer to a children's trust cannot be seized by your creditors. It also won't be included in your taxable estate. Income from the trust would be taxed at the children's lower income tax rates. These are the reasons for the children's trust.

The ICT (or Section 2503 Minor's Trust) by its terms, controls the taxation and asset protection benefits of this trust. While the trust is in effect – and the beneficiary is under 21 – neither the grantors nor the child's creditors can claim the trust assets.

There is one disadvantage with the children's trust. When your child reaches 21, your child can demand the trust assets. Since it is an irrevocable trust, the grantor cannot withhold distributions from the trust. You cannot thus prevent your child from receiving the assets that are then owned by the trust. You can only extend the trust until a later age if your child – at age 21 – consents in writing. So, carefully consider whether your child(ren) at that young age can properly handle the trust assets. You no more want to lose the trust assets to an irresponsible 21-year-old than to your creditors.

> An irrevocable children's trust reduces taxes and provides asset protection.

Charitable Remainder Trusts

Gifting your assets to charity may seem an extreme way to gain creditor-protection, however, our tax laws allow you to give away your property to charity, achieve asset protection, and use these same assets to generate income for you during your lifetime. For asset protection, as well as the tax advantages from gifting assets during your lifetime, the Charitable Remainder Trust (CRT) can be your answer.

Here's a snapshot of how the CRT works. As the grantor, you select a tax-exempt charity as the beneficiary of your irrevocable trust. When you create and fund the CRT, you make a charitable donation and can claim an immediate tax deduction for the value of the assets contributed to the trust. Although you have gifted the 'principal,' you would be the income beneficiary. Over your lifetime your trust would pay you a fixed annual income. You thus get an immediate tax deduction and future income from the donated assets.

> CRTs allow you to give away your property to charity, achieve asset protection, and use these same assets to generate income for you during your lifetime.

Assume that you have $200,000 in stocks purchased 15 years ago for $60,000. If you sold the stock to invest in treasury bonds (for a more stable retirement income) you would pay $21,000 in capital gains taxes on the profit (15% x $140,000 gain). If your treasury bonds are worth $200,000 when you die, your estate may then pay another $88,000 in estate taxes (although future estate taxes are uncertain). Your heirs would inherit, after taxes, only $91,000 from the original $200,000.

Suppose you don't sell your stocks. Instead you transfer them to a CRT. You would get the same annual income as from treasury bonds for the remainder of your life because you could be the CRT's income beneficiary. You would deduct your $200,000 donation as an immediate charitable contribution. With the income from the tax savings from your charitable deduction, you can buy $91,000 worth of life insurance to cover the $91,000 that your beneficiaries would have received had you not donated your stock to the CRT. The net result: You get a large tax deduction this year, the same perpetual fixed retirement income as with treasury bonds, you donate to your favorite charity and the donated trust assets are lawsuit-proof.

Do you have appreciated assets? Do you want a fixed lifetime income? Would the CRT's fixed income satisfy your retirement needs (adjusted for inflation)? If so, a CRT may be a good asset protection strategy for you – particularly if it can help you achieve your philanthropic goals. Income from the CRT can be seized by your creditors, but even then we have solutions. For example, we can protect your income through a charitable remainder annuity trust (CRAT), if your state exempts annuities from creditor seizure. There are other trusts that you can use as a variation on this theme.

Qualified Personal Residence Trusts

Have you heard about the Qualified Personal Residence Trust? A Qualified Personal Residence Trust (QPRT) is a special trust. You transfer your residence to the trust and retain a tenancy for ten years. At the end of the term, your residence passes to your beneficiaries. Your objective is to transfer your residence now at its lower value (basis), rather than when you die and it has a greater value. The QPRT thus reduces estate taxes.

A QPRT can also lawsuit-protect your home. Your creditors can only claim your right to use the property for the remaining term of years (or the rental value for those years). However, your creditor cannot attach or seize the home because it would be owned by the trust. The beneficial remainder interest can be claimed by your beneficiaries' creditors, unless your trust includes those all important spendthrift provisions. At the end of the term, the trustee must distribute the assets (the residence or cash proceeds from its sale) or convert the QPRT assets into an annuity. This is a more desirable alternative in those states that creditor-protect annuities.

> The QPRT allows you to transfer your residence to the trust and retain a tenancy for ten years.

Q-TIP Trusts

If you are in a second (or third, fourth or fifth marriage), the Q-TIP (Qualified Terminable Interest Property) trust may interest you. The Q-TIP ensures that your spouse will receive a lifetime income from the trust. The trust principal will then pass to your children (or an alternative beneficiary) after your spouse dies or remarries.

Q-TIPs are common with second marriages because they preserve your assets for the benefit of the children from a prior marriage rather than the spouse's children or family, who would become the probable beneficiaries of an estate bequeathed outright to a surviving spouse. Q-TIPs can also protect a spouse when the grantor believes that the spouse may waste the assets during the spouse's lifetime. A Q-TIP is essentially a spendthrift trust to shelter your assets from your spouse's creditors or subsequent mates.

Income from the Q-TIP trust must be used solely to benefit the surviving spouse during the spouse's lifetime, or if the trust won't qualify for the unlimited marital deduction. Estate taxes on the principal are deferred until the surviving spouse dies.

A Q-TIP trust won't protect your assets against your creditors, because the Q-TIP is a testamentary trust. It takes effect only upon your death. However, a Q-TIP trust can shelter your wealth from a spendthrift spouse, a spouse who may have future financial or legal difficulties or a spouse who will want to leave your money to his or her children.

The Q-TIP's trust principal will be safe from your spouse's creditors, though the income to your spouse would be unprotected. Moreover, the trust income must be distributed as it is earned. The trustee cannot withhold distributions.

You can use a similar irrevocable intervivos marital deduction trust for asset protection. The objective is to shift marital assets from the higher-risk spouse to the less-at-risk spouse.

Of course, this is only another form of lifetime gifting, and these transfers are subject to fraudulent transfer claims. A spouse who makes an outright gift must understand that the transferred assets may be lost by a surviving spouse in a later lawsuit or in divorce. It can also be lost to the spouse's spendthrift spending.

Land Trusts

Land trusts, widely used in Illinois, Florida, Georgia, California, Colorado and a few other states, can partially insulate real estate from lawsuits.

The land trust can own any real estate, including the family home. A bank is normally the trustee. The land trust will protect the beneficiaries' interest in the real estate only if the trust has the proper spendthrift and anti-alienation provisions.

As the trust beneficiary, you wouldn't directly own the real estate. The real estate would be titled to the trustee. You instead own only a beneficial interest in the trust. This interest would be personal property, not real property.

Owning a beneficial interest in a land trust is not, in itself, sufficiently protective. Your creditors can possibly seize your beneficial interest. You need more protection. One option is to title your beneficial interest to a limited partnership, LLC or to an irrevocable trust.

Land trusts have two disadvantages. It is frequently difficult to finance land trust property as it's necessary to temporarily re-convey the property out of the trust to its grantors or beneficiaries to complete the financing. Also, a beneficiary wanting a Section 1031 tax-free, like-kind exchange, must again transfer the property from the trust, since a land trust is not a beneficial interest in real property but an interest in personal property.

Privacy – not asset protection – is the land trust's major advantage. The name of the beneficial owner won't appear on the public records because the property is titled to the trustee. To the extent secrecy can aid protection, the land trust can be helpful.

Medicaid Trusts

Nursing home costs can impoverish you as quickly as a lawsuit. Hence, the Medicaid trust. This special purpose trust shelters assets so the grantor can qualify for Medicaid to pay their nursing home costs. Medicaid trusts, of course, chiefly interest those who prefer to leave their money to their children rather than spend it on their own long-term care.

A Medicaid trust is similar to other irrevocable trusts. The grantor (as an individual or couple) transfers their assets to an irrevocable trust. However, unlike other irrevocable trusts, the grantor can

> Privacy – not asset protection – is the land trust's major advantage.

be the income beneficiary. Their children or spouse would be the residual beneficiaries. The grantor can receive income from the trust to the maximum amount allowed by Medicaid. But the now, asset-free grantor can qualify for Medicaid nursing home assistance.

The Medicaid trust offers about the same asset protection as any other irrevocable trust. Medicaid trusts prohibit using the trust assets for other health care purposes, and it also limits the beneficiaries' income to those income limits set by Medicaid. You must create and fund your Medicaid trust 60 months before you apply for Medicaid. That's its one disadvantage: Few people can – or will – anticipate their long-term care needs that far in advance.

Alaska and Delaware Trusts

Books and articles on asset protection have hyped Alaska and Delaware trusts. Alaska and Delaware have enacted legislation to encourage 'special' trusts in their jurisdictions. Their trusts promise more estate planning and asset protection benefits. You should explore their estate tax advantages if your state has an inheritance tax. Alaska and Delaware primarily promote their trusts as an alternative to the offshore trust. Undoubtedly, many Americans would be more comfortable with a US-based trust, rather than a foreign trust. This is their selling point.

Though Alaska and Delaware trusts are highly publicized, other states have comparable trust laws – including Rhode Island, Colorado and Nevada. I consider the Nevada trust the most protective domestic trust, by comparing the laws of these competing trust jurisdictions. For example, Nevada trusts have the shortest statute of limitations for a creditor to file suit. The settlor of a Nevada trust can also be a beneficiary and retain more control without reducing trust protection. Delaware's, Rhode Island's and Alaska's trusts are not quite as debtor-friendly as Nevada's.

A key question to answer before you form an asset protection trust in any state is whether their trust laws will give you significantly greater protection than what you would get from a comparable trust in your own state? (I compare domestic trusts to offshore trusts in Chapter 11.)

A trust in any state won't give you adequate protection against a fraudulent transfer claim (even when the trust is more protective than an irrevocable trust in your own state). The trust laws from these states may give you estate planning advantages, but not enough added creditor protection. For estate planning, have your estate planning attorney check the benefits of a Nevada, Alaska or Delaware trust.

To totally lawsuit-proof a client, I seldom use any domestic trusts. I want an offshore trust.

A trust from any of these 'protective' states won't fully protect you against a present creditor. They certainly will be less protective than an offshore trust. Alaska, Delaware, Nevada and every other state must constitutionally recognize and enforce the judgments and court orders from other states. For example, if you fraudulently transfer assets into a trust set up in another state, it can be recovered by your creditor.

> **Explore the estate tax advantages of Alaska and Delaware if your state has an inheritance tax.**

Other states will promote trust legislation. Yet the number of trusts set up for asset protection purposes in these more 'protective' jurisdictions has not grown dramatically. Conversely, the number of offshore trusts continues to rise. They create a far more formidable barrier against lawsuits and creditors.

Avoid Trust Shams

You must also know which trusts to avoid. For example, promoters of 'pure trusts', 'common law trusts' or 'constitutional trusts' ensnare a gullible public. These promoters claim that these trusts predate our tax laws and are immune from taxation. They also claim these trusts can lawsuit-proof your assets. The tax claims are nearly always bogus.

'Pure' trusts are 'shams'. They won't give you a legitimate tax benefit or other benefits beyond what you could get from other trusts. The IRS has challenged these 'abusive trusts' and penalized their promoters and taxpayers who unlawfully – if unwittingly – used these trusts to avoid taxes. A grantor trust requires the grantor to pay taxes on the trust income. An irrevocable trust pays the taxes on its income. In either case, taxes are payable on trust earnings. A trust is generally not the way to avoid income taxes.

Can a pure trust creditor-proof your assets? Possibly. The answer depends on whether the trust is irrevocable and whether you surrendered control over the trust. The asset protection and tax benefits that one can derive from any trust will be based solely on its terms and characteristics – not the name of the trust.

Most pure trusts are simple, revocable grantor or nominee trusts. They compare to living trusts. They will give you neither asset protection nor tax benefits. Avoid organizations or promoters who claim their trust enjoys special powers or immunities. Have

> Most pure trusts are simple, revocable grantor or nominee trusts. They compare to living trusts.

your attorney prepare or review your trusts. You want your trust to give you every benefit that you expect – not huge tax troubles.

Gifting For Asset Protection

Gifting can be a sensible strategy to reduce estate taxes and protect your assets – especially when you gift assets to a less liability-prone recipient.

For example, you may save income taxes by transferring income-producing assets to a recipient in a lower tax bracket. Gifts can also reduce your taxable estate (and estate taxes) while you simultaneously reduce the assets exposed to your creditors.

The annual gift tax exclusion currently lets you transfer $12,000 annually per recipient, tax-free – provided your gift is immediately available to the recipient. If you and your spouse jointly own and gift property, your combined annual exclusion doubles to $24,000 per recipient. A couple with three children can gift $72,000 annually, tax-free. You can accelerate your gifting to more rapidly shift vulnerable assets out of your name.

- One option is to transfer your property in exchange for an installment sale note payable over a number of years. You can forgive $12,000 installments per recipient annually, without tax consequences. Your promissory note would be self-liquidating and your transfer would be a 'fair consideration' exchange (the note) and therefore not fraudulent. To protect your note from your creditors, title it to a limited partnership or LLC.

- A bypass-generation gift can accelerate your gifting. These gifts, however, may impose a generation-skipping transfer tax of 50 percent (plus the gift tax that applies to larger gifts). To avoid this tax, use a generation-skipping trust.

- Gift whatever assets are most vulnerable to creditors. Retain those assets that are exempt from creditor claims or are otherwise protected.

- Another option is to transfer property to a minor child through a children's or minor's trust. Or make gifts under the Uniform Transfers to Minors Act. But you won't get absolute protection if your transfer is fraudulent. Your beneficiaries' creditors, however, cannot seize the funds until distributed to the beneficiaries.

Lawsuit-Proof Your Estate

It happens. Seniors can have more debts than assets when they die. An indebted testator will naturally want to bequeath their estate to their heirs free of creditors' claims – to the extent possible. While most people fully pay their debts from their estates, how can you protect yourself if your debts exceed your assets when you die? Or what if you are sued after you die? People do get sued after they die. You must arrange your affairs so that your assets will pass to your heirs free of lawsuits or creditor claims. Consider several strategies:

- Title your property jointly with right of survivorship to your intended heir (or as tenancy-by-the-entirety). Jointly owned property passes to the surviving joint owner free of creditor claims against the deceased owner. (This is one exception to my prior advice not to own property jointly.)

- Title your property to an irrevocable trust funded during your lifetime (before you have creditors).

- Accelerate your lifetime gifts to deplete your estate (but avoid fraudulent gifts).

- Invest in fixed annuities or other financial investments, which will transform your wealth into an income stream which will pass debt-free to your survivors.

While your living trust won't insulate your estate from your creditors, your living trust can give you limited protection. For instance, each state sets a time limit for creditors to file claims against an estate. With your assets titled to a living trust, you avoid probate. By avoiding probate, your creditors – including potential litigants – may be less aware of your death. They are then less likely to file a timely claim.

Disclaiming Inheritances

You may anticipate a big inheritance and have a judgment creditor. How can you judgment-proof your inheritance? One solution is to disclaim your inheritance. Any beneficiary can disclaim their inheritance and this passes the inheritance on to the next generation. A disclaimer is a particularly good strategy when you prefer your children to receive your inheritance rather than risk losing it to your creditor.

A disclaimer is a complete and unqualified refusal to accept rights or property. You can disclaim both gifts and inheritances. Your alternate beneficiaries may be your children, spouse or anyone else you designate to receive the gift. For a disclaimer to be effective, you must observe several requirements: 1) Your disclaimer must be in writing, 2) You must not have previously accepted any part of the property (or any benefits of ownership) and 3) Your disclaimer must be received by the transferor within 9 months from the date of the transfer or the date the document creating the interest (the bequeath or gift) is made.

If you want to bequeath wealth and want to protect your beneficiaries, change your will. Direct inheritances to a protective entity that would insulate the inheritance from the beneficiaries' creditors. For example, you may direct the inheritance to 1) a domestic testamentary trust with spendthrift, anti-alienation and discretionary provisions, 2) an offshore asset protection trust or 3) a limited partnership or LLC. The legacy directed to a protective entity can be structured so that the full benefits of the gift or bequest can still be enjoyed by the beneficiaries.

> A disclaimer is a complete and unqualified refusal to accept rights or property.

Six Tips to Build Trust Protection

No matter the type trust, there are many opportunities to increase trust protection. Here are six:

- Never put your eggs in one basket. Use multiple trusts and different trustees for different assets. Your creditor will have more difficulty challenging several trusts. Multiple trusts also give you more flexibility to accommodate multiple objectives, beneficiaries or financial objectives.

- Use a foreign or offshore trust (not a domestic US trust). This will further discourage litigation and maximize your protection.

- Incrementally transfer assets to your trusts. Smaller, staggered transfers suggest transfers that were not intended to defraud creditors.

- Add 'innocent' preambles to your trust. For example, your trust may state an estate planning purpose.

- Include one or two beneficiaries other than yourself in your trust. A trust that will only benefit you won't protect you against either your present or future creditors.

- Don't control your trust. If you control the trust, your creditor can claim its assets.

Update Your Estate Plan

We can't leave the important subject of protecting your estate without a reminder that is vital to keep your estate plan current. If you die without a current estate plan, you invite more legal problems:

- You need an up-to-date will (and/or living trust). Your estate won't then pass by intestacy to unintended beneficiaries. Unfortunately, only one in five Americans has a current will. Don't be one of them.

- Review your will and/or living trust at least annually. Your estate planning needs will change as rapidly as your asset protection needs. An outdated will can cause you even more legal problems than dying without a will.

- In addition to your will or living trust, you also need a durable power of attorney (one for healthcare and one for your financial/legal affairs). Appoint someone who can immediately represent you should you become incapacitated. You also need a living will to indicate if you want your life artificially prolonged.

- Find a good estate planner. You will need one if you have a taxable or complex estate. A good estate planner can save you a fortune in estate taxes (Uncle Sam may be your biggest creditor). A good estate planner can also show you many other ways to combine estate planning with asset protection.

Wealthsaver Tips

1. Trusts can help you to achieve a number of tax, estate planning, gifting and asset protection objectives.

2. For asset protection, your trust must be irrevocable and presently funded.

3. A revocable living trust won't shield assets from your creditors.

4. Use spendthrift trusts to protect your children's inheritance from their lawsuits and financial problems.

5. If you have considerable wealth, investigate the offshore trust. It will give you and your heirs more protection.

6. You cannot control the trust if it is to insulate your assets from your creditors.

7. You can combine trusts with other protective entities (LPs, LLCs, etc.) to accomplish a wide variety of objectives.

8. Design your trust with as many protective provisions as possible.

ELEVEN

The Offshore Advantage

Your money is never safer than when it's outside the country and beyond the reach of the American courts. Your strongest asset protection strategy may be to move your money to a foreign jurisdiction. This estate and family wealth planning strategy has been popular since those olden days when Roman emperors relocated their fortunes to foreign lands to preserve their riches for their descendants. Not surprisingly, with the onset of the lawsuit explosion, offshore wealth protection has become far more popular.

About $5 trillion is now protected in the numerous offshore financial centers (OFCs). OFCs feature favorable tax, banking, privacy, estate planning, and, most importantly, powerful asset protection laws. Those are the reasons so many wealthy individuals and families from every country send their money offshore. But only within the last decade or two have so many Americans taken advantage of offshore asset protection and investment opportunities. The number of Americans with their wealth offshore is expected to grow in the years ahead and particularly as creditor remedies expand domestically.

Untouchable Offshore Wealth

From my years of experience as an asset protection and wealth preservation lawyer, I have learned that the safest wealth is offshore wealth.

> **The safest wealth is offshore wealth.**

I have created offshore asset protection programs for hundreds of clients, and I know of none who has lost their offshore assets to any litigant. Not only are these individuals more financially secure, but they also enjoy far greater financial privacy. They also oftentimes find more profitable investments as international investors.

Of course, you will have questions: Is protecting your money offshore safe? Yes, your money will be far safer offshore than here in lawsuit-crazy America.

Can you legally move your money offshore? Yes, but you must follow the tax reporting rules and pay your taxes.

Americans have been programmed to believe that offshore finance is only for the crooks, frauds, drug peddlers, money launderers – or the super-rich. Perhaps your own financial planner, lawyer or accountant has advised you not to 'go offshore' because it's 'too risky, too expensive or too bothersome.' They would be wrong.

Offshore wealth protection is popular as an asset protection strategy today – and will continue to be – because the more sophisticated financial and legal professionals know that it is a better way to protect their clients' wealth. Unfortunately, too many American lawyers still rely entirely upon domestic asset protection strategies when their clients' net worth could be considerably better sheltered offshore. Asset protection plans for my wealthier clients usually mix domestic and offshore strategies. Their domestic component shelters their US-based assets – real estate and businesses. Their offshore structures protect their nest egg or liquid assets. When we blend the two, we create the most effective overall protection. You need an asset protection planner who is familiar and comfortable with offshore strategies. A planner who uses only domestic planning inevitably shortchanges the client who needs stronger protection.

Powerful Offshore Protection

Why do you get the best protection when your assets are offshore?

There are several reasons. First, asset protection jurisdictions won't recognize or enforce US judgments or administrative orders (such as from the IRS). You therefore have jurisdictional immunity. Of course, no foreign country can ignore every legal order from another country; some countries won't enforce US civil decrees. These countries would be used for lawsuit protection.

> **Asset protection jurisdictions won't recognize or enforce US judgments or administrative orders.**

Because these protective countries won't enforce an American judgment or civil decree, the creditor must re-litigate their case within that foreign jurisdiction. However, this is usually impractical – if not impossible – for different reasons. For example, the statute of limitations to commence suit within that jurisdiction may have expired. Or the offshore financial center may not recognize the plaintiff's underlying liability claim. The best offshore financial centers impose other procedural obstacles to effectively block creditors and litigation. Asset protection jurisdictions are debtor-oriented. They try hard to protect their customers' wealth because wealth protection is their business.

These asset protection jurisdictions have special laws that allow you to form unusually protective asset protection structures and entities within their country. Offshore asset protection trusts, limited liability companies, limited partnerships, foundations,captive insurance companies, international business companies and hybrid companies are a few examples. Each entity, in its own way, gives you far more protection than you could obtain through a comparable US entity.

Finally, asset protection jurisdictions are also good privacy havens – though a good privacy jurisdiction is not always good for asset protection.

The ultimate advantage from an offshore protection plan over a domestic asset protection plan is that whatever assets you fraudulently transfer to a US entity would be easily recovered through the US courts because the US courts have continued jurisdiction over these assets. An American court would have no jurisdiction over offshore assets. This explains why your offshore assets will be better protected than would your US-based assets which would remain susceptible to fraudulent transfer claims and other creditor challenges that could be enforced through the US courts.

> Your offshore assets will be better protected than would your US-based assets which would remain susceptible to fraudulent transfer claims and other creditor challenges.

Keep in mind that you never know when someone will sue you on a claim from the past. Your asset protection plan must then withstand a potential fraudulent transfer claim. And in many instances, a creditor can persuasively argue that there was a fraudulent conveyance. You avoid this vulnerability and uncertainty when your money is offshore.

OFCs can give you enormous debtor protection through these and still other legal and procedural obstacles which few creditors can or will attempt to overcome. I mentioned their short statute of limitations. For example, an offshore lawsuit must usually be filed within 2 years from when you transferred your assets offshore. Few creditors can file such a timely challenge to an offshore transfer. Another obstacle is that your creditor must *prove beyond a reasonable doubt* that your transfer offshore was fraudulent. This is an extremely difficult standard to prove. There are other obstacles.

Nevis – a particularly good asset protection jurisdiction – requires that a creditor post a $25,000 cash bond to cover the defendant's legal fees before the creditor can commence litigation. Another roadblock is that the creditor must retain Nevis counsel on a fee-only basis and not a contingent fee arrangement.

An even more formidable procedural obstacle is that an American creditor who holds a US judgment must nevertheless re-litigate their case within that offshore jurisdiction – and win a judgment from *their* courts – before the creditor can even attempt to recover a fraudulently transferred asset. And the creditor cannot re-litigate the case unless the claim follows rules of liability recognized by that country. For example, your creditor probably could not file a discrimination, anti-trust or one of the many other lawsuits that are based on American law. If so, the creditor cannot re-litigate.

Still other requirements effectively filter most prospective claims against a defendant's offshore assets. While no worthwhile asset protection country would completely disregard fraudulent transfer claims, these financial centers can and do make it difficult – *exceptionally* difficult – to pursue such claims.

Another formidable obstacle facing a determined creditor who attempts to recover your offshore assets is that your trustee can relocate your offshore assets to yet another trust or protective entity in another asset protection haven. The creditor must then start new legal proceedings in that OFC. This 'flee' provision is found in most offshore trusts. Creditors can tire from the chase as you continuously move your assets between countries and structures. This flee provision, or 'Cuba clause,' is only one more of the many powerful asset protection provisions found in any well-drafted offshore trust. Other provisions can effectively deprive your creditor of any practical opportunity to seize your offshore assets.

> Your trustee can relocate your offshore assets to yet another trust or protective entity in another asset protection haven.

These barriers to recovery explain why fewer than 3 out of 100 judgment creditors even attempt to recover offshore wealth. And these few cases are usually settled for pennies on the dollar. Without offshore protection, these creditors would undoubtedly have recovered considerably more. The fact that 97 out of 100 creditors *won't* attempt to seize offshore wealth strongly endorses the OFC's protective powers.

Many a creditor has the legal right to recover offshore assets as a fraudulent transfer, and yet this same creditor won't attempt recovery only because it's impractical. A creditor can spend enormous legal fees and recover nothing, though the creditor has the legal remedy. Offshore asset protection makes it impractical for all but the most determined creditor to pursue their claim. A creditor's legal recourse indeed becomes academic when your creditor *won't* assert his remedy.

Select The Right Offshore Financial Center

Another common question is which is the best OFC? There is no one best OFC. Many offshore jurisdictions can give you excellent protection. But when you choose a country you should focus on 5 criteria. You want a country that has:

- Strong asset protection laws and pro-debtor policies
- A predictable and sound legal and political system
- No taxes on foreign capital
- Financial privacy and confidentiality
- No exchange controls.

Other criteria and reasons to have your wealth offshore can influence your choice. Choose the OFC which best satisfies those needs. But for asset protection, the most important criteria is whether the OFC can and will protect your assets. All else is secondary. There are about twenty OFCs which specialize in asset protection, but you would also closely investigate 5 more features when you select your OFC:

- **What is their Statute of Limitation?** Your creditor should have the *shortest* time to challenge a fraudulent transfer. Only then are you safe. OFC statutes of limitations range from an unlimited duration to 1 year (Nevis).

- **Will they enforce a foreign judgment?** Your OFC must neither recognize nor enforce a foreign civil judgment. Your creditor *must* be forced to re-litigate their case in that OFC.

- **What is the burden of proof to recover a fraudulent transfer?** Must your creditor allege your fraudulent transfer was made with fraudulent *intent?* That can be a helpful standard.

- **What is the standard of proof?** You also want a rigid standard of proof on fraudulent intent. Some OFCs require that the creditor establish fraud by a mere preponderance of the evidence and others want fraud to be proven beyond a *reasonable doubt.* This, of course, is a more difficult standard.

- **Will they freeze your assets?** You do not want an OFC that will allow your creditor to attach your assets before your creditor obtains judgment from that OFC. Few OFCs will.

OFCs come in every size, variety and political persuasion. OFCs are located throughout the world. Bermuda, the British Virgin Islands and the Bahamas hug America's southeast coast. The Cayman Islands, Turks and Caicos, Nevis and Antigua dot the

Caribbean. The Isle of Man, Channel Islands, Jersey and Guernsey shadow England. Switzerland, Liechtenstein, Luxembourg, Hungary and Austria are good European havens. The Philippine, Singapore and Hong Kong serve the Pacific Rim. Cyprus, Malta and Gibraltar are Mediterranean OFCs. The Cook Islands, near New Zealand, is another favorite.

OFCs are clustered nearby the industrialized countries whose arcane laws force their wealthier citizens to find friendlier environments for their money. The world is shrinking so your choice of OFC no longer depends upon geography. With electronic banking, you can easily move your money to whatever country best satisfies your needs. You can easily bank in another hemisphere as next door.

> With electronic banking, you can easily move your money to whatever country best satisfies your needs.

OFCs rapidly rise and fall. Newer, more competitive OFCs continue to arise. Gibraltar, the Cook Islands, Nevis, the Marianas, Belize, the Turks and Caicos and Montserrat are relatively new offshore contenders. Other bright stars are on the horizon. Nevis and the Cook Islands are 2 of the more protective foreign asset protection jurisdictions and are my favorites. Yet, every asset protection lawyer has their own favorite jurisdiction and affiliations (trustees, protectors, banks, etc.). You won't get a unanimous opinion when you ask about which OFC is the *best*.

Your offshore asset protection plan will also be multi-national. For example, you may have a Nevis trust as your primary protective shield, but your trust may bank or invest its funds in Switzerland, Panama, Singapore or elsewhere.

The Asset Protection Trust

The traditional offshore protective entity is the offshore asset protection trust (OAPT), though you may have heard it called by other names – creditor protection trust, offshore trust, international trust, asset conservation trust, foreign trust or foreign grantor trust.

The offshore trust is a comparatively new twist to the trust's long heritage. But only in the 1980s have certain foreign countries enacted laws creating the asset protection trust. That's why offshore trusts have only within the past decade or so become one of the most popular trusts. This reflects the increased need and demand for asset protection.

Yet you can use an offshore trust for reasons other than lawsuit protection. They can avoid forced heirship laws, protect premarital assets, be useful for estate planning, Medicaid planning, international business planning and for regulatory avoidance purposes.

The offshore trust compares to the domestic irrevocable trust, though for many reasons the offshore trust is considerably more protective – if only because the offshore trust is a *foreign* trust. Where your irrevocable US trust is vulnerable to your existing creditors and the creditor-friendly US courts, your OAPT has immunity. The offshore trust has other uniquely protective features: 1) The debtor-friendly laws of the OFC govern its enforcement, 2) If a US court orders you to repatriate the trust assets, the offshore trustee must refuse your demand. Your trust funds will *not* be turned over to your creditor, 3) Your trustee can relocate the trust assets to another OFC if your trust becomes endangered and 4) Your trustee can – if necessary – withhold distributions to a beneficiary who has creditors.

In all other respects, the OAPT compares to the US irrevocable trust which is widely used for estate planning. For example, offshore trusts have a *grantor* (or settlor, donor or trustor) who creates and funds the trust, appoints the trustees and protector and names the beneficiaries. The *trustee* manages the trust for the benefit of the beneficiaries. (This is ordinarily a foreign trustee firm.) The *beneficiaries* receive the trust's income and/or assets.

Unlike the US trust, the OAPT has a *protector* who oversees the trustee. The protector has the power to replace the trustee and must approve major actions by the trustee. The grantor appoints the initial protector (who should not be an American resident subject to US court directives).

> **Parents or grandparents oftentimes create an OAPT to protect their wealth for their families.**

Any adult or legal entity can be the trust grantor and create and fund the trust. Parents or grandparents oftentimes create an OAPT to protect their wealth for their families. Or the spouses can be the co-grantors and combine their wealth into one trust. Or each spouse may establish separate trusts. Who becomes the grantor will depend upon tax, asset protection, estate planning, business and personal considerations.

For confidentiality purposes, we may interpose an offshore corporation or foreign LLC as the trust's nominee grantor. And offshore trusts in some OFCs do not require you to name the grantor or that you publicly record the trust, which also helps to protect the grantor's identity.

Controlling Your offshore Wealth

More people don't safeguard their money offshore because they have concerns about relinquishing control over their money to a foreign trustee. How can you be certain that your trustee won't steal or squander your money?

The trust gives your trustee broad powers to do whatever is necessary to protect or enhance the trust assets. These same powers found in *any* irrevocable trust include the right to sell, buy, lease, encumber or invest trust assets, defend or prosecute claims, pay debts and taxes, hire other professionals, make loans and/or distribute income or principal to beneficiaries, and so forth.

The trust purposely grants the trustee broad powers while the grantor retains no or negligible authority. A grantor who retains too much control loses asset protection. However, delegating control over your wealth to a foreign trustee will become far less frightening once you realize that foreign trustees will comply with a grantor's *voluntary* wishes. Moreover, they are exceptionally trustworthy based on their track record for honesty and fidelity.

You can allay some concerns about losing control through a number of strategies, and thus balance asset protection against your natural desire to retain control over your offshore funds. However, your attorney must tell you precisely *how much* control you can safely retain without jeopardizing your asset protection.

You have options. For example, whomever you appoint as your protector will logically follow your directions to block trustee actions or replace the trustee. Through your protector you have *alter ego* control. Or you can make your offshore trust *revocable* until a specified event – such as a lawsuit – when your trust would automatically become irrevocable. Or your limited partnership can be owned by an offshore trust as its limited partner. You would be the general partner and stay in control of the partnership assets within the US *until* you are sued, when you would transfer the partnership assets to the trust. Or you can be the managing director of an IBC (foreign company), which would be owned by the trust. The trust funds can be invested in the IBC which would be under your control. Or you can control the trusteeship until threatened by creditors. For instance, you and/or your spouse – or another US designee – can be the co-trustees with your foreign trustee. Or you and/or your protector can be co-signers on the trust bank accounts. Or you can keep your trust unfunded until you are sued. Other control retention techniques are available to you.

While you have these and other safeguards to insure that your assets will be handled properly, your worries about losing direct control over your wealth is understandable. But you have little cause for concern. These professionals are bonded, licensed and backed by the reputation of their own OFCs.

You will find long established and excellent trustee firms within every OFC. Most are lawyers or chartered accountants. Your

> You will find long established and excellent trustee firms within every OFC.

trustee should be well-established and administer many trusts and offshore entities. An active trustee firm can provide you with a wide range of services and effectively deliver those services. Your advisor who sets up your trust can probably recommend a trustee who has provided other clients good service.

Of course, you should check your trustee's references. How many clients do they have? Are these clients satisfied? How long has their firm been in business? Who within their firm will handle your account? Will they provide bank references? Bonding? Can they deliver the services you need? Are they accessible? Responsive? What are their fees?

Avoid Fatal Errors

If your offshore trust is to be effective for asset protection, it must be correctly structured and administered. Several celebrated cases have illustrated that offshore trusts *can* fail. Those few cases highlighted fatal planning errors that you must avoid.

- **Rule # 1: Don't retain control.** If a US court determines that your trust is only a sham, you will lose your protection. Your trustee must control your trust both in form and in practice.

- **Rule # 2: Keep your trust assets offshore and not within the United States.** Trust assets located within or tied to the US can be seized by a US court if your transfer to the trust is fraudulent.

- **Rule # 3: Your trust must include every protective safeguard.** A trust that is improperly drafted can be technically defective. You need a trust prepared by an experienced professional.

In those few cases of failed trusts, one or more of these basic rules were not followed. The debtor-grantor was then ordered by a US court to repatriate the trust assets for the benefit of the creditor. Several grantors who failed or refused to do so were jailed for contempt. This court ruled correctly when the grantor had *defacto* control over their trust. One defendant set up his trust only days before his trial. But ordinarily a court won't hold you in contempt if you *can't* repatriate your trust funds because you truly lack the power or authority to comply with the court order. That's why you need a properly structured and administrated trust and not a last-minute effort to place your assets beyond the court's reach.

Timing and relinquishing control over your assets are both vital to offshore success. Don't wait until the last moment to protect yourself. Set up your offshore entities before you incur a liability, and certainly before you are sued. Nor should you control your trust or the court may conclude that you can repatriate your money and then force you to turnover the money to your creditor.

The Formidable Nevis LLC

The offshore trust has been the traditional protective entity, but now it is only one of several protective entities that you can use. For example, I frequently use a Nevis LLC to protect my offshore clients. However, the offshore trust is still useful for clients who need offshore estate planning, want to avoid the tax problems from transferring appreciated assets to other offshore entities or in other special circumstances. In some situations, we use both the offshore trust and a Nevis LLC as its subsidiary.

> The offshore trust has been the traditional protective entity, but now it is only one of several protective entities you can use.

The Nevis LLC is one of the most powerful wealth protectors. It can give you more protection than the OAPT and at less cost.

Nevis is a small Caribbean British Commonwealth nation located in the Leeward Islands. Nevis gained its international reputation for financial privacy and asset protection because of its progressive and debtor-friendly laws. The Nevis LLC demonstrates this tiny jurisdiction's innovation for wealth protection.

The United States and other foreign jurisdictions have limited liability companies, however the Nevis LLC is particularly good for asset protection because it has features that you won't find with other LLCs. The Nevis LLC uniquely combines the most protective features of the offshore trust, limited partnership and Nevada corporation into one remarkably protective entity.

A Nevis LLC can be either member-directed or managed by a foreign director. However, for asset protection your LLC should be controlled by a foreign (Nevis) managing director. You contribute your assets to the LLC and become the LLC member. Your rights then compare to the rights of a member of a domestic LLC, corporate stockholder or limited partner of a limited partnership. As a member you would own – but not manage – the LLC. Management would rest with the managing director. Through this transfer of control you protect the LLC assets from US court orders.

> As an LLC member you no longer directly own the contributed assets. These assets would instead be owned by the LLC.

As an LLC member you no longer directly own the contributed assets. These assets would instead be owned by the LLC. A US court cannot order you, as the LLC member, to repatriate the LLC assets because the manager, not you, controls the LLC assets. Moreover, a foreign managing director would be beyond US court jurisdiction. Your creditor would be limited to a charging order against your LLC interest, which would give your creditor *only* the right to claim profits or liquidation distributions due you from the LLC. Your creditor cannot seize your membership interest, nor can your creditor vote or exercise your other membership rights – such as the right to inspect books and records. Thus, the Nevis LLC compares to a US limited partnership or LLC. A US court order to transfer or seize your LLC interest would be ignored by the managing director who, under Nevis law, need only recognize a creditor's charging order which can only be obtained through the Nevis courts.

Suppose you are a debtor-member who owns a substantial interest in the Nevis LLC. Your managing director would withhold profit distribution that could be seized by your charging order creditor. If you own a minority interest, and if withholding distributions would conflict with the interests of the other debtor-members, you can title your LLC interest to another self-owned Nevis LLC. This would then safely receive your distributed profits. As you have seen with an American LLC or LP, a debtor-member of a Nevis LLC can access funds that are not a 'distribution of profits.' Thus, the charging order would not apply to salaries (e.g. as investment advisor), loans, etc. made to you from the Nevis LLC.

Under certain circumstances, Nevis law and IRS regulations impose US income tax liability on a charging order creditor for LLC profits that are attributable to the debtor-member. Your charging order creditor can thus possibly incur a tax liability even if your creditor recovered no distribution. You have seen this same 'poison pill' feature with the US limited partnerships and LLCs (but not other offshore entities). This is still another protective feature of the Nevis LLC.

Your Nevis LLC would delegate the important powers to your managing director who would ignore US court repatriation orders. If your LLC has multiple members, which we recommend, your operating agreement should require a unanimous vote to change the managing director. This would overcome a US court order to compel a single debtor-member to replace the manager with a manager appointed by the court to repatriate the LLC assets. The Nevis LLC can be structured with similar protective 'duress' provisions that you would find with the offshore trust – except that the debtor-member of an LLC retains a membership interest in the LLC and, derivatively, its assets.

A Nevis LLC is significantly more protective than the offshore trust if you already have creditors and a transfer of assets to your trust would be a fraudulent conveyance contestable in the trust jurisdiction.

Here's why. If a Nevis LLC member has an existing creditor, the Nevis LLC ordinances allow the member to transfer his or her assets to the LLC without it constituting a fraudulent conveyance – if the debtor-member's interest is proportionate to the capital contributed. This transfer is then a 'fair value' exchange and one expressly exempt from the Nevis fraudulent transfer statutes. Interestingly, under Nevis law a mere promise of a future investment by an existing or future incoming LLC member can be used to measure this proportionality. Thus, a debtor-member can own a small interest in the LLC subject to the charging order, although this member contributed all or most of the LLC's assets. Through this dilution strategy, you can further discourage a creditor from obtaining a charging order. This is only one of several features that are unique to the Nevis LLC.

US limited partnership and LLC law remain unsettled on the question of whether your present creditor can recover assets that you transfer to a limited partnership or LLC, even when you receive in exchange for your contributed assets, a proportionate share in the limited partnership or LLC. (Some courts have ruled that 'impairing' a creditor is sufficient for a transfer to be fraudulent.) However, you have no such ambiguity or uncertainty under Nevis law. Whatever money you invest in your Nevis LLC will not be a fraudulent transfer, nor one challengeable by even an existing creditor.

It is for that reason that I say the Nevis LLC is more protective than a foreign trust or domestic limited partnership or LLC. You can legally and ethically invest in the Nevis LLC, regardless of your financial situation. Nor can we overlook this important point at a time when offshore trusts are increasingly challenged and subject to stern court sanctions against their grantors.

The Nevis LLC is also a more attractive option for the attorney whose clients have existing creditors and where the attorney or professional advisor has concerns about their own professional liability from a fraudulent transfer. And, as mentioned, in more serious cases, we can maximize your protection by having a Nevis LLC as a subsidiary to an offshore trust. 'Layering' your protection combines the strength of both entities.

The Nevis LLC has several other benefits over the offshore trust:

- The Nevis LLC provides you minimal IRS reporting requirements. And you are not subject to US foreign trust reporting requirements. If you are a US member who owns 10 percent or more of an LLC interest, you must follow the IRS' foreign corporation ownership reporting requirements.

- Although the Nevis LLC is tax neutral, you can elect to have it taxed as a partnership or C corporation.

- Nevis imposes no taxes on their LLCs.

- You can structure your Nevis LLC so that its profits flow to its members in whatever proportions are specified in its operating agreement. This may differ from the actual ownership interest.

- You can appoint a protector to oversee the managing director as you can with an OAPT.

- Your LLC agreement can include the same anti-creditor 'poison pills' which you can adopt with a domestic LLC. For example, a member's interests can be assessed by the managing director. These same assessment rights would apply against a charging order creditor.

- Your LLC operating agreement can include a 'flight' or 'Cuba clause' so that your manager can expatriate threatened LLC assets to another protective entity in another OFC.

- The managing directors and members of the Nevis LLC are immune from company liabilities.

- Nevis LLCs do not require minute books, annual director or member meetings or compliance with other customary corporate formalities.

- You can have your Nevis LLC owned by an offshore trust or combine it with domestic entities – FLPs, LLCs and irrevocable trusts. These multi-entity arrangements can strengthen and coordinate your domestic and offshore estate planning and asset protection.

- A Nevis LLC is less costly to organize and maintain than an offshore asset protection trust.

You can see why the Nevis LLC is rapidly replacing the offshore asset protection trust. However, the offshore trust is still useful for those select offshore wealth protection purposes – estate planning, forced heirship avoidance and other special purposes that you can only achieve with a trust.

> Unquestionably, the Nevis LLC is more protective than a foreign international business corporation (IBC). The IBC gives you considerably less safety and no corresponding advantages.

Unquestionably, the Nevis LLC is more protective than a foreign international business corporation (IBC). The IBC gives you considerably less safety and no corresponding advantages.

Other OFCs are developing new protective entities. For example, the Bahamas limited partnership closely parallels the Nevis LLC. Liechtenstein's and Panama's private foundations compare to the offshore trust. St. Vincent and the Isle of Man hybrid companies are oftentimes substituted for an offshore trust or Nevis LLC. Asset protection OFCs are always in search for 'that better mousetrap', however, only an exceptionally innovative 'mousetrap' can beat the Nevis LLC when you want to safeguard your wealth.

Offshore Insurance Companies

I oftentimes speak to business and professional groups about asset protection and tax-favored wealth planning. Invariably I am asked about the offshore captive insurance company.

'Captives' or tax-exempt closely held insurance companies (CICs) can give you both asset protection and tax deferral – if you set it up and maintain it properly. If it meets your economic needs, you might qualify for significant tax benefits.

The CIC is licensed to write insurance in the US and registered with the IRS. Captives are chiefly formed in such offshore jurisdictions

> **The CIC is licensed to write insurance in the US and registered with the IRS.**

as Bermuda or the British Virgin Islands (2 jurisdictions which require a small capitalization and have favorable insurance and tax laws). Offshore CICs are multiplying and over 4,000 CICs writing $60 billion in premiums annually. This is more than one-third of the total commercial insurance sold in the United States. Fortune 500 companies use CICs to protect their excess cash as well as for tax advantages. Only within the last decade or so have individuals, small business owners and professionals used CICs for these same reasons.

With your own CIC you can fully or partially insure your business or professional practice from malpractice and other liabilities or losses for which you would carry insurance through other underwriters.

When you insure yourself for insurable risks through your own CIC, you get a present year tax deduction and pay claims with pre-tax dollars from your CICs loss reserves. Your CIC can insure low liability risks or your CIC can transfer risks to a reinsurer so your CIC would have little economic risk and you would still enjoy its significant tax benefits.

Premiums that you pay to your insurance company would be deductible as an ordinary business expense. You may deduct premiums up to $1 million or more annually, depending upon the type CIC that you establish.

Aside from annual income tax savings, you gain other tax benefits:

1) You can possibly postpone capital gains on appreciated assets owned by the CIC.

2) You enjoy tax-free growth of your CIC assets.

3) The CIC can reduce – or eliminate – estate taxes on assets that you transfer to your children.

The specific CIC tax benefits are too technical to be fully covered here; however, these tax benefits are supported by Congress to provide substantial tax incentives to professionals and small insurance companies that have high earnings and taxable profits.

Whether you own your own CIC as a single professional or business owner, or through a group, you can deduct your insurance premiums each year and grow your funds in the CIC tax-free. Or you can reclaim the funds and pay only a long-term capital gains tax. This three-tier tax advantage is not available through your pension, IRA or other retirement plans.

The CIC also offers you superb asset protection. For instance, your CIC can supplement your other liability policies. This 'excess' liability protection will give you more security that you won't be financially ruined by a judgment in excess of your present coverage.

Your pre-tax premiums to your own CIC will also be protected from your personal creditors, as well as the liabilities of your business or professional practice. And you can accomplish all this without losing control of the funds in your CIC.

Do you own a business or professional practice whose profits are above $300,000 annually? Then owning your own captive insurance company may be your answer to lower taxes and improved protection. www.asgoldstein.com has more information on this.

IBCs and Foreign Corporations

I also wonder why offshore promoters continue to sell international business corporations (IBC) to safeguard wealth from lawsuits. An IBC is a bad choice when you want solid protection. An IBC is a foreign corporation that is exempt from taxation in that country because it is owned by non-residents. An IBC otherwise compares to a US corporation.

An IBC can privatize your offshore wealth; but, as you know, privacy is not asset protection. When your creditor discovers your money is sheltered in an offshore company (or IBC), they can have a US court compel you to transfer your IBC ownership shares to your creditor. Or the court can force you to liquidate your IBC and repatriate its assets for the benefit of your creditor. Courts won't believe stories that you 'gifted' your money to the IBC or that your money somehow 'disappeared.' For solid asset protection, your entity must be specifically designed for this purpose. And that entity would not be an IBC. IBC promoters should never sell IBCs for asset protection.

Nor should you mistakenly believe that you can hide your money in a privacy haven bank account. Yes, some people do – and some people succeed. But it's poor protection because your judgment creditor can force you to disclose your offshore assets. If you lie, you commit perjury. If you disclose your offshore assets, a US court can order you to repatriate your money to your creditor. So a foreign bank account, whether in your own name or in the name of an IBC, is not creditor-protected. In either instance the money is under your control and you can comply with a court's repatriation and turnover order or be held in contempt. Never rely on an IBC when you want asset protection. The IBC can play some secondary role in your offshore plan, but it can never be your primary offshore firewall.

Protect 100% of Your Wealth Offshore

It may become necessary to protect everything that you own offshore, though it is easiest to protect liquid assets – cash, securities and collectibles (gold and jewelry) which can be physically relocated offshore. Real estate, cars, boats, US securities and other US-based assets necessarily remain within US court jurisdiction and are thus recoverable by a creditor through US courts if you fraudulently transfer them to an offshore entity.

> For maximum creditor protection, your trustees, protectors and fiduciaries, as well as your assets must be physically offshore.

For maximum creditor protection, your trustees, protectors and fiduciaries, as well as your assets must be *physically* offshore. This is the only way to put them beyond the control and recovery powers of the US courts.

A crisis lawsuit-proofing strategy would shift as much of your wealth as possible to one or more offshore asset protection entities. For example, you might mortgage or sell every US-based asset and transfer the proceeds offshore. Your creditors' only recourse would then be to seize equity-stripped assets, which would have little or no value to your creditor.

It's not difficult to transfer assets offshore. You follow essentially the same procedures that you would use to transfer your assets to a domestic entity. You would wire transfer funds. Your stockbroker can transfer your securities. You would transfer your personal property by a bill of sale or assignment and you convey real estate with a deed.

If your lawsuit has not reached crisis stage, you may only invest offshore your nest egg or any excess wealth that you do not foreseeably need.

Some people prefer to start small and test their offshore arrangement. They set up and nominally fund their offshore entities. Once they are comfortable with their offshore fiduciaries, banks, investments, etc., they add more funds. If it later becomes necessary for them to transfer their entire wealth, they already have their wealth protection system in place and can, more confidently, transfer their remaining wealth offshore.

If you have a judgment creditor and need continued asset protection, you could repatriate your funds through a protective stateside entity. For example, you can repatriate your funds through a Nevada or Wyoming corporation, a family limited partnership or conduit your funds to your spouse's account or domestic spendthrift trust where you would be a beneficiary. You can access your offshore funds even when you have creditors. You will eventually solve your legal problems and you may need your wealth protected offshore for only a short time.

> If you have a judgment creditor and need continued asset protection, you could repatriate your funds through a protective stateside entity

Pay Your Taxes

Let me make another point absolutely clear. You go offshore with your money for asset protection – not to avoid taxes. It's that simple! Your offshore trust will be a grantor trust and is thus tax neutral. Your trust will pay no taxes. The trust income will be taxed directly to you as its grantor in the year the income was earned. You therefore do not defer or save taxes. A grantor trust is taxed as an S corporation, limited partnership or living trust. American taxpayers will find that their offshore trust will give them neither a tax advantage nor disadvantage.

The Nevis LLC, IBC and other offshore entities (except the CIC) are also tax neutral. They cannot save you US income taxes. Offshore promoters may suggest that you can avoid US income taxes by going offshore with your income or money, but they would be misleading you. Only certain tax qualified insurance and annuity programs can defer or save you taxes. Whatever income that you or your entities earn offshore is fully taxable in the year that this income is earned, whether or not you repatriate it. You must also report to the IRS your offshore entities or bank accounts. And these reporting requirements can be complex, so review these requirements with a tax advisor experienced in these matters. For more information on reporting requirements, visit www.asgoldstein.com.

Privatize Your Finances Offshore

When you are sued, your US bank or any other party must provide your opponent whatever financial records they subpoena. However, your offshore banking and financial records would stay fully privacy-protected against US court orders or subpoenas because OFC banks are jurisdictionally immune to service of process. An offshore bank in a good OFC cannot legally deliver or disclose your financial information to a third party except as permitted under narrow treaty provisions.

Because offshore banks are jurisdictionally immune, they ignore US writs of execution or attachment orders. Thus, the secrecy laws of most financial centers will protect your entrusted funds from creditor seizure and protect the confidentiality of your financial transactions. However, you nevertheless need a protective entity (i.e. an offshore trust, Nevis LLC, etc.) to protect your offshore wealth from a US turnover order or from creditor seizure.

For maximum privacy, you should use an offshore bank with no American-based branch. Offshore banks with a US branch will be within the jurisdiction of American courts.

The offshore banks jurisdictional immunity guards you against unwanted intrusions into your financial privacy. It is comforting to know that your financial records – which are otherwise so readily obtainable by your creditors – are beyond their view when your funds are in the right offshore financial center.

Privacy is a major benefit from offshore banking and one too many American investors overlook. With your financial affairs needlessly exposed, you get into trouble. The privacy advantage will become more important as the number of lawsuits proliferate.

For more offshore privacy, you can convert titled assets – real estate or stocks and bonds into bearer investments (i.e. gold, diamonds, art, stamp collections, coins and similar collectibles). Bearer investments offshore will remain confidential and private. For still more privacy, you can buy and sell your collectibles through a third party, such as your own offshore corporation or Nevis LLC. Or you can reconvert these assets to cash with complete confidentiality and privacy. Private vaults are plentiful in foreign countries and can provide you still greater secrecy.

For true financial privacy, you must create two separate financial worlds. Your public world is your home country. This is where you work, pay taxes, maintain your bank accounts and investments and expose whatever financial affairs that you expect the world to know about.

> For true financial privacy, you must create two separate financial worlds. Your public world is your home country. Your private world is offshore.

Your private world is off-shore. This is where you keep your 'invisible money', those assets that only you (and the IRS) know about. In this private world you shelter your major bank accounts, investments, etc. that you want to keep invisible and private.

Never mix these two worlds. You will want to avoid direct transactions between them. For example, you should not directly transfer your funds between your onshore (public world) and your offshore (private world) when you can instead transfer your funds through intermediary entities in other OFCs with privacy laws.

Privacy is every citizen's basic right. The fact that so many Americans seek more privacy doesn't speak against them but against those who have stripped them of their privacy. Financial privacy should be every American's goal and your first line of defense against litigation.

Is Offshore Your Right Solution?

For all its benefits, offshore wealth protection isn't for everyone. You must realistically assess what offshore asset protection can do for you. And what it can accomplish for you may not justify its cost or effort. So discuss your situation with the right professional for a professional evaluation.

> You probably aren't a good offshore candidate if you cannot become comfortable with your assets offshore and controlled by third parties.

You probably aren't a good offshore candidate if you cannot become comfortable with your assets offshore and controlled by third parties. Many people who can otherwise greatly benefit from offshore protection, refuse it for this one reason. Some eventually overcome their fears. Or they may have no alternative but to put their wealth offshore to save it. They take the plunge. Yet not everyone can be coaxed to expatriate their money. You must decide whether your discomfort with having your wealth offshore is only a matter of learning more or one of chronic insecurity. If you refuse offshore protection, you may exchange it for a far less protective domestic protection plan. This may be costly.

Before you 'go offshore' with your assets, talk to others who have shared your same questions, experiences and fears. How safe will my money be? Will the trustee run away with my money or lose it on some investment? Will I really get my money back when I need it? These undoubtedly exemplify your many questions. So let others who once shared your same concerns share their experiences.

One client recently commented, "You never realize how vulnerable your wealth is in the US until it goes offshore." And a Los Angeles physician admits, "I was nervous with my money offshore. But I'm more nervous when I think about how easily it could have been lost here."

Knowledge builds confidence and confidence prompts action. That's why I must educate my clients. It builds their confidence. When you have your fears calmed, you too can get your offshore program under way more enthusiastically. And it will function more smoothly.

So educate yourself. Learn what you can. Request a free copy of my book *How to Protect Your Money Offshore* (Garrett Publishing). This helpful educational tool will answer many more of your questions about the offshore advantage.

Wealthsaver Tips

1. Protecting your assets offshore can be your safest lawsuit-proofing option.

2. For maximum protection, your offshore assets should have no connection to the US.

3. A number of jurisdictions and entities can be used to shelter your wealth offshore.

4. The Nevis LLC is one of the most protective entities – and one gaining in popularity.

5. An international business corporation (IBC) can privatize your offshore finances – but it is not recommended for asset protection.

6. You can combine your offshore and domestic entities to gain greater control and added protection.

7. Do not go offshore for secrecy. You need a fully protective arrangement that can safely be disclosed to your creditor.

8. Do not go offshore to evade taxes. Stay tax compliant.

TWELVE

Debt-Shield Strategies

You can't always entirely rely on the exemption laws or that you have titled your assets to one or more protective entities. You may need an additional firewall. That firewall is to 'strip the equity' from *everything* you own – both your real and personal property. Your goal: Convert your unencumbered assets into debt-ridden assets which would be worthless to a plaintiff.

You can accomplish this using many different types of mortgages and liens. A lien is a mortgage or security interest filed against a debtor's real estate or personal property. As the property owner, you retain ownership of the property, but you transfer the *economic* value of your property to the mortgage holder. This will reduce your equity in your property and the equity that a creditor or litigant can seize.

It's an easy concept to understand. Suppose your home is worth more than what you owe on the mortgages (or liens) against it. You then have *equity* in your property which your litigant can claim. To protect your home, you would reduce (or 'strip') your equity by *increasing* the amount of mortgages or liens against your home. Though this strategy is simple, some terminology may make it less confusing.

You are probably familiar with 'mortgages.' This is a voluntary lien on real estate to secure a debt that you owe. Some western states call it a 'deed of trust' instead of 'mortgage.' Instead of giving the lender a mortgage, the borrower deeds the property to a third party trustee. The borrower can occupy the property as long as the debt is paid. The only difference then between a mortgage and a deed of trust is that a trustee can sell your property at public auction if you default, while a mortgage holder must go through a court foreclosure to auction your property.

> **A lien on personal property is called a security agreement.**

Different terminology applies to personal property. A lien on personal property is called a security agreement. Or you may pledge your personal property to secure your debt. The personal property may then remain in the possession of the secured party (i.e. pledged jewelry to a pawn shop). But more typically, the debtor continues to possess the collateral. The secured party only files a notice of lien (a financing statement) in a public recording office so third parties have notice that the property is encumbered.

There are, of course, specific drafting and recording requirements to create these liens; but let's leave the mechanics to the lawyers. Or you may place *multiple* liens against one property. The priority of each lien is then determined by their priority of filing in the public records.

The point is that when you have valid liens (whether through a mortgage or deed of trust in the case of real estate – or a security agreement in the case of personal property) – a future claimant can only seize whatever equity you have left in the property (the difference between the resale value of the asset and the liens). For asset protection, of course, you would want to have little or no equity exposed. If you own a $300,000 home with a $300,000 mortgage against it, it is worth *nothing* to a litigant. Your goal is to have *every* asset worth nothing to your litigant.

Big Mortgages Discourage Lawsuits

The computer has demolished your financial privacy. When you have *exposed* wealth, you are an easy lawsuit target.

Any lawyer can get an instant electronic asset search and financial profile on you. This online asset search will, in seconds, reveal whatever real estate, business, auto, boat, etc. that you now own or have ever owned. Asset searches will also disclose mortgages or liens against your property. So, you want it to appear that everything that you own is mortgaged 'to the hilt.' In our debt-ridden America, it is not unusual for people to owe as much or more than they own.

Nothing will discourage a prospective litigant faster than finding that a would-be defendant is mortgaged to the eyebrows. You can own millions in assets, but when they are fully mortgaged, you are a poor lawsuit candidate. Litigants want assets with equity. When your assets can be claimed first by *other* creditors, you are poor. 'Poverty' becomes negotiating power.

Get a Line Of Credit

Let's start with this question: *When* should you mortgage yourself to the hilt? My advice? *Always* keep your real estate fully encumbered. Keep mortgages filed against your property for as long as you own it – even if you must periodically refinance your mortgages to cover the equity that you build as your property increases in value.

You may say, "But I don't want a big mortgage. Why pay interest on a loan that I don't need only to protect myself against a lawsuit that may never happen?"

Good question! Refinancing your real estate to 'strip the equity' may not seemingly make *financial* sense, even when it makes *legal* sense. But a *home equity* loan or line of credit will always make sense. If your home is worth $200,000 and has no mortgage, you might arrange for a $150,000 home equity loan or line of credit against your home. You would owe your lender nothing until you actually draw down your credit line, and you would do this only when you are sued. Still, a prospective litigant who searches for your assets would see only $50,000 equity in your home because our $150,000 mortgage would be on public record. You will then be a considerably less attractive lawsuit candidate because you have reduced your apparent net worth. You not only lower your exposure to *future* lawsuits, but gain leverage to negotiate a lower settlement if you do get sued.

If you own *any* real estate, then get an equity loan or line of credit to cover as much of your equity in your properties as possible. With that accomplished, you should arrange for standby second or third mortgages to encumber whatever remaining equity you still have exposed. You will pay a few dollars for loan fees, but this is great lawsuit protection.

Encumber Everything

Your first goal is to encumber your real estate now because you want a 'poverty' profile to discourage lawsuits. However, once you are sued (or threatened with a lawsuit), you would encumber every asset. Remember, you can use any asset as security for a loan.

Put liens against your second homes, investment properties, stocks, bonds, art, jewelry, collectibles, business ownership, vehicles, retirement accounts, inheritances – every other asset you own.

You can lien your assets separately or 'blanket' lien them to one creditor. This is typically our strategy once a big judgment appears likely. Similarly equity strip your business or professional practice. Your goal: Leave no asset unencumbered and exposed!

Find Friendly Lenders

How do you find a lender who will help you to equity strip your assets?

Countless asset-based lender(s) lend money and lien assets as collateral. For example, virtually any bank will give you a home equity loan or refinance your home. Plenty of lenders will refinance your business, autos or boats. You can borrow and pledge as collateral *any* asset to virtually *any* lender.

If you have good credit, you can probably borrow about 80 percent of the value of your assets from conventional lenders (banks, finance companies, etc.). If you have poor credit, you can still find 'hard money' lenders who may give you a higher interest loan, but paying steeper finance charges is preferable to losing your assets in the lawsuit.

You probably understand the concept of 'equity stripping' for asset protection. Your problem may be in its implementation. You and your advisors may not know how, or where, to find the right lenders. Or you may not know about the many other possible strategies to 'defensively position' your assets.

We have engineered a number of creative ways to structure secured loans to maximize our client's protection. And we have arranged loans and debt-shields for even the poorest credit risks. Our financing arrangements may have involved third party guarantees

> We have engineered a number of creative ways to structure secured loans to maximize our client's protection. And we have arranged loans and debt-shields for even the poorest credit risks.

or we may have used the loan proceeds as collateral for a 'back-to-back' loan or we may have obtained loans from offshore lenders. We have encumbered assets and estates worth many millions through more complex insurance/financing arrangements – financial deals which fully encumbered all our clients' assets. Sometimes these same financing arrangements also helped to save taxes.

For instance, one car dealer involved in heavy litigation fully encumbered his $2 million home, vacation home and car dealership worth over $6 million through a crazy patchwork of loans. Because his assets were fully encumbered, we could settle a multi-million dollar lawsuit filed against him for under $100,000. Without these mortgages shielding his equity, the lawsuit would have dragged on and it would have undoubtedly cost him far more to settle.

Debt-shielding is usually simpler. Banks, finance companies and other conventional asset-based lenders can usually handle the job. Or a family member or affiliated company may become 'your lender' if you have more modest assets to protect.

A debtor's family – parents, siblings and other relatives – may encumber the debtor's property since a close relative is nevertheless a legally distinct party. Liens or security interests between related parties are enforceable if fair consideration was provided for the loan. Yet, a loan from family members or an affiliated party will make a fraudulent transfer claim more likely because 'insider' loans are more closely scrutinized by other creditors. And if a court determines that your loan is a sham or one not adequately supported by fair consideration (you have not received money, property or services whose value equals the loan), the court will cancel the mortgage which will again expose your assets.

You may even have your spouse encumber your separately owned property in those states that follow 'common law' property rules. Community property states allow property owned and held separately to be granted as security to a spouse. Although one spouse may encumber the other's assets, state fraudulent transfer laws frequently void such loans granted *after* the claim arose. Or you may have an affiliated business lien your personal property; however, this security interest will also less likely be upheld by the courts if you own or control that business.

Nevertheless, no rule prevents you from forming a corporation, limited partnership or limited liability company and granting to that entity a mortgage or security interest against your other assets. Although this mortgage may be challenged in court, an asset search would nevertheless not reveal your relationship to that entity. Therefore, a 'friendly' lien held by your entity (or one that you directly or indirectly control) may give you some level of protection to the extent it deters a plaintiff seeking unencumbered assets to target.

An aggressive asset protection specialist may use other creative planning techniques to reduce the visibility of their clients' ownership in a lender entity. Or you may own a minority share in the business that holds the mortgage. As the owner of only a minority interest, you wouldn't 'control' the corporation or LLC and the lien is more likely to survive a challenge.

More sophisticated arrangements are too complex to discuss here, but for example, you may use a foreign corporation (an international business corporation, IBC) or a foreign LLC, which is de-controlled and would not be directly owned by you as the lender. This foreign IBC or LLC can encumber your assets. But you must carefully structure your foreign entity to minimize the federal tax reporting requirements and to comply with the special anti-deferral tax rules that apply to foreign corporations, trusts and partnerships.

Only the right professional can give you guidance here. A more complex case can utilize several levels of customized foreign trusts, corporations, LLC's, charitable organizations, private foundations or other entities. Each – in its own way – would provide one more layer of privacy, anonymity and protection. But don't use these techniques for tax evasion.

Frequently, our foreign entities are mere 'shells,' or IBCs or LLCs with neither shareholders nor capital. Only through intense investigation can a creditor distinguish a shell entity from an actual operating foreign entity. Therefore,

> Frequently, our foreign entities are mere 'shells', or IBCs or LLCs with neither shareholders nor capital.

a foreign shell entity may give you reasonably good asset protection when used to encumber your property. However, for more bullet-proof protection, your foreign entity must be prepared to document and defend your mortgage before a US judge who must – if the mortgage is challenged – determine the priorities among competing lien holders or judgment creditors.

The success behind this type arrangement lies in the absolute privacy that is only available from certain offshore financial centers which would deny a plaintiff's attorney access to records. The complexities of multiple layer foreign entities can completely sever the relationships between the US property owner and the foreign IBC or LLC which holds a lien against this property.

On the other hand, you can sometimes create your 'friendly lien' simply by giving a mortgage to a relative, friend or favored creditor to whom you owe money. What is important is that if your lien is later challenged you can show that you *do* owe the money and that you indeed owe an enforceable debt.

Friendly Judgments

Not every mortgage or lien filed against your property need be consensual. For example, a relative, friend or some other 'friendly' adversary may have a claim against you. If they should sue you and win a judgment before a hostile creditor wins *their* judgment; then your 'friendly' creditor would have priority claim to your assets.

'Friendly' lawsuits can range from defamation to breach of contract. But whatever the nature of the lawsuit, it can nevertheless result in a massive judgment against you which would effectively blockade your assets against a subsequent judgment creditor who may be less friendly. This strategy, however, requires a claim 'with substance'. You do not want to use the courts to perpetrate a fraud on your other creditors.

Mortgage Your Business

Nor should you forget to mortgage your business. Debt-shielding your business is as vital as shielding your personal assets.

A mortgage against your business can indeed be your best friend if you must combat your business creditors. When you encumber your business to a

A mortgage against your business can indeed be your best friend if you must combat your business creditors.

friendly lender you position yourself so that your lender can – as an alternative to bankruptcy – foreclose on your business and sell you back its assets to start fresh.

For example, if your business assets are valued at $100,000 and you have a 'friendly' $100,000 mortgage against these assets and your business owes $200,000 to unsecured creditors, your friendly mortgage will then have priority – whether in bankruptcy or under any other liquidation. Your unsecured creditors would then recover nothing. Without this protective mortgage, your unsecured creditors could claim your business' assets.

Through your 'friendly' mortgage, you can also effectively control your own business. Should a litigant or unsecured creditor attempt to collect on their judgment, your friendly mortgagee can intervene and, if necessary, foreclose and re-sell back to you your own business. And no funds need change hands since your mortgage holder can finance you with a new loan. Again, avoid sham mortgages. You want a friendly mortgage that can withstand close scrutiny.

Perhaps your friendly creditor is a relative who loaned you money to start your business. One client started his publishing firm with a $250,000 loan from his uncle. His business is successful, but why not give his uncle a mortgage on the assets of the business? The uncle's mortgage now serves as an effective barrier against lawsuits or creditor claims.

If you have a friendly supplier, you may give this favored supplier a mortgage against your business, if you're confident this supplier will cooperate with you in the tough times. Meanwhile, if your business is sued, this mortgage can keep your business protected.

You can even become your own mortgage holder if you do it correctly. Entrepreneurs oftentimes set up Nevada corporations as a 'supplier' to their own companies. The Nevada corporation could indirectly be owned by the entrepreneur, but operated through 'nominee' officers and directors so that the owners affiliation and the true ownership of the lender corporation is undetectable. Or for further privacy, the Nevada corporation may be owned by an offshore company.

You need to do more than give a mortgage to your 'friendly' mortgage holder. You must be prepared to validate your mortgage and prove that you actually owe the money. Perhaps consulting or other services were provided by the Nevada corporation. Can you document that these services were actually rendered and are worth what you say you owe?

Self-Finance Your Business

> You can reduce, or even totally eliminate, the risk of losing your investment in your business and simultaneously create a defensible mortgage against your business.

Whatever money you lend to your business is money that you can easily lose. You can reduce, or even totally eliminate, the risk of losing your investment in your business and simultaneously create a defensible mortgage against your business.

The *wrong* way to finance your business is to *directly* invest in your business – whether to buy the corporate shares (equity) or as a loan to your business. If your business fails, you would then be a stockholder or an unsecured creditor. In either instance, you would probably reclaim little or none of your investment. The bankruptcy court may even cancel your claim or subordinate your claim to the claims of the 'arms-length' creditors.

You can nevertheless secure yourself with the assets of the business so your claim has priority to the claims of the business' other creditors. To solidify your mortgage against your business requires additional steps. For instance, a bank could directly loan your business. Your business would pledge its assets to the bank as collateral. Your bank will lend to your business if you pledge sufficient personal assets to collateralize the loan. As a fully secured loan, your bank has no risk. If your business fails, your bank as its secured party would be the first creditor to be repaid from the liquidation. With the bank repaid, your bank would release back to you whatever personal assets you pledged to the bank as security.

Don't invest or lend money to your corporation without reviewing this strategy with your attorney. Your investment structured in this manner gives you two advantages: 1) Whatever you invest in your business will be better protected, 2) you would indirectly control the mortgage against your business – and thus indirectly protect your business against lawsuits.

The Obligation-Based Lien Alternative

As we've seen, cash loans can effectively equity strip your assets, but they are not without their drawbacks. One is that your lender must pay taxes on the interest payments. Also, you may not be able to completely encumber your assets through commercial lending. You will also be forced to make interest payments. Finally, you may not have enough cash to sufficiently fund a decontrolled entity, in order to completely equity strip a target asset.

> As we've seen, cash loans can effectively equity strip your assets, but they are not without their drawbacks.

Fortunately, the law allows other obligations – as well as cash loans – to serve as the basis for a lien. Liens are commonly used to secure obligations in the normal course of business, and are every bit as valid as cash loans. Furthermore a lien securing an obligation may be superior in some ways to a lien securing a loan.

For example, there is generally no negative tax or economic consequence to fulfilling an obligation. Nor do you worry whether your interest payments are tax-deductible. You have no interest expenses at all, for that matter.

And it's very easy to structure a security agreement so that the lien is not reduced or paid down until your obligation is completed in full. You can even structure the agreement so that the lien *grows* until the obligation is fulfilled. If you or your entity is owed the secured obligation, it will have little value to a creditor, whereas the cash proceeds of a loan have value to a creditor. You then have to protect the loan proceeds.

Moreover, if you have creditors, you may not have the cash assets to pay the loan and your 'protected' property will then be in danger of foreclosure. However, cash shortages should not affect your ability to fulfill non-monetary obligations, (or rather we could arrange a monetary obligation with a 'friendly' entity) so foreclosure is not a problem.

Nor do you have to worry about how you will get $500,000 to equity strip your $500,000 home. Cash loans are easy to quantify and you cannot get a 'large' lien to secure a small loan. However, certain obligations can be difficult to quantify so you have more leeway when you structure an obligation of 'equivalent value' to the cash value of a lien.

With the above in mind, let's examine a few ways to create a bona fide obligation to justify a valid lien on your property.

The LLC Capitalization Tactic

One such advanced and innovative method to equity strip is via the LLC capitalization technique. The concept goes like this: Two people form a limited liability company (LLC) in order to run a business (which could be some legitimate, yet easy-to-do activity, such as investing in stocks and bonds). Under the LLC Acts of every state, each member (member being the LLC equivalent to partner) can obligate the other, per a written agreement, to contribute capital (assets) to the company so that it has a means to operate. One of the members contributes a smaller amount of assets up front to capitalize the company, in exchange for a small but significant ownership interest (usually 1-5%). The other member promises to make a large capital contribution over time, in exchange for an upfront large interest in the company (95-99%). Because the first member contributed his capital up front, but the second member did not, the LLC places a lien on the second member's property to ensure that he fulfills his obligation to capitalize the LLC over time. As long as the LLC is not considered an insider under applicable fraudulent transfer law and the obligation is valid, its fulfillment demonstrable and it 'makes sense' in a business context, we create a rock solid lien against the second member's property.

It's important to note in this scenario that the second members promised contribution could take many forms. It could be a promise to contribute cash, services, equipment or other property. And after the lien expires, the members could dissolve the LLC and typically return their capital back to them – tax free. Furthermore, you can equity strip almost any asset via this method – whether it be accounts receivable, real estate or personal property. Indeed, you have maximum flexibility when equity stripping via an LLC capitalization and you can set practically any terms to fit within the realm of normal business practice.

> You have maximum flexibility when equity stripping via an LLC capitalization and you can set practically any terms to fit within the realm of normal business practice.

The Lessor's Lien

I am a corporate officer and lawyer of several companies and I am often tasked with reviewing various real estate lease agreements. Most of these lease agreements contain a lessor's lien clause. These liens that I periodically review are not part of an intentional asset protection program; rather they are liens that arise in the normal course of business. As I mentioned previously, a lien may be used to ensure that someone meets an obligation. In this instance, the lessor wants to make sure that the lessee fulfills his lease obligations so the lessor oftentimes encumbers the lessee's accounts receivable, furniture, equipment, inventory and other assets. Of course, in this situation, the lessor is not attempting to protect the lessee's assets against other creditors – yet that is exactly what the lessor is accomplishing.

The best asset protection planners understand how liens are used in such everyday business arrangements, and the planner capitalizes on such processes. Utilizing a standard business arrangement for asset protection is especially desirable because it appears that there was no intentional asset protection scheme. Because normal business arrangements often use accounts receivable to secure a lease agreement, a lessor's lien is an especially good way to protect this valuable asset.

> The best type of lessor's lien, of course, is one that is held by a company who is friendly towards the lessee, because we can then draft the lease and lien terms to best suit our needs.

The best type of lessor's lien, of course, is one that is held by a company who is friendly towards the lessee, because we can then draft the lease and lien terms to best suit our needs. Oftentimes I will take property from a business, sell it to another business and then lease it back to the original business. This 'lease-back' arrangement has two benefits: First you protect one piece of property by titling it to a separate entity and when you lease back the property to the original entity, you put a lessor's lien on a second asset. For example, an LLC could sell an office building to a second LLC, lease the building back to the first LLC and subsequently place a lessor's lien on the first LLC's accounts receivable. As simple as the concept sounds, a lessor's lien in this or similar circumstances still requires a high degree of skill to do correctly. The trick is to transfer the original asset into a separate entity in a manner that won't be considered a fraudulent transfer. Also, you must structure each entity so that they'll be respected as separate entities if challenged in court. For example, sometimes if one entity is sued and the managers of that entity also happen to manage the second entity, both entities may be considered 'one entity' under the 'theory of interlocking directors'. This will 'pierce the veil' of the second LLC which will not only avail the first LLC's creditor of the second LLC's assets and also invalidate the reason for a lien on the company's accounts receivable. Therefore if you want a lessor's lien between friendly companies – hire a skilled professional to assist you.

Avoid Sham Mortgages

You can discourage a lawsuit with a mortgage recorded against your assets because your creditor may simply assume that the mortgage is bona-fide. As noted, even a 'paper' mortgage can discourage a would-be litigant. Don't rely on sham mortgages though. Always assume that your creditor will challenge the validity of your mortgage. You must then be prepared to satisfy the court that you owe an enforceable debt for the amount of the mortgage. When your mortgage holder is a friend, relative or affiliate, the mortgage can expect close scrutiny. A more inquisitive or aggressive creditor may challenge the validity of your mortgage. If you borrowed money, do you have the cancelled checks to prove the loan? If you gave the mortgage to secure a debt for services, can you prove that the services were actually rendered and were reasonably priced?

Another limitation of third party liens is that the total value of the secured party's claim against the collateral may still leave an exposed equity. For example, a real estate developer who owns separate parcels of land may arrange for a mortgage to be held by a third party in order to reduce her equity in the land. The mortgage granted by the developer to the third party and recorded on the county records offers no protective value until a cash loan or other value is given to the developer. If a plaintiff wins a lawsuit against the developer, the plaintiff can have the county sheriff attach and sell the property to satisfy the judgment. While the sheriff's sale will not extinguish the mortgage held by the third party, it would be cold comfort to the developer, who nevertheless lost her property.

Except for the appearance of a lien against the developer's properties, the developer's arrangement will not withstand a plaintiff's attorney who wants to sell the developer's property to satisfy the judgment unless a valid debt is *presently* owed to the third party mortgage holder. The difficulty for the asset protection planner is to show actual cash loans to the developer to create that valid lien.

And what will the developer do to protect the cash received from the lender? If the transaction is small enough, this presents less of a problem. However, you may need complex arrangements to protect property worth several hundred thousand dollars or more. The challenge for clients with millions to protect can usually only be met with creative and aggressive planning. Usually this calls for transferring the loan proceeds to one or more offshore entities, investing the proceeds in exempt assets or to buy offshore annuities or some other sophisticated insurance-based product or to secure an obligation-based lien.

Another challenge when planning complex third party liens involves the federal tax law. Not every asset protection consultant, attorney or CPA has adequate knowledge of the federal income, gift and estate tax laws to safely apply these arrangements. There are common tax traps that apply to third party liens held by decontrolled entities or some other third party. Because of its tax complexities, many asset protection specialists avoid using foreign entities in their plans. On the other hand, the most effective asset protection transactions may require a foreign corporation, trust or other foreign entities for tax and privacy purposes and to remove the liquid assets from the grasp of predatory litigants.

Structuring secured liens on your personal assets or the assets of your business can be effectively accomplished only with careful planning, attention to detail and by observing the applicable laws involved over the life of the lien. You must clear a number of hurdles in order to avoid problems with the lien itself, such as the fraudulent transfer laws and tax concerns. This complexity creates a two-edged sword: It requires a high degree of knowledge and skill in several different legal areas to succeed. The costs involved can be significant when you consider the legal fees, taxes and special business services, such as foreign managers. Yet, done properly, the complexity of the transaction can impose a formidable barrier to the average plaintiff looking for a fast lawsuit recovery. As more Americans enter the ranks of those concerned about lawsuits, and as they educate themselves on asset protection, there will be more demand for sophisticated asset protection strategies. Third party secured lien arrangements will be high on that list.

Protect the Loan Proceeds

Protecting the cash proceeds from your loan is usually an easier task than structuring the mortgages. Usually we won't equity strip a client until we are in crisis mode and a judgment looms. Then we will complete the loan and transfer the proceeds – together with the client's other liquid assets – into offshore protective entities or into exempt assets. We would not normally use domestic FLPs or LLCs at that point because such transfers would be susceptible to creditor challenge as fraudulent transfers.

Ultimately, your end game plan – once you are in a crisis mode – is to transfer your domestic (US-based) assets to some protective entity (i.e., FLP, LLC, etc.) *and* to fully secure those assets to one or more mortgage holders so you have no equity exposed to your creditor. The loan proceeds would then be moved to an offshore trust, Nevis LLC or a self-protected investment (such as certain foreign annuities). Or we may combine or layer these entities, investments and strategies to maximize your protection.

Covering Your Loan Payments

One obvious drawback to borrowing to create a funded lien is that you pay interest on your loan. But bear two points in mind. First, your loan proceeds would earn you money as they are invested (albeit through a protective entity). Your real cost then is the 'spread' – or difference – between your interest charges and your yield on the investment – or between what your money earns and your interest payment. You will probably need your liens (and loan) in place for only a short period while your judgment creditor attempts collection. As a practical matter, most judgments are either resolved through settlement or bankruptcy within 1 or 2 years and therefore you probably won't require a long-term loan.

Wealthsaver Tips

1. It is oftentimes necessary to 'equity strip' or 'debt-shield' your assets to keep them safe from creditor seizure.

2. You can get mortgages to equal or exceed the value of your property – and thus leave nothing exposed.

3. In a crisis situation, you can encumber everything you own – both your real and personal property.

4. Equity stripping can be the most effective way to discourage a lawsuit from being filed against you.

5. Get a line of credit against your business and your real estate. It will give you that 'poorer profile' at little or no cost.

6. Who can be the friendly lender who will encumber your assets? You have countless ways to structure loans and mortgage shields.

7. Avoid sham mortgages. It is important that your encumbrances be fully defensible.

8. You can create liens without cash and without interest payments by using executory obligations.

THIRTEEN

A Final Word About Insurance

Now that we have covered the specific firewalls that we use to protect assets from lawsuits, let me make a few final comments about the importance of liability insurance in your planning.

Insurance is a critical asset protection tool to shift the risk of loss on a liability claim from yourself to your insurance company. This is no small consideration in an era of rampant litigation. It is comforting to know that you will be covered against at least *some* liabilities and lawsuits.

Unfortunately, liability insurance won't be your complete answer. Insurance covers far fewer lawsuits than you might expect. That doesn't suggest that you should forego buying liability insurance. Liability insurance is the *starting* point for asset protection. But even when you rely on insurance as your first line of defense 1) you must have the *right* insurance, 2) you must carry *enough* insurance and, most importantly, 3) you must understand that insurance is *only* your starting point. It is not your ending point.

For the reasons we will discuss, you can't fully rely on liability insurance. You must *supplement* your insurance with the other lawsuit protection strategies that I discussed in this book.

Liability insurance, in fact, can create questionable security. Many people don't further protect themselves against liability because they mistakenly believe that their liability insurance will safeguard them. Still, no matter how much insurance you carry, you can only transfer *some* risks to your insurance company; you can't transfer *every* risk.

In fairness, the insurance industry didn't perpetrate the hoax that insurance is a liability cure-all. The hoax is largely self-inflicted. People *want* to believe that insurance is their solution to a lawsuit because insurance is easy to buy. Sign a form, write a check and you have no more lawsuit worries. You can buy millions in homeowners', malpractice and business' premises liability – even umbrella coverage – to protect yourself against lawsuits, but: *It's not enough! Insurance won't fully protect you.*

Laced With Loopholes

> **Even with the right insurance, plenty of loopholes can render your insurance useless.**

Even with the right insurance, plenty of loopholes can render your insurance useless. Consider the three most common liability insurance policies; 1) general business insurance, 2) professional liability insurance and 3) personal liability insurance.

Your general business policy covers specified risks or claims that arise on your business' premises. But its exclusions extend to intentional torts (such as assault and battery, drunk driving, etc.), to acts outside the scope of employment, contract claims, discrimination claims and acts that occur outside the premises (such as working from home). These are only a *few* examples.

Your medical or professional liability policy will insure you against *most* forms of negligent omission or commission, yet it won't cover you for gross negligence, acts where you violate the law, punitive damages, fines, penalties, product liability, contract claims and services that you provide to institutions (hospital, HMOs, etc.). These exclusions must be of great concern to you as a professional because these are precisely the things that may cause you liability.

Then we have the personal liability insurance; 1) auto liability 2) homeowners and 3) umbrella policies. Each has its own long list of exclusions. For example, your auto policy probably won't cover an underage family driver. Or you won't be covered for a DUI accident. Your homeowner's policy may not even insure you on a routine 'slip and fall' case. Your umbrella policy won't insure you from sporting accidents, liability from dangerous instruments (guns, etc.), dog bites, intentional wrongs, business-related claims and an ever-expanding list of other exclusions.

One young attorney complained to me that he pays $15,000 a year for his malpractice insurance, and was never sued until this year when he was sued by a disgruntled employee on a $100,000 wrongful termination claim. For that, he was uninsured. We don't always foresee the less obvious lawsuit threats.

Professionals are 'deep pocket' defendants and they are frequently blamed when things go wrong. They understand they need protection and that's why they spend tens of thousands each year to buy malpractice insurance. Yet every professional is exposed to more than malpractice claims. They are businesspeople with the same hazards as *anyone* in business – partnership suits, employee claims, lawsuits from contracts, etc. In fact, today's professional has more chance of getting sued for something the professional is *not* insured against than for something for which the professional *is* insured.

This is true of everyone. The reasons you can get sued are limitless. And new theories of liability are invented daily by creative lawyers. On the other hand, liability policies are narrowly construed, and they progressively limit *which* lawsuits they cover.

> The reasons you can get sued are limitless. On the other hand, liability policies are narrowly construed, and they progressively limit which lawsuits they cover.

To illustrate this point, 1 in 3 federal civil suits is a sexual harassment claim. Yet only one defendant in 20 has insurance for this type claim. Nor will your insurance protect you from divorce, tax claims, debts or a breach of contract. Insurance also won't safeguard what you leave to your children.

People who believe that they are insured against a certain claim are always surprised when their insurance company points out their ominous 'fine print' exclusion. For example, one client was sued for $500,000 resulting from his teenage daughter's car accident. He *assumed* that his auto insurance policy would cover his daughter's accident until his insurance agent notified him that his policy didn't cover his daughter because she moved out of his house to attend college. He paid over $150,000 to settle. You too have endless ways to get into trouble, and your insurance won't always come to your rescue. I repeat: *Buy insurance – don't rely upon it.*

Maximize Your Insurance Protection

To the extent you rely upon insurance, you need *enough* insurance. Too little coverage will still expose you to a judgment in excess of your coverage. And a good plaintiff's lawyer can manipulate a jury to make an outlandish award far beyond your policy limits.

Do you remember the 'runaway jury' in John Grisham's novel? We joke about crazy multi-million dollar verdicts, but ridiculously high verdicts for even minor injuries are *not* anomalies.

You can't predict what you can lose once you are sued. Years ago we could, with reasonable accuracy, predict the outcome of a lawsuit. Juries were sane. Judges cut excessive awards. 'Punitive' damage claims which awarded a plaintiff millions for no damages were unheard of. That was then. The courts compensated *actual* losses. Not today. Courtrooms now redistribute wealth. *You* can't be confident that your million – or multi-million dollar policy – is *enough.* No matter how much liability insurance you carry, some litigant will sue you for more.

Most cases do settle within the policy limits. But until you do settle, you will anguish that possibly – just possibly – you will be hit with a judgment that will *exceed* your coverage. You will then lose your assets despite your insurance. You will also have to hire your own lawyer to defend yourself against your potential *excess* liability.

How much liability insurance is enough? That's a tough question to answer. If insurance was free, I would say to buy 'all you can'. But insurance isn't free. The more you buy the more you pay. You must then balance the cost of increased coverage against the risks from having less coverage. You must not only consider the probability of an excess judgment against you, but also what you could lose if you did face a judgment beyond your policy limits. Since you can never buy enough coverage to insulate yourself against today's insatiable litigation demands, your only solution is to protect yourself by means other than insurance.

> Since you can never buy enough coverage to insulate yourself against today's insatiable litigation demands, your only solution is to protect yourself by means other than insurance.

How Deep Are Your Insurer's Pockets?

Insurance companies also go bankrupt. Whenever an insurance company fails, it strands tens of thousands of insureds who relied upon their insurer's financial stability to protect them against lawsuits.

One insurance company insured hundreds of physicians for malpractice. They filed bankruptcy last year and abandoned scores of doctors with claims against them. These doctors were suddenly exposed both on their pending lawsuits and on future claims that could arise before they purchased new insurance. Their state insurance commission paid a small portion of their claims, yet a number of doctors lost their entire net worth. They never thought this could happen to them. Even the venerable Lloyds of London nearly stumbled into oblivion. So, ask yourself, can you be certain that *your* insurance company will be in business when you most need them? Check your insurer's financial stability. Unless your insurer is highly-rated, you have *much* less protection than you think. *Standard and Poors* or *Best* can give you your insurer's financial rating, as can your insurance agent. You want an insurer with no less than an A-rating.

Running Your Case

Another huge problem with liability insurance is that you lose control over your case. Your insurance company – not you – decides whether to settle, and for how much. Perhaps this is unimportant with an automobile accident, but it can be enormously important to you if the lawsuit involves your professional competence or impacts upon your personal reputation.

For example, a doctor or another professional may be convinced that they are 'in the right' and want their day in court. However, their insurance company may consider it cheaper to settle. Or you may want to quickly settle your case to avoid adverse publicity while your insurer insists that your case goes to trial.

> Once you are sued, your premiums will rise. With multiple lawsuits over your lifetime — win or lose — your insurance premiums will increase with each new lawsuit.

You and your insurer can have different agendas. If you force your insurance company to resolve your case as you want, you can forfeit the insurance protection for which you paid hefty premiums.

Once you are sued, your premiums will rise. With multiple lawsuits over your lifetime – win or lose – your insurance premiums will increase with each new lawsuit.

One physician friend relied on her malpractice insurance for years until her insurance company defended her on 4 lawsuits. They hiked her premiums to $250,000 a year. She pays more for her insurance than she would likely be forced to pay on any one lawsuit. This isn't unusual.

Insurance = Lawsuit Target

I have my own opinion on how we can solve the lawsuit epidemic, though I disagree with Shakespeare's admonition that we 'kill all the lawyers'. A far less gruesome solution would be to shut down every liability insurer and instead compel everyone to fully protect their assets. In short, we would create a nation of untouchable wealth.

Liability insurance is the major impetus behind many costly and frivolous lawsuits. When you are well-insured, you have 'deep pockets'. This can only attract lawsuits. Whether you are rich or poor, a prospective litigant knows that your insurance company has tons of money. Plaintiffs' lawyers know that insurers will settle even a frivolous lawsuit rather than fight, because it is less costly. It is insurance that has greatly contributed to our transformation into a nation of litigants.

Because insurance attracts lawsuits, and because of fast-rising insurance costs, more and more professionals and businesspeople now 'go bare' or without insurance.

'Going bare' is particularly common with physicians who have been hardest hit by malpractice suits and exorbitant malpractice premiums. High-risk specialists, obstetricians, orthopedic surgeons and others pay $100,000 or more annually for their malpractice coverage. Physicians in the litigious states of California, New York and Florida pay 2 or 3 times that amount for the same coverage. A general practitioner in a low litigation state will still pay $20,000 or more annually for insurance. And this won't buy much coverage.

Insurance costs dig deeply into every medical professional's earnings already hammered by reimbursement cutbacks and managed care programs. Nor are unaffordable premiums only a doctor's problem. The litigation explosion has impacted every profession and business. 'Going bare' is gaining traction in even such 'lower risk' occupations as law, financial services and architecture.

Premium costs are only one reason so many professional and business owners are abandoning insurance. Doctors, other high-risk professionals and business owners understand that they greatly increase their chances of getting sued only because they are insured. Without liability insurance they wouldn't be 'deep pocket' defendants – particularly if their assets were well-protected.

> Premium costs are only one reason so many professional and business owners are abandoning insurance.

I have scores of doctor clients who now practice without liability insurance. However, you can't always avoid insurance. Physicians, by state regulation, must oftentimes carry malpractice insurance. HMOs and hospitals frequently require their affiliated doctors to carry liability insurance. Most other professionals consider insurance an option. However, 'going bare' can only make sense if you have few assets – or your assets are *very* well-protected.

'Going bare' discourages lawsuits. I can illustrate this with the case of a cosmetic surgeon who was threatened with 5 malpractice suits in 3 years (not one case had apparent merit). In each case we pointed out to the patient's attorney that our doctor client had no insurance and that his assets were protected. Not one patient sued. If this doctor had insurance, he would undoubtedly have been sued several times.

One dilemma of 'going bare' is that you must pay your own defense costs or face a default judgment if you don't defend the case. This quandary is particularly undesirable when you know that you have done nothing wrong. Nor do defense costs come cheap. It can cost $100,000 or more to defend against even a routine liability or malpractice suit.

One compromise solution is to retain a law firm to defend you if you are sued. Your annual retainer would cover the litigation costs. A number of professional and business clients retain us to keep them completely judgment-proof (we continuously monitor their finances to make certain they stay fully protected). These professionals have their defense costs covered through a malpractice defense firm whose fee is paid through a separate 'defense-only' policy. These professionals practice with confidence that they won't lose their assets even if they are sued and lose. Of course, the uninsured professional or business owner should announce to their clients that they have no coverage so their client or patient will have dampened enthusiasm to sue.

More legal defense fund insurers are popping up. They insure *only* the defense costs. But when you couple good legal defense coverage with a good asset protection plan, you may have a smart alternative to huge insurance premiums and an insurance policy that will only magnetize lawsuits.

Still, self-insurance isn't for everybody. Your insurance premiums may be a bargain, considering your risks. Or you may prefer insurance if only for your own peace of mind. Some people aren't comfortable unless they are insured against every possible lawsuit, no matter how remote the odds. You must assess your own comfort level to decide upon *your* best alternative.

Insure Yourself

Physicians and other professionals in a group practice have other options that fall somewhere between buying expensive insurance and 'going bare.' Sole practitioners or smaller groups frequently benefit from 'insurance alternative' programs. For instance, they may join or form purchasing cooperatives or IPAs (Independent Physician Associations).

Another popular option is to form your own captive insurance company. Particularly investigate this if your premiums are over $200,000 annually. As mentioned earlier, the Captive Insurance Company (CIC) is an insurance company licensed to write insurance in the US, registered with the IRS and based offshore in jurisdictions such as Bermuda or the British Virgin Islands. Whatever premiums that you pay to your CIC can be maintained and managed in the US. Over 4,000 CICs now write about one-third of the total commercial insurance sold in the United States.

With your own CIC you can customize your insurance in ways that are not possible with commercial third party insurers. For example, a professional can customize their malpractice policy to pay only the professional's legal fees (with choice of attorneys). Their policy wouldn't pay claimants (these are 'shallow pockets' policies). As a prospective defendant, you won't then have 'deep pockets' which is, in itself, a necessary asset protection strategy. Or your CIC can cover you for claims for which you cannot buy insurance or claims which are not covered through traditional policies. Even when you can buy a comparably broad coverage policy from a traditional insurer, you would lose the CIC's powerful tax advantages. If you want insurance, why give away the profits and tax benefits to a commercial insurance company? Consider forming your own insurance company.

Is Your Employer's Insurance Enough?

Your employer's insurance also may *not* adequately protect you. For example, an employer's insurer may not be obliged to defend or pay a judgment against the employee. Employers ordinarily and automatically share liability with their negligent employee; therefore, a judgment against the employee usually brings a simultaneous judgment against the employer. The employer's liability would be paid by the insurer, which would normally cover the employee. That's the theory. Nevertheless, employees who rely solely on their employer's coverage run several risks. One risk is that you have no protection if your employer is *not* liable for an error or omission that occurred *outside* the scope of employment. Or you lose your protection if your employer's policy is terminated without your knowledge. Or your employer may have inadequate insurance. Or too many employees may be sued on the same claim (as is often the case) and the shared liability limits are too low. Or your employer's plan may be a claims-made policy which will cover you only for claims made during the policy period. But you may change jobs *before* a lawsuit is filed. Or lose your job. If you are sued *after* your employment ends, you have no coverage.

Review your employer's policy. Your employer's insurer must defend and protect you *and* your employer. Evaluate your employer's financial sta-

> **Your employer's insurer must defend and protect you and your employer.**

bility. A company in financial difficulty may lose, reduce or cancel their insurance. That's why every employee should buy their own supplemental insurance. It's inexpensive and essential.

Assert Your Rights

Insurance means nothing unless you also know how to protect yourself against your own insurer. For example, if you are sued, your insurer must defend you in good faith or you can sue your insurer for any judgment awarded against you above your coverage. Your insurance company can also incur liability to you for any excessive award against you unless your insurer notifies you of the excess claim and settles – or attempts to settle – in good faith and *within* the policy limits. Your insurer *cannot* refuse a reasonable settlement offer if their refusal will expose you to excess liability.

Your insurance company may also decline to cover a claim. When your coverage is questionable, *demand* that your insurance company defend and indemnify you. Your insurer may then defend the lawsuit and reserve their rights not to pay any judgment. Or your insurer may litigate its liability to insure you under the policy. If there is *any* possible question about whether a claim should be covered by your insurer, hire your own attorney to represent *your* interests. Don't rely on the attorney retained by the insurance company. Your interests and your insurer's may not coincide. You want an attorney *on your side*.

Slash Your Premiums

Despite the high costs of insurance, you may need or want insurance. The trick is to buy *more* coverage at *less* cost. I don't sell insurance, but I can tell you about the common mistakes that many people make when they do buy liability insurance. Some tips:

- **Use one insurance agent.** You need an agent who understands *your* business or profession, its special risks, the coverage you really need and how to buy it most economically. Insurance is complex. You need an agent who can handle your insurance needs as professionally as you would expect your asset protection lawyer to handle your asset protection planning. Buy your liability insurance through one agent. It will help avoid insurance gaps and coverage overlaps.

- **Buy enough coverage.** If you have significant assets, you need at least $1 million coverage per claim. Less coverage isn't meaningful protection against today's high awards. Check what it will cost to increase your coverage. A $3 million policy may not cost considerably more. To save money, increase your deductibles (or the share of the claim that you are obligated to pay).

- **Buy an umbrella policy.** Umbrella insurance is your *best* insurance value. It will cover you against many liability claims that won't be covered (or will be inadequately covered) under a general liability policy. For example,

State Farm's Umbrella Insurance paid President Clinton's defense costs, as well as the settlement on the Paula Jones case. Many claims that are not covered by regular policies *are* covered through an umbrella policy.

Transferring your liability risk to an insurance underwriter is a *first* step toward creating *untouchable wealth,* yet it is not always the most cost-efficient way. As one architect explained, "I paid $70,000 a year to buy a comprehensive professional liability policy to protect my $2 million net worth. I have since slashed my insurance costs by re-titling my assets to keep them safe from lawsuits – no matter how large the claim. This protection cost me $10,000 to set up. And I pay another thousand a year to maintain this protection. I now carry *less* insurance, save $50,000 a year and improved my protection."

Wealthsaver Tips

1. Buy as much liability insurance as you can reasonably afford – but don't rely solely on insurance to protect you.

2. Understand precisely what your insurance will – and won't – protect you against. There are many exclusions.

3. Buy only from well-rated companies. You can't afford the risk of a bankrupt insurance company.

4. Insurance makes you a more attractive lawsuit target. This is one disadvantage with insurance.

5. Consider forming your own offshore insurance company. It might pay big dividends and give you even better protection.

6. As an employee, you need your own coverage to supplement your employer's.

7. Your insurer will not always do what is in your own best interests. Know how to assert your rights against your insurer.

8. You can lower your premiums for liability insurance and frequently get superior coverage.

FOURTEEN ■ ■ ■

Your Next...
(and Most Important) Step

I can go on and on with hundreds of additional asset protection strategies but I think you now know enough about the basics to get you started on your asset protection plan. Make no mistake about it, reading and learning whatever you can about asset protection through this or any other book is a great way to begin the process. But it's not enough. You must do more. You must act today to implement your plan. Otherwise, reading this or any other book is only a gesture in the right direction. So I urge you to protect yourself as soon as you finish this book.

Contact us today for your complimentary, confidential Wealthsaver analysis.

As with any goal, you must commit to action. Protecting yourself is not something to do next month...or next year. It may then be too late. Set a deadline and timetable to complete this important financial goal.

Here's how to start. Call us at 561-953-1050 or e-mail us at asgoldstein@asgoldstein.com and mention that you have read this book and want your own complimentary and confidential Wealthsaver audit.

We will send you our Wealthsaver audit questionnaire. Take a few moments to complete it and return it to us.

Our professional staff will review your questionnaire and return to you, a full report which will indicate:

1. The assets you own that are now unprotected and

2. The options that you can choose from to improve your financial protection.

It's that easy!

And remember this service is absolutely FREE to you. Of course, your information will be held by us in strict confidence.

[Note: this report shall not constitute legal advice and no lawyer-client relationship is established by your taking advantage of this offer. We shall have no liability for any actions taken or not taken as a result of the Wealthsaver audit.]

If, after you review the audit report, you would then like to proceed further, we would be pleased to schedule a direct telephone or office conference with Dr. Goldstein and/or our other professional asset protection planners. We would be delighted to help you with your asset protection planning needs.

Index

401K plans 85, 86
529 plans 96

actual fraud 58, 59
administrative orders 233
affiliated corporation 137
Aid to Families with Dependent Children 92
alimony 92
annual gift tax exclusion 224
annuities 101, 104, 106, 226
anti-alienation 209, 210, 212, 220
anti-deferral tax rules 265
anti-trust 235
Antigua 237
antiques 60, 115
appreciating assets 156
architects 131, 178
Arizona 109, 113, 195
asset-based lender 263
Austria 238

badges of fraud 58, 59, 69
Bahamas 95, 237, 248
bankruptcy 13, 19, 64, 73, 77, 86, 93, 96, 167, 170, 196, 210, 267, 283
bankruptcy courts 111, 139
bankruptcy trustee 66, 73, 111, 167, 170, 196
bank account 101, 117, 134, 251, 255
bank records 75
Belize 238
benefit 41, 50, 56, 67, 83, 85, 93, 120, 125, 239, 242, 250, 255, 156, 179, 197, 199, 204, 214, 221, 223, 228, 272, 287
Bermuda 237, 249, 287
boat 70, 80, 101, 113, 116
breach of warranty 139
British Virgin Islands 237, 249, 287

burial plots 96
business-related claims 281

capital gains 125, 156, 187, 199, 217, 250
captive insurance companies 51, 233
cash surrender value 94
Cayman Islands 237
certificate of limited partnership 153
Channel Islands 238
Chapter 11 32, 47, 139, 222
charitable remainder annuity trust 218
Charitable Remainder Trust 217
charter 153
checking account 109
child support 92, 98
Child Support Enforcement Act of 1975 92
civil decree 233
claims-made policy 289
co-owned assets 42, 101, 106, 116
co-ownership 101, 106, 111, 113, 116, 213
collectibles 155, 252, 262
commercial property 116, 157
common law 223, 264
common law trusts 223
community debts 113
community property 113, 114, 115
constitutional trusts 223
constructive fraud 58, 65
Consumer Credit Protection Act 91
control-retention techniques 48, 241
Cook Islands 207
corporate records 133, 134, 152
corporate shareholders 120, 142, 152
corporate trustee 207
corporation 56, 92, 117, 247, 251, 253, 255, 265, 268
county records 274

court order 67
credit-equivalent bypass trust 176
creditors 25, 31, 42, 50, 56, 70, 77, 92, 98, 101, 105, 106, 108, 115, 122, 126, 133, 137, 149, 151, 160, 164, 176, 178,183, 188, 195, 204, 205, 206, 214, 216, 218, 219, 223, 226, 245, 255, 267
Creditor Protection Trust 238
Creditor Remedies 231
credit applications 75
credit line 261
criminal penalties 67
CRT 217, 218
Cuba clause 235, 247
Cyprus 238
C corporation 125, 126, 128, 129, 181, 184, 247

debt-shielding 264, 266
declaration of homestead 82
decontrolled entities 275
deeds of trust 83
deep pockets 285, 288,
defacto control 242
default judgment 286
defense costs 286, 291
defined benefit plans 85
defined contribution plans 85
Delaware 145, 146, 190, 221, 222
Delaware trusts 221
depositions 75
de facto control 206
dilution strategy 246
directors 120, 121, 128, 134, 143, 146,192,193
disclaimer 226
discounted valuation 176, 190, 198
discovery 12, 74, 140
discretionary clause 210
discrimination 135, 235, 280,
disregarded entity 128, 156, 186, 187, 188, 199
distributed profits 130, 160, 245
divorce 18, 19, 95, 98, 105, 112, 113, 210, 281
domestic trusts 222

double taxation 126, 128, 142, 181
due diligence 45
durable power of attorney 109, 228

encumbrances 42, 66
England 238
equity 23, 42, 80, 81, 122, 130, 145, 262, 269
equity-strip 31, 252
ERISA 85, 86, 87, 88, 93
ex-spouses 72, 112, 208
exempt assets 31, 46, 62, 84, 93, 98,274

family limited partnership 89, 130, 140, 149, 150, 173, 174, 175, 193, 198, 199, 200, 201, 253
family trust 176
federal laws 77
financial goals 49, 150, 212
financial services 285
fines 280
fixed annuities 226
flee provision 235
flexible Plan 43, 44
Florida 46, 63, 77, 81, 91, 98, 109, 111
Florida Supreme Court 67
foreclosure 139
foreign corporation 143, 247, 265, 275
foreign grantor trust 238
foreign trust 239, 246
Fortune 500 119
foundations 233, 248, 265
fraud 12, 44, 58, 59, 65, 69, 73, 58, 59, 266, 271
fraudulent transfers 55, 56, 57, 59
friendly mortgage 145, 267
funded intervivos trust 202
future services 64

general partnership 107, 121, 122, 150, 179
Gibraltar 238
Gifting 57, 85
going bare 285, 286
grantor 158, 176, 188, 191, 197, 200, 203, 204, 206, 211, 216, 217, 221, 223, 238, 240, 25
grantor trust 188, 253

gross negligence 191
Guernsey 238

holding corporation 142
Homestead Protection 80, 81, 213
Hong Kong 238
household furniture 96
Hungary 238
hybrid companies 248
hybrid entity 202

illegal tax schemes 50
indemnification 139, 146
Individual Retirement Accounts 85
inheritance 113, 207, 208, 209, 212,
        221, 226
Insider loans 262
installment sale note 224
insurance 15, 16, 17, 29, 51, 75, 77, 86,
        94, 95, 97, 98, 129, 131, 146,
        177, 179, 214, 216, 279, 280,
        281, 288, 291
insurance company 215, 249, 251, 279,
        282, 283, 284, 288, 289
insurance trust funds 146
integrated plan 35
intentional torts 280
international business companies 233
interrogatories 74
IPAs (Independent Physician Associa-
        tions) 287
irrevocable intervivos trust 200, 204,
        205, 206, 214
irrevocable life insurance trust 94, 95
irrevocable trusts 207, 208, 221, 248
IRS 245, 249, 254, 287
IRS reporting requirements 247
IRS Revenue Rule 163
Isle of Man 89, 95, 238, 248
Jersey 238
jointly and severally liable 107, 109
joint account 101, 109, 122
joint tenants 101, 104
JTWROS 104
judgment-proofing 47
judgment creditors 56, 57, 67, 75, 112,
        236
jurisdictional immunity 233, 255

jurisdiction shop 98
Justice Antonin Scalia 67

Keogh plans 86

Land trusts 158,220
legal defense fund insurers 287
liability-producing assets 111, 182
libel 83
Liechtenstein 238, 248
liens 42, 165, 201, 259, 260, 254, 269,
        272, 275
limited liability 182, 183, 185
Limited Liability Company 181-185,
        192, 196-198, 201
limited liability partnerships 183
Line of Credit 261
living trust 82, 108, 176
living will 228
Lloyds of London 283
Luxembourg 238

maintenance costs 158
Malta 238
Marianas 238
marital assets 72, 98
marital trust 176
Massachusetts 81, 96, 111
Medicaid planning 239
Medicaid trust 221
Microsoft 119
money laundering 44, 45
mortgage 64, 71, 73, 84, 103, 104, 138,
        145, 200, 255, 260, 262, 264,
        266, 267, 269, 273
multiple liens 260
multiple trusts 227

negligence 131, 135, 189
negligent omission 280
Nevada Corporate Planners 147
Nevada corporation 140, 146, 189, 244,
        268
Nevada trust 222
Nevis 235-238, 244, 246
Nevis LLC 243-247, 254
New Zealand 238
nominee trusts 223

298 So Sue Me!

non-exempt assets 46
non-voting shares 144

O.J. Simpson. 77
officers 120, 121, 134, 136, 143, 146, 184, 192, 268
offshore financial centers 231, 233, 266
offshore trusts 37, 49, 51, 171, 186, 197, 222-235, 239, 246
option to purchase 173
out-of-state corporation 145

Panama 238, 248
Patterson v. Shumate 85
penalties 67, 280
pension plans 85, 131
perjury 143, 251
permanent separation 113
personally guaranteed debts 136, 138
phantom income 174
Philippines 238
poison pill 144, 194, 245, 247
predatory litigants 275
present liability 61, 62, 76, 187, 199
primary residence 80
privacy havens 234
Private vaults 255
probate 82, 102, 107, 109, 117
procedural obstacles 57, 233
product liability 124, 135, 280
product liability claims 135
professional associations 131
professional corporation 131
profit-sharing plans 95
protective entities 26, 31, 33, 106, 142, 243, 248, 275
protector 162, 169, 175, 238, 239, 241, 243, 247, 252
proxy 144
publicly traded corporations 60
public assistance payments 93
public recording office 260
public registry 114
purchasing cooperatives 287
pure trusts 45, 50

Q-TIP Trusts 219

Qualified Domestic Relations Order 98
Qualified Personal Residence Trust 218

registration statement 153
Revised Uniform Limited Partnership Act 179
revocable trust 205, 206, 207
rights of survivorship 108

SBA 116
secrecy 44, 220
Secretary of State's 153
security interest 137, 139, 146, 259, 264
seizure 66, 77, 79, 90, 92, 94, 96, 142, 160, 164, 201, 254
self-insurance 287
self-settled trusts 206
SEP-IRA 89
separate debts 113
separate property 113, 114, 115
settlor 203, 222
sham Mortgages 267
shell entity 265
Singapore 238
single-member limited liability companies 189, 199, 200
Social Security 93, 125
sole proprietorship 121, 128, 150, 198
spendthrift clause 210
spendthrift trust 85, 219
spousal communication 74
sprinkling provisions 211
Standard and Poors 284
State Farm 291
state insurance commission 283
stockholders 120, 128, 146, 158, 192
straw 55, 71-74, 143
subpoenas 254
substitute partner 160
Swiss annuities 95
Switzerland 238
S corporation 126, 127, 130, 253

tax consequences 41, 50, 119, 142, 224
tax laws 216, 249
tax lien 117
tax returns 93, 188

tenants by the entirety 42, 110
tenants-in-common 101, 105, 116
testamentary trust 204-207
Texas 81, 84, 91, 98, 113
tort claims 135, 179
transfer restrictions 143
transmutation agreements 114
treasury bonds 217
trustees 227, 238, 239
trustee firms 241
Trusts 158, 175, 176, 186, 190, 197,
        203, 205, 212, 214, 216, 218,
        220, 227, 229
trust company 207
Turks and Caicos 237

umbrella policies 280
undivided interest 103
Uniform Fraudulent Conveyance Act
        (UFCA) 55
Uniform Fraudulent Transfer Act (UFTA)
        55
Uniform Gifts to Minors Act 96
Uniform Limited Liability Company Act
        (ULLCA) 185

Uniform Limited Partnership Act 149,
        153
unlimited marital deduction 176, 219
untouchable wealth 23, 24, 27, 285, 291
US Supreme Court 67, 68, 84

vehicles 60, 102, 262
voluntary lien 259
voting powers 144
voting shares 144

wage exemption 91, 92
wage garnishment 91
war-chest 43
wedding rings 96
welfare payments 92, 93
will 212, 213, 227, 228
Writ of Execution 67
yacht 80

zero percent money purchase plans 88

Complimentary, Confidential WEALTHSAVER® Audit

Give us 15 minutes of your time and our
professional staff will identify every asset that you own that is now
vulnerable to lawsuits…and what you can do to protect them.

It's free and always confidential

Call 561-953-1050
or e-mail
asgoldstein@asgoldstein.com

Note: This is not an offer to provide legal
advice and no lawyer-client relationship shall
be created by you participating in this audit.

Are you ready for your very own financial protection plan? Give my office a call and let's arrange a personal consultation to put together a plan that will give you the best protection possible against any financial or legal problem.

Whether you have few assets or enjoy considerable wealth...you'll have the confidence that what you own is more safe and secure once we meet and begin to safeguard your future.

It's easy to arrange. Simply phone our office. There's never an obligation when you call and, of course, upon request, we will send you a brochure describing our firm's services.

We serve individuals and businesses nationwide.

Arnold S. Goldstein & Associates, LLC
Telephone: 561-953-1050
Fax: 561-953-1940
e-mail: asgoldstein@asgoldstein.com
Visit our website: www.asgoldstein.com

ABOUT THE AUTHOR

One of America's leading wealth protection specialists, Arnold S. Goldstein Ph.D. has helped thousands of individuals, families and organizations gain complete lawsuit protection.

You may have seen or heard Dr. Goldstein discuss his powerful financial strategies on radio and TV talk shows (including CNN, CNBC and NBC's Today Show), or as a seminar and meeting speaker.

You could have read about his wealth preservation concepts in numerous business and finance magazines: *INC, Fortune, Money, CFO, Entrepreneur, Success, Venture, Business Week, Bottom Line,* to name a few.

Possibly you may have found your path to financial security from his best-selling books, *Offshore Havens* or *Asset Protection Secrets,* or his more than fifty other books on wealth protection.

A veteran wealth preservation specialist, Dr. Goldstein is founder of the Florida and Massachusetts firm of Arnold S. Goldstein & Associates. He is a member of the Massachusetts and federal Bars and a member of the Bar of the US First Circuit Court and US Supreme Court.

He holds five academic degrees (including graduate law degrees, an MBA and a Ph.D. in economic and business policy from Northeastern University, where he is professor emeritus). He has served on the faculty at several other universities and as a post-doctoral research scholar on offshore trusts at the London School of Economics. He now also holds the distinguished professorship of management at Lynn University. Dr. Goldstein resides in Delray Beach, Florida with his wife Marlene and their two labs, Shadow and Coco.